True Blue

Inspired by true events and experiences

By

Jeanette McConnell

Copyright © 2025 Jeanette McConnell

All rights reserved, including the right to reproduce this book, or portions thereof in any form. No part of this text may be reproduced, transmitted, downloaded, decompiled, reverse engineered, or stored, in any form or introduced into any information storage and retrieval system, in any form or by any means, whether electronic or mechanical without the express written permission of the author.

ISBN: 9781918038095

PROLOGUE

Madeleine swallowed the lump in her throat and blinked rapidly, holding back her tears. The past thirty-four years had been filled with a series of ups and downs, uncertainty, and despair.

She walked with her friend along the path toward the church's ancient porch. It had been many years since she stepped inside a place of worship, but she felt comfortable with Jane by her side. Their friendship had endured for many years. Although she experienced a sense of peace, she felt drained, and her emotions were tied to her past and all her tomorrows.

The gathering was small, but the feeling of love, sharing, and understanding was immensely overwhelming. She felt as if the sermon had been prepared solely for her. Then, taking her turn in communion, eating of His flesh and drinking of His blood, she felt at peace while listening to the softness of the minister's voice. Madeline was alone with her thoughts, pain, and hope for the future. They sang hymns she had never heard before, but she found the tune and embraced the words.

The Minister invited everyone to go forth and be healed, to ask for the reclamation of their selves or others. Madeleine's voice told her to appeal for the healing of her friends, her enemies, and all those who needed His help more than she did, but a voice inside her, far stronger than her own, nudged her to ask for assistance in saving her soul. For the healing of all the pain of yesteryears and for giving her the strength to carry her through to fulfil the hopes and dreams for the future.

With her friend by her side, she slowly made her way to the place of healing. Kneeling at the altar, they bowed their heads, waiting as the minister spoke to each of his followers. Then, looking up, Madeleine saw his kindly face, eyes searching hers. He asked her what she needed to be healed.

Tears welled, but Madeleine could not find an answer. She needed to release all the burdens of her past to deal with today and have faith that the happiness she had found was here to stay. She felt afraid.

Then, she felt his hand gently resting on her head as he asked that she be reconciled through him. She felt humble, trying to pray as he spoke and to put forth all the reasons for wanting this healing. She found none but was comforted by his words.

Arriving back at her seat, she sat with her eyes closed, feeling so close to that 'power above.' As she prayed for all those in need of her prayers and healing, it was as if a beautiful light was glowing and drawing her towards an eternal tunnel.

Finally, all her fears were released, and she could move forward with hope.

Childhood adventures
1919

Daisy woke up. It was still dark, but far below in the kitchen, she could hear some movement and smell the aroma of bacon and eggs cooking.

'Why so early? 'Then she remembered—they were going to Granny and Grandpa's farm for a holiday. The door opened, and Mary, the housemaid, told her to dress quickly as the taxi would soon arrive to take them to the station.

Breakfast wouldn't go down Daisy's throat; there were so many butterflies in her tummy from anticipating the exciting train journey ahead.

A few hours later, her eyes were glued to the carriage window as they sped towards Scotland, changing trains twice, eating sandwiches and cake from the basket her mummy had brought, and thinking of Aunties Net, Violet, Nan, and Uncles Jock and Parker, who would be waiting for their arrival. Poor Daddy was home with only the maids and Paddy, their mischievous terrier.

The train steamed into the station. As they alighted, a porter approached. Loading their cases onto a wooden trolley, he wheeled it to where Grandpa was waiting with the trap to escort them the four miles to the farm. Daisy sat in the back while her mother rode beside Grandpa, and within minutes, they were on their way.

As they rattled into the cobbled yard, Aunty Violet ran out of the house to embrace Daisy with a big hug and a kiss.

'Come away in, we're all waiting for tea,' she said.

Grannie was there, sitting in her black, high-necked dress with a white lace collar. Her grey hair was piled high on her head in a sort of cottage loaf. After hugging Daisy to her bosom, she gently pushed her away.

'Off you go and get your coats off. Tea will be ready as soon as you've washed your hands.'

Soon, nine family members gathered around the large table in the dining room, enjoying a delectable spread of ham and salad, scones, pancakes, cream sponges, and a giant fruitcake. After working steadily through almost everything, Daisy asked permission to leave the table.

'Off you go,' said Granny.

'And don't get y'rself into any mischief,' called Mama.

Having just turned seven, Daisy was spirited and headstrong, often driving her mother to distraction. She dashed into the cobbled yard, hollering as she went:

'I won't, Mama; I'm just going to talk to the horses and visit the smelly pigs.'

Daisy watched as the cows emerged from the byre in a steady stream, returning to the field. She decided to visit all the loose boxes. There was 'King of Diamonds', who had brought them home in the trap, 'Cut-the-wind', another chestnut mare; then, to her delight, she discovered a beautiful foal just big enough to put its head over the half door of the loose-box. Daisy explored the stables where the three big Clydesdales were munching away at their hay and whinnied softly as she stroked their velvety noses. She climbed the ladder into the hayloft, rolling over and over. She loved the scent of hay, the horses, and the bags of grain and meal.

Next, she found the mill and watched the water cascade over the wheel. Lastly, she visited the pigs, who were snorting, squealing, and lapping the smelly mixture in their troughs.

By now, dusk was falling, and Daisy could hear Aunty Violet calling her name. It was nearly bedtime, and all the lamps in the house were lit, while the curtains were drawn. She was chased upstairs for a bath and then allowed back down for a cup of hot cocoa – all milky and sweet- and some bread and butter before bedtime. After kissing everyone goodnight, Aunty Nan tucked her into bed upstairs. It was some time before she fell asleep, reflecting on the day's adventures and imagining what the next day could bring.

When she woke in the morning, the sun shone on her bed. There were many different noises: cows mooing in the dairy, the clip-clop of the Clydesdale being led out to the trough for a drink, the milking machines, and the clatter of pails. From the kitchen, much chatter drifted, along with the delicious smell of bacon and scrambled eggs.

'Daisy, hurry up, or you won't get breakfast.' It was Uncle Jock at the back door.

Granny was sitting at the big table, with Grandpa at the other end, while Aunties Violet, Nan, Net, and Uncle Parker were also there. Mama had breakfast in bed because she needed to rest, as Daisy would shortly have a baby brother or sister.

If Daisy hurried, she could coax old Jock into letting her lead one of the horses back to the stables, and then she could quickly head over to the dairy to watch the milk gushing into the big vat, ready to be made into cheese.

During the morning, Daisy enjoyed a long walk across the fields to visit the ploughman's wife, Annie, in her little cottage, which always smelled of baking scones and oatcakes. Annie showed her the six puppies that their collie had in the woodshed.

'How I would love to take them home!' thought Daisy.

In the afternoon, Auntie Nan called for Daisy to help carry the big basket of scones, fruit cake, and cans of hot tea to the men in the harvest field. They sat down and talked while the men had their tea, and Daisy watched the reaper rotate as it cut the golden corn. As it reached the last section in the middle, the men stood around with big sticks, trying to catch the rabbits as they ran out. She was always glad when they missed, and the bunnies escaped.

Daisy stayed behind after Aunt Nan returned with the empty basket and billy cans. When the work was finished, she coaxed Willie, the farmhand, into letting her ride back to the stables on one of the mares. She helped push the hay down from the hayloft into the racks for the horses to eat. All the animals were her friends when the grown-ups were too busy to play with her, and the other children of the farm workers were at school. She could talk to them or take long walks with one of the dogs across the fields to the woods by the millstream, stopping to watch the ducks in the pond.

One day, the stable door blew shut while Daisy was inside. She wasn't tall enough to reach the handle to open it. The men were all working, and no one heard her banging. She felt worried as she pondered what to do.

Most of the windows were too high, except for one small one through which she could see the immense waterwheel outside, turning the massive stone discs that ground the corn. It was stationary, so she bravely wrapped her hand in her smock and smashed one of the small panes of glass, just managing to squeeze out onto the wheel and climb down. Having cut herself in a few places, she feared she would be in trouble for tearing her dress when she returned to the house.

Later, Daisy realised she had frightened everyone – the wheel could have started up and thrown her into the millstream! Hence, she was sent in disgrace to her bedroom for the rest of the afternoon. There was nothing she could do but lie in bed and plan tomorrow's adventure. She'd heard Auntie Net say she was allowed to go into town to do some shopping. Daisy snuggled down in bed, her thoughts on the following day.

'Maybe if I were good 'til then, she'd take me with her in the pony trap, and we'd have ice creams in the dairy, and then I know old Mr Campbell in the grocers would say 'Hey, lassie! So, you've come back to see us all.'

And then he'd push a small paper bag of liquorice all sorts over the counter. With those happy thoughts, she drifted off to sleep...

1934

Since graduating from Commercial College, Daisy worked as a shorthand typist for a well-known company for two years. Her daily routine had become monotonous, and she yearned to face new challenges. Despite her sheltered upbringing and expensive education, she had never been a conventional young lady. After searching the vacant columns of many papers, she was about to give up when... There it was! Just what she wanted.

Educated young gentlewoman to train as a Land Girl on a smallholding in Sussex. To look after a herd of pedigree goats, poultry and learn market gardening. Live with the lady. References exchanged. Please apply in writing.'

A few weeks later, as the successful applicant, Daisy settled in a small village in Sussex. Her home was a stone cottage sitting on a few acres of land. Her new employer managed a small holding with a herd of six pedigree Toggenburg goats, named after the region in Switzerland, where the breed originated, two dozen hens, and a small market garden.

Miss James was a tall, weather-beaten, energetic woman of about fifty-five. Daisy lived with their family and soon found a helpful friend in Gladys, the country girl, who did all the housework and cooking each morning. Daisy had to rise at six o'clock and then milk the goats. Each stall was expected to be spotlessly clean, with fresh hay added to their manger every morning. It took her a few days to master the art of milking, but the goats were very patient and gentle. Each had a name, and after putting the milk in containers for sale in the village, she opened the hen house and collected the eggs. Then, she walked the goats into the woods to eat the young leaves on the hazelnut trees. They would follow her quite docilely in a single file.

Daisy faced a steep learning curve. She learned new things, such as Toggenburgs being the aristocrats of the goat world. If any of their hay dropped on the floor, they refused to eat it. The Billy goat was different because he was kept solely for breeding in his sturdy wooden shed. The only way Daisy could feed him was to open the door quickly, shove the food in, and retreat hastily, for the moment he saw her, he would charge at her. She could hear his massive horns crashing against the wood whenever she closed the door.

One day, she was sent to catch a calf in the paddock. She went forth gaily, taking a rope. But ten minutes later, she was still breathlessly tearing around, trying to get the rope around his neck. Once lassoed, the fun began! Off he galloped around the paddock with Daisy grimly hanging on and breaking all speed records. She tripped on a tussock of grass and was dragged along the ground, stubbornly refusing to let go until the angry calf finally tired.

Daisy's employer was a tough, hard-working country woman who presumed Daisy would be the same. She expected Daisy to dig the plots for planting, keep them weed-free, and harvest potatoes for sale on market days. Often before dawn, Daisy had to break the ice on a large tub of water and clean the bunches of celery, cut and pack cabbages, and anything else that needed doing. After breakfast, Mrs. James piled into her Ute and drove off to the local open market with the day's produce to sell.

On one such day, Mrs. James asked Daisy to cut back the red creeper on the side of the house. Daisy was busily clipping away up the ladder when she decided to stop for a breather. As she reached the ladder's bottom rung, she looked around at the piles of creeper on the lawn and noticed a wire hanging down.

'*What could it be?*' she wondered.

Suddenly, the awful truth dawned on her: she had severed the telephone wire attached to the house!

The maid, Gladys, and Daisy spent the rest of the day in fear and trembling, waiting for the return of the 'Boss.' There was no hope of getting it repaired in time. Daisy was sure she would not be popular for a day or two!

Despite a few hitches, Daisy enjoyed her year working outdoors. There, she became strong and healthy, thanks to a diet of goat's milk and cream, fresh eggs, and vegetables. She was extremely fit and learned many new skills, fostering her resilience and independence.

She became very friendly with the family who ran the neighbouring farm and eventually moved to live and work for them. She rose at four in the morning with the men to milk her share of the cows by hand, muck out the milking shed after the cows had been taken to the field, and then went into the house to share an enormous breakfast of bacon, eggs, toast, and tea.

She was kept busy all day and learned to harrow the fields with a team of two horses, cut hay in the stockyard, and take turnips out in the cart to throw them to the cows in winter. The farmer taught her to drive his two-seater Morris. They practised driving around the yard, down the hill to the gate, around the pond, and back until Daisy mastered changing gears and steering.

She loved her experiences as a land girl and novel encounters, such as holding a cow while the bull was brought out to 'service' her. However, Daisy was easily embarrassed, and much to the amusement of the men, she would blush from the roots of her hair.

Eventually, upon returning home to Lancashire, she found a job in a radiology department where she also worked as the doctor's chauffeur.

Daisy, now twenty-five, decided to resign from her job and travel home to Swindon to spend the holiday with her parents.

1941 – 1944

Daisy and her brother Ken enjoyed a privileged upbringing, living in a majestic late nineteenth-century Victorian house on the outskirts of Manchester. Their father, James, ran a very successful drapery business in the city, while their mother, Jeannie, spent many hours socialising with the community's elite. Jeannie, a social climber, viewed herself as far superior to many of her husband's associates. She carefully sought out members of society who were considered essential and influential. Her husband abhorred snobbery, frequently telling Jeannie he had no time for her hoity-toity friends.

Daisy adored her father, with whom she shared a unique and loving relationship. Her mother, in contrast, was present but emotionally distant. They were passionate about different things and held numerous opposing values.

Consequently, from an early age, Daisy developed a strong sense of self and independence. She had a sense of adventure and loved embracing new challenges. She was never happier than when she was out enjoying herself. Daisy was strikingly attractive rather than beautiful. She dressed in the most modern styles, accentuating her curvaceous figure and extremely slim waist. She was exceptionally gregarious and flirtatious!

Daisy celebrated her twenty-seventh birthday a few months after Britain declared war on Germany. At that time, she was working as a secretary for a legal firm in Manchester. However, she soon grew increasingly frustrated with the predictable routine and longed for change and adventure. Many of her friends were married and had children, while her relationships were limited to brief flings or one-night stands.

These were stark and uncertain times, as no one knew what would happen, and the fears of repeating the events of the First World War were ever-present. Her parents frequently entertained officers from the large British Army camp stationed nearby, and on one such occasion, they had the honour of welcoming Major Appleby. During the evening, Daisy mentioned to him that she hoped to move to London and apply for work with the War Department.

'Remarkable and quite commendable,' replied the Major. 'If you are serious, Daisy, then I may be able to help.' He suddenly commanded their attention, and the anticipation of what he might offer was palpable. 'It just so happens that I have a flat in the city. If you wish, you can use it at a reasonable rent, of course.'

Her mother cast an imploring glance at her husband, who merely shrugged his shoulders and said:

'Daisy, my dear, I will not stand in your way if that is your wish. You are at an age where you must make your own decisions.' Then, turning to the Major, he responded graciously, 'Major, I am extremely grateful to you for the offer of help. Knowing she has somewhere to go will put my wife and me at ease. I appreciate your kindness.'

Daisy eagerly accepted the Major's offer, and before long, she secured a secretarial job at the Ministry of Information. Many months later, the Major, who was on a few days' leave, took her out for dinner at a fashionable West End restaurant. An orchestra called the Falkmans was playing. The Major was friends with one of the musicians, a Belgian named Stephane, who asked to be introduced to Daisy. They shared an instant and easy rapport.

Over the next few months, Daisy visited the restaurant many times, and her friendship with Stephane blossomed. He was clearly smitten and would bribe one of the servers to reserve a small table for her in a corner near the band. Between sessions, he would sit with her and later walk her home before travelling on the underground to his own home, where he lived with his Spanish wife and a twelve-year-old daughter, whom he adored.

Stephane was tall and well-built, his dark hair always carefully brushed back from his high forehead and just above his upper lip, a pencil-thin moustache that he kept neatly trimmed. His bespectacled face conveyed a degree of seriousness, but he could also be quite mischievous. When he smiled, his entire face would light up. He was charming and charismatic, and when he wanted to impress, he wore the most magnificent black cape lined with crimson silk, which swished from side to side as he walked. He appeared flamboyant and exuded confidence.

From the beginning of their romance, Stephane was honest with Daisy. He explained that he was married to Helena and had a twelve-year-old daughter named Jacqueline. Additionally, at thirty-nine, he was twelve years older than Daisy.

The prospect of an older, married lover did not deter Daisy. However, after nearly two years, the reality of a disenfranchised relationship and constantly being in the shadows became disheartening. She wanted Stephane for herself. She knew of one way to force the issue. Daisy had always used precautions during all the wonderful nights they spent together in each other's arms. She understood the risk she would be taking if she ceased using the diaphragm. Many frowned upon unmarried mothers; however, she was prepared to take that chance.

It wasn't long before Daisy knew she was carrying Stephane's child. Although shocked by her pregnancy, he was delighted at the thought of becoming a father again. He acknowledged that this would further complicate his life, recognising that the scandal could potentially destroy his career. Stephane was never going to desert his wife and daughter.

Daisy was devastated, as she was certain he would divorce Helena so they could build a life together. After spending many hours pleading with him, Daisy realised that Stephane was not going to change his mind. She decided to conceal her pregnancy even from her parents, believing that having a baby out of wedlock was a disgrace. She hoped to protect them from scandal and shame.

Daisy visited a charity called 'The Society for the Unmarried Woman and her Child', which was located in a large house near Hyde Park. She was interviewed by a kind and pleasant woman who arranged for her to reside at the home during the seventh month of her pregnancy. The home, run by nuns, served as a refuge for single mothers. At the time, only twenty young ladies from good families were residing there, each paying a weekly board of five pounds. The young women slept in large communal dormitories, attended daily prayers, and assisted the domestic staff with their duties.

Daisy knew the time had come to tell her boss that she was having a baby, but upon telling him, she was amazed when he simply smiled and told her.

'I knew almost as soon as you did. You can trust me to keep your confidence.' Unfortunately, a month later, the Ministry of

Labour transferred her to the Air Ministry in Whitehall, as all single women had to do war work. She maintained a flat stomach and a slim silhouette, allowing her to continue working without arousing concern from her colleagues.

The day before her baby was due, Daisy sat writing a letter to her father when suddenly she felt like her insides had dropped to the bottom of her belly. The pains she had experienced for the last couple of hours were now excruciating. The home called a taxi, instructing the driver to take her to Queen Charlotte's Hospital as quickly as possible. A staff member contacted the hospital to inform them that Daisy was coming.

A foggy night made the trip slow and hazardous. Daisy was convinced that her baby would be born in the taxi, as it was taking all her strength not to push down hard. She was willing the taxi driver to speed up!

Upon arriving at the hospital, to the taxi driver's amazement, Daisy jumped from the car, raced up the steps, and bypassed the nurse waiting at the entrance. Within minutes, Daisy was whisked away on a trolley to the delivery room, and in less than half an hour, she was holding her baby, swaddled in a pink blanket. She was recovering in the hospital when she received a letter from Stephane,

Liverpool Jan 1944
'Greetings, little mother! And with them, an expression of my happiness at the news that all went well.
So, that little devil J.J. crossed us at the last moment and decided to make his arrival into the world as 'Madeleine'! Well, it only goes to prove once more that one should always provide for the unexpected! To think that we left her name almost out of calculations just through the sheer 'dashed sureness' that she would be a he!
Maddie, the Child of Mischief, our mischief! I dare say she'll probably develop into a bundle of tricks, after all those we have been up to for the past three and a half years. What does the little rat look like? I am simply dying to have a peep at her. Do let me know, as soon as you can, how everything went and how you are now.

Beloved, I am very happy about it all, especially that you made up your mind to keep that little monkey! A Girl! I got the news just a few minutes before my train left this morning, so you can well imagine that the unexpected change of sex gave me plenty of matter for thought during my trip. Still, it made me a very proud Papa, and I felt like passing the news on to everyone who spoke to me. Luckily for me, my exuberance was tempered by the fact that they were the usual uninteresting and sometimes distasteful Ensa party, and I have now regained my sangfroid.

Au revoir, my beloved sweetheart, this brings us more together than ever before. I pray that I might always have you both by my side.
    Stephane

Stephane visited Daisy that evening, carrying a huge bouquet. His long black cape flung over his shoulder, revealing the crimson silk lining. He nearly hugged and kissed the breath out of her in his passionate embrace!

The following week, when Daisy went to register her daughter's birth, 'Madeleine Jeanette,' she was asked to provide the father's name. Since Stephane had insisted that he would not be cited as the child's father, she reluctantly wrote *'Unknown'*! Despite his denial and later reassurances, Daisy realised Stephane would not have to accept parental responsibility for his child.

When Daisy was discharged from the hospital, she returned to the home for an additional six weeks, during which she received support and guidance on caring for her baby. Her next challenge was finding a place to live. She knew she had to obtain employment as soon as possible to support herself and her infant daughter. Additionally, she needed to find someone to look after her daughter while she worked. Fortunately, Stephane had found a young couple, Cliff and Susan, who were eager to have someone share their house in Chiswick. They lived on the first floor with their two-year-old daughter and offered the top floor to Daisy.

Cliff insisted they buy a Morrison Shelter – a large metal cage a bit higher than a dinner table to protect them from the many bombs falling all over London. It had a hefty iron frame with a sheet steel ceiling secured with chunky nuts and bolts. The structure was large and angular, occupying most of the dining room. Under the table lay a crude wire mattress, with just enough space for all of them to lie. On quiet nights, when they could sleep in their beds, Daisy would place her daughter in one of the large chest drawers and push it under the bed to ensure her safety.

When Maddie was six weeks old, Daisy secured a position as a shorthand typist with ENSA at the Theatre Royal. ENSA was an organisation that provided entertainment to the Forces at home and overseas, where actors and actresses offered their services for free. Every morning before going to work, Daisy took Maddie to the day nursery, then travelled to the underground railway and journeyed to the West End. A few times a week, Susan cared for Maddie, allowing Daisy to visit the nightclub where Stephane played. Stephane would join her during the intervals. At the end of the evening, he would occasionally walk her home, but most nights she took the train alone.

One evening, when Daisy got off the train and left the station, walking the short distance home, she noticed flames shooting up. She quickened her pace and soon felt out of breath, stumbling and running, dreading the worst. Rounding the corner, her fears were realised when she saw that the police had cordoned off the entire area.

Daisy's heart turned to stone as black smoke billowed skyward. The fractured vista consisted of glass, rubble, and crackling flames, pierced by the yells of firefighters battling to extinguish the fire. In her acute distress, Daisy pushed a policeman out of her way, screaming and shouting.

'My baby's in there! Please, please let me through.'

He firmly took hold of her arm and told her.

'No, Mam... I'm sorry, but it's not safe. You will have to wait until we get everything clear." Daisy stood there motionless with fear. Overwhelmed by shock and unable to shed a tear.

She was sure her daughter, a child conceived out of love, was probably dead.

The buildings on both sides still stood. One had a massive hole in its roof, and the windows were blown out. The façade of the other had vanished. You could see into the exposed sitting room and the upstairs bedroom, as the entire side of the house had been demolished, leaving a pile of rubble. Suddenly, it began to rain. The drops, darkened by the bombing, extinguished what remained of the flames. Daisy was rooted to the spot, soaked to the skin, shivering from the cold, and unable to move, paralysed by the fear that her baby girl was almost certainly dead; however, she was not going to give up hope of finding her daughter alive.

One of the volunteer wardens shouted to Daisy.

'Okay, miss, you can pass through now, but mind where you walk. It's still unsafe in parts.' Then, gently placing his hand on Daisy's shoulder, he confided,

'I'm sorry, but there is nothing that can be salvaged since the fire destroyed what little remained after the bomb struck.'

Daisy barely heard him as she stumbled over debris and shattered glass. She tripped over a splintered chair when she heard someone call her name.

'DAISY- DAISY!'

Looking up, she was relieved to see her friend walking over the ruins toward her.

'Susan... Thank God you're alive. B-but the..." Daisy was shaking so hard that she could hardly get her words out. Tears were tumbling down her cheeks. Her voice – nothing but a whisper. 'Oh my God! The children! Where are the children? Please tell me...'

Susan stumbled through the wreckage to reach her friend and hugged her tightly.

'They're safe and unharmed. Eunice, at number sixty-three, is taking care of them. If it were not for the Morrison Shelter, none of us would have survived!'

Daisy broke down, sobbing uncontrollably. Her baby was alive.

1947

Daisy was happy working at the Theatre for ENSA, remaining until it disbanded in 1946 when CSE Forces Entertainment took it over. Despite the devastation in the City of London, she relished the excitement and camaraderie of the war years. Civilians and soldiers alike sought to cope with the fear and monotony of a prolonged battle. Poignant bonds were essential for people to maintain if they were to feel a sense of safety amid chaos, and numerous organisations were established to foster connections of emotion and intellect during that time. Every day, life continued, even amid the madness. People were acutely aware of the need to preserve the ordinary pleasures of daily existence, even as the relentless march of the war's shocking events intruded.

Daisy met with Stéphane whenever an opportunity arose for him to slip away from home. He was purportedly estranged from his wife, Helen Royer, yet they continued to share their East Acton home. He always insisted that he and Daisy take a bus to Hyde Park, as it was far enough away from his home for him not to be recognised. Their time together was becoming increasingly infrequent. Eventually, one day, Stéphane contacted Daisy to tell her he could no longer see her, as he felt it necessary to maintain his reputation. He provided Daisy with details of his bank, assuring her that she could always contact him through the manager.

Maddie had recently turned three, and like countless unattached women in the immediate post-war period, Daisy appreciated the company of many American soldiers. They offered respite from the privations of that time. She had a brief engagement with an American lieutenant. However, as time passed, she felt the need to start anew and seek work elsewhere.

The time came when she felt anxious to reconnect with her father, as she had never told him he was a grandfather and felt guilty that he would never know about many of the most precious moments in his granddaughter's life.

She called her father one evening after returning from work.

'Hello Papa_'

'Daisy… Is that you, Daisy?'

'Yes, Papa… I'm so sorry that I haven't been in touch for a while; I…" Her voice trailed off.

'My dear child, when are you coming to see me? You seldom write. I have been so worried about you.'

Daisy reassured him:

Everything is fine, Papa. I've left my job in London and thought I might come and spend some time with you and, hopefully, find work while I'm there. Is Mama keeping busy with all her highfalutin friends? Hopefully, she will be happy to have me home for a while?

'My darling daughter, don't worry about that now, just let me know when you are coming to see me. It's been so long since you visited, and I miss you dearly.'

Daisy noted that his voice held a tinge of sadness and was worried that all was not well.

'I'll phone you again in a couple of days, Papa. I must hang up now because I'm using someone else's phone. I love you and will see you very soon.'

Jimmie offered to collect her from the station, but Daisy insisted on taking a taxi because she was unsure which train to take. She also thought it would be wiser to be greeted at the family home rather than in public—she anticipated her father's shock upon seeing his daughter accompanied by a young child.

When Daisy arrived at Manchester Central Station, she hailed a cab to continue her journey. Daisy glanced nervously at Maddie as they drove up the long driveway toward her father's magnificent Georgian house.

'You be a good little girl for mummy and give your grandpop one of your BIG hugs.' Maddie twisted a strand of hair in her chubby fingers and chewed on the end.

'Mama.' Daisy took her daughter's hand, brushing the hair from her mouth. 'Don't do that, sweetheart.'

As they exited the cab, Daisy bent down to smooth the skirt of her daughter's dress and adjusted the ribbon that held the child's beautiful blonde curls. She took Maddie by the hand and almost ran toward her beloved father, who was making his way along the driveway.

Despite being amazed to see a child holding his daughter's hand, Jimmie instantly recognised that the beautiful, chubby little girl was his granddaughter.

'Daisy, my darling daughter…'

'Papa…before you say anything…I, I…'

He took her in his arms, hugging her closely with relief. Daisy clung to her beloved father's warm embrace. She realised he was overwhelmed with joy rather than anger, as she had feared.

'Come now. We have been standing outside long enough, and I'm sure you're both hungry, so I've asked Pearl, my housekeeper, to prepare a light meal for us. There is so much news for us to catch up on!'

As her father took hold of his granddaughter's little hand, Daisy stood watching them, tears of happiness filling her eyes. She realised that she should not have waited so long. Reflecting on the precious years with her daughter, which circumstances and guilt had taken from him.

Jimmie was happier than he had been in a very long time and found it hard to believe that this chubby little girl with big blue eyes was the grandchild he had longed for so long.

After enjoying lunch and putting her daughter to rest, Daisy and her father sat on the sofa in the lounge. They both still felt emotional and had much they wanted to say to each other. Her father spoke first:

'I don't wish to be called granddad or grandfather – it makes me feel very old. Would you allow her to call me Jimmie, please?'

Daisy smiled, took his hand and nodded.

'Of course she can.' Then she asked: 'Papa, where is Mama today? Has she gone to one of her luncheons?'

Jimmie's shoulders slumped, his eyes downcast as he struggled to find the needed words.

'She's moved away, gone to live with your brother.'

Daisy frowned with consternation.

'Gone where?' Although Daisy knew her parents hadn't been getting along for many years, she could not believe that her mother would walk out like this, leaving her father to fend for himself. 'But why, Papa? Why?'

He took her hand in his and said:

'My darling, please just leave it be. It was for the best. Maybe one day we can speak about it, but for now… let's enjoy our time together.'

Daisy hugged her father, telling him she loved the idea of extending her visit so he and Maddie could get to know one another. He was delighted and told Daisy she could stay as long as she wished.

It was a wonderful time for them all, especially Maddie, who became a constant companion at her grandfather's side. Daisy reflected joyfully on the adventures Maddie was sharing with her grandfather.

In one of the large fields, there was a pretty pond where watercress grew. Daisy remembered collecting it as a child and putting it between two slices of fresh bread. The stables at the top of another long driveway winding up past the gatehouse housed two horses when they were not out in the field: Chorister, a beautiful Cleveland Bay that Jimmie rode when out hunting, and Kitty, a Welsh Mountain pony he bought so that he could spend time teaching his granddaughter to ride.

For several months, Maddie spent time with her grandfather, watching him groom the horses. She chatted away and repeatedly asked when he would take her for a ride. Each morning, as he saddled the pony, Maddie sat hunched on the ground, watching and hoping this would be the one.

One day, after Jimmie groomed the horse and saddled it, he told her that she was going to have her first lesson. She instantly sprang to her feet and began jumping up and down excitedly until her grandfather reminded her to be careful not to frighten the horses. Scooping her into his arms, he gently lifted her onto the saddle. Maddie squealed in delight! Grasping the reins in her little chubby hands, her grandfather led her around the field. When Daisy called them in for lunch, Maddie clung tightly to the horse's mane and refused to get down until Jimmie promised she could ride him again the following day.

Daisy watched in wonder at the attachment that had grown between the two, but she knew that she could no longer delay a visit to her mother. Although she was not looking forward to it, as they had never shared a close or loving relationship, her sense of obligation and family duty prevailed.

When she called the number her father had given, her brother Ken answered and informed Daisy that they now lived in Devon, where he and their mother had purchased a large country house hotel. Daisy was astonished that they had managed to obtain the funds to buy such a property.

'You have bought *what*? Where did you get the money to buy such a large place?'

Ken chuckled in reply.

'Mother was able to extort it from father after they parted. She told me she had convinced him that she had to keep up appearances and was entitled to continue leading the life she was accustomed to.'

Daisy gasped.

'Mother almost sent him bankrupt twice with her constant demands for the best of everything. What about poor Papa? Don't you have any feelings for him?'

She interrogated her brother, wanting to understand what had happened between their parents. Ken told her that, as far as he knew, an estrangement had arisen when the uncles and aunts whispered behind closed doors and fell silent immediately whenever anyone entered the room.

Daisy slammed the phone down on her brother, but not before telling him she had planned to drive to Devon to see them.

Two days before she was due to leave her father, he presented her with a car.

'It's not new, but it's reliable and will last a long time if you take care of it. You can't keep travelling on trains and buses, carrying all your possessions *and* a young child.'

His generosity deeply moved Daisy.

'Thank you, Papa. Thank you so much for the car and for being so understanding. I should have brought Maddie to see you sooner, but I was worried you'd disown me!'

Her father hugged her close.

'I wish you well with your mother and hope she doesn't cause too much fuss learning she has a granddaughter, especially since she knew nothing about her until now! We all know what she can be like. She won't be pleased. But her main concern will be whether her posh friends learn that her daughter has had a child out of wedlock. She would be aghast if anything were to taint her reputation.'

'I know,' sighed Daisy. 'That is why I'm dreading this visit, but it would be even worse if she found out from someone else. I'm sure you'll agree?'

'Don't fret, dear child,' her father reassured her. 'I'm sure everything will be ok in the end. I love you dearly, and you have given me a wonderful gift in Maddie. I will always be here for you and my beautiful granddaughter.'

After loading the car with their possessions and safely stowing the food and drink for the journey in the boot, Daisy was ready for the long journey ahead. Jimmie had no idea how long it would be before he saw them again or where his daughter's travels would take her and Maddie. He was concerned for her and imagined a long and bumpy road ahead.

It was already getting late when Daisy drove around the circular driveway leading to the front entrance of her mother's new home, a magnificent three-story building. She was about to leave the car when she saw a smartly dressed man emerging from the front door in a fashionable navy-blue uniform. Daisy watched him move swiftly down the steps toward her car and open the door for her.

As she alighted, he tipped his hand to the brim of his cap.

'Welcome, Miss Daisy. Alfred at your service. I will accompany you to the drawing room, where your mother and Mr. McConnell await you.

'Thank you so much, Alfred. I appreciate your help, but prefer to make my way.'

'Very well, Miss. I will ensure that your luggage is taken to your room.'

Daisy thanked him with a smile and helped Maddie out of the passenger seat. She paused to straighten her clothes, hoping they would make a good impression on her mother's critical eye. At that moment, her brother Ken bounded down the steps, arms outstretched, ready to welcome his sister.

And then he pulled back suddenly with a look of utter shock.

'What… Who the dickens is THAT?' he exclaimed.

'This is my daughter. Maddie, say hello to your Uncle Ken, sweetheart.'

Ken looked horrified.

'Oh, my God! What on earth is Mama going to say? Why haven't you told us before? Does father know?'

Ignoring him, Daisy scooped Maddie into her arms and followed Ken as he ran up the steps, taking two at a time and quickly making his way to the sitting room, where his mother sat, absorbed in tatting lace.

'Mummy, there is_'

Daisy had reached the doorway.

'Hello, Mummy,' she said.

As Daisy had foreseen, her mother was furious.

'You bring shame to the family. You and your father are both a disgrace.'

Daisy was astonished and confused by her mother's outburst.

'My Father! What do you mean? Why do you say this about him?'

Her mother did not reply, turned her back on her children and grandchild, and strode out of the room, slamming the door behind her. The subject was not broached again.

As her savings had diminished, Daisy needed to find work as soon as possible. She asked her mother if they could stay for a while. Jeannie agreed, stressing that it would only be temporary, to which Daisy was more than happy to agree, especially since she knew it would not be long before they were at each other's throats!

Maddie loved the long, curved staircase leading up to the bedrooms and was often caught sliding down the bannister, usually landing with a thump at the bottom. Occasionally, the butler would be there to break her fall, but if her grandmother were around, they would both receive a stern telling off.

Most mornings, Uncle Ken would let Maddie call the residents to breakfast by striking the large brass gong with a wooden stick covered in cotton to muffle the sound. Maddie had a spacious bedroom with a large bed all to herself. She loved the soft Eiderdown pillows and the lovely warm blankets that enveloped her as she snuggled down under them. Opposite her bed was a large bay window with a padded seat adorned with cushions. She loved sitting there and watching the parachutes slowly drifting into view as they landed at the nearby Chivenor airfield. She would wait for the chutes to unfold and would laugh when they burst open, floating like feathers as they descended to the ground.

One morning, while Daisy was walking to the village to buy some cigarettes from the little local store, she stopped to talk with two men working on the overhead telephone wires. The younger of the two slid down the telegraph pole, nimbly jumping the last four or five feet. They introduced themselves as Peter and Ron. Daisy liked the look of Ron, who seemed to be the younger of the two and was appraising her keenly. She thought he was quite handsome and had the most amazing light blue eyes. After chatting for a few minutes, Daisy continued on her way.

One sunny Sunday morning, Maddie, who had recently turned four, was pushing her legs backwards and forward on a swing that her uncle Ken had hung from one of the large trees on the front lawn. She rose higher and higher. Her mother was stretched out on the lawn, soaking up the early summer sun, when she heard the roar of a motorbike coming around the driveway. Then it stopped abruptly at the entrance of the hotel. Daisy quickly sat up and watched as a smartly dressed young man made his way over to her. When he was close enough, she recognised that it was Ron, one of the two men with whom she had spoken a few days earlier.

'Mmm, he certainly scrubs up well!' she thought.

Dressed smartly in tan trousers and a light blue open-neck shirt, his blonde hair slicked down with Brylcreem, she hadn't noticed how neatly built he was when she saw him before. He exhibited a slightly cocky attitude, as without saying a word, he eased himself onto the ground so close to Daisy that their thighs touched!

After chatting for a while, Daisy invited him into the guesthouse as it was nearly time for afternoon tea. As they made their way into the lobby, Jeannie emerged from the library and, upon seeing Daisy with Ron, bestowed upon him her darkest glare. Before Daisy could introduce him to her mother, she heard her sharp remark.

'Good afternoon, Ron. I see you have met my daughter, Daisy. Tell me, how is Rene? Is she well?'

Ron nodded.

'She is. Thank you, Mrs McConnell.' Then, with his arm around Daisy's waist, he guided her along the hallway to the drawing room.

'I see you know your way around here. And what was that all about?' Daisy asked. 'I wasn't aware you knew my mother. She didn't appear happy to see you here.'

Without answering her questions, Ron exclaimed:

'Wow! I didn't realise that old bat was your mother! I thought you were here for a holiday, not that you were related to her! I take it then that Ken is your brother?'

By now, Daisy was giggling, thinking it was funny that he referred to her mother as 'the old bat'!

'Yes, on both counts, but please don't hold that against me, as I hope I am nothing like my mother. Ken is fine on his own, but my mother controls his life pretty well, even though he is nearly thirty years old.'

The following evening, Ron invited Daisy to a small pub on the far side of town, where they stayed until closing time. They continued to meet regularly, often going to the cinema or racing around the countryside on his early model Triumph. They quickly became ardent lovers.

Jeannie was displeased with Ron, especially knowing he was engaged to Rene, who lived in the next village. She was appalled at how Daisy flaunted herself without considering the impact of her behaviour on Rene. Jeannie also felt aggrieved by Ron's duplicity and believed that he wouldn't be dating Daisy if he loved Rene.

Eventually, Ron broke up with Rene, telling her that he and Daisy were getting married. Subsequently, they married quietly in the local Registry Office, with two of Ron's friends as witnesses. Their relationship was passionate but extremely volatile. When they weren't making love, they were fighting violently. Therefore, the marriage didn't last, and in less than a year, they had parted ways, allowing Ron to resume his relationship with Rene.

Daisy and Maddie moved away, and many years passed before Daisy and Ron crossed paths again.

Daisy secured a live-in position shortly after in a small village near Banbury. She lived in the central part of the house with her new employer, Mrs. Clarke. Inside, a narrow stairway led from the kitchen down to a small flat where the O'Donovans lived with their twenty-seven-year-old son, Bernard. Mrs. O'Donovan assisted Daisy with the housekeeping while her husband and son worked in the extensive grounds, tending to the stables where the horses were housed.

Mrs. Clark was part of the local hunting fraternity. The hunters usually met in the large courtyard surrounding the house. The riders wore tailored red coats, white pants, and black equestrian boots, mounted on impeccably groomed quarter horses and thoroughbreds. The morning always started with a traditional stirrup cup toast of port, so named because riders drank the toast while in their stirrups as they prepared for the long day ahead. The hounds dashed around the horses with their noses to the ground, hoping to pick up a scent and waiting impatiently to start. Occasionally, one or two would stray from the pack, eager to explore the rest of the yard, but the Master of the hounds would crack his whip, commanding them to return.

Maddie loved observing the horses, their ears perked in anticipation, as they snorted and danced from side to side. Everyone waited excitedly for the call of the Hunter's Horn telling them to be off for the hunt.

Maddie spent many hours in the stables, engulfed in the bittersweet smell of hay, horse sweat, and steamy manure. She spoke to the horses as she blew ever so softly into their nostrils, attempting to mimic their gentle neighing. Often, the son or the father would come into the stalls, linger for a while, and encourage her to stay. Maddie felt wary of their approaches and didn't particularly like their attempts to fondle and touch her. It felt wrong, so she stopped visiting the stables. She was warned she had to keep their secret or she would get into a lot of trouble if anyone found out she had been a very naughty girl.

Daisy and Maddie had been there for just over a year when, early one morning, Maddie was awakened from a deep sleep by the sound of people shouting. She got up, straining to hear where

the noise was coming from. She tiptoed out onto the landing, crouched next to the wooden balustrade, and peered through the gaps. She tried to listen to the quarrel; she didn't understand why, but heard, *'Conor'*, which she knew was Mr. O'Donovan's name, then, *'sordid affair...'*
Maddie was about to return to her bed when she overheard Mrs. Clark telling her mother that she could no longer stay and had three weeks to find another position. Maddie had witnessed enough to understand they would soon be moving again.

Every week, Daisy bought a magazine called 'The Lady', which featured everything from fashion and fiction to music and biographies, along with the Domestic Service pages. She started scanning the job listings and sent off several handwritten applications. She didn't have to wait long before she received a reply. It was postmarked Stratford-upon-Avon and came from a widower asking her to attend an interview at her earliest convenience. Shortly thereafter, Daisy received a letter informing her that she had been selected as the successful applicant. The letter summarised some of her employment conditions.

Holidays – 3 weeks in the year. Time off – two half days a week (one fixed and one by arrangement to suit myself) other than the weekdays, unless by special arrangement. A car is available and usually at your disposal if you are a competent driver. All food for yourself and one child can be taken in the house and a studio flat at your disposal. Laundry sent out. Commencing salary £150 per year, less insurance.

Mr. Thompson lived with his teenage son in a lovely fourteenth-century thatched house in a picturesque village, just a short distance from the town. Daisy was delighted when shown their accommodation, which was accessed by a gate at the end of a large, picturesque garden. The open living and dining room was spacious, featuring two small bedrooms, a small kitchen, and a bathroom, all of which led off the main room. In the courtyard, there was a garage next to the building, where a new Morris Traveller was kept for Daisy's use.

Mr. Thompson's wife had died at the age of thirty-five when their son Anthony was just nine years old. Since then, he had employed a housekeeper to care for them. Daisy found him pleasant, rather handsome, tall, physically fit, and well-groomed. The man had a certain presence about him.

There were several large, thatched houses similar to Mr Thompson's home, all with beautifully manicured gardens. It was a five-minute walk from their apartment to the local primary school and St Andrew's Church and vicarage. Around the corner from the school, a long row of early-century council houses flanked a high archway, where many years ago, stagecoaches drove through into a courtyard. The horsemen would leave their horses to recover after the long journey and make their way across the road to the Bell Inn. After devouring a hearty meal and a few ales, the men would collect their steeds and continue on their journey.

After passing her Eleven Plus exam, Maddie graduated to the local Grammar School, a short walk across the fields from where she lived. Still with a marked stammer, her mother was concerned, so she sought guidance from the school. The name of a speech therapist in the town was recommended for Maddie, who struggled with the sessions during which she had to *'hissss'* like a snake and talk funnily while she was trying to make the complex syllables sound soft. After several weeks, it was reported to Daisy that Maddie had not improved with the therapy. Daisy was advised to seek help elsewhere.

Subsequently, Maddie was sent to a hypnotist. After one session, he told Daisy that her daughter was unresponsive and unwilling to enter a state of hypnosis. Daisy, feeling frustrated, asked Maddie why she wouldn't let him help her.

'Don't you want to be able to speak like your friends?'

Maddie responded, tears streaming down her face:

'I tried, mum. I did try. The therapist said he was going to put me into a deep sleep, that I was to close my eyes and think of nothing other than walking down a lot of steps as I counted backwards from 100… I was still awake when I got to the bottom!'

Nothing more was said. Daisy tried to be patient as Maddie stumbled over her words, but it only irritated her. She didn't have the time or the patience to understand or empathise with the challenges posed by her daughter's speech impediment.

Maddie spent much of her school holidays with her grandfather, riding together over the downs and helping him weed the large garden. Jimmie had a gardener since the grounds were too expansive for him to manage alone, but he loved to potter, enjoying Maddie's company as she sat making long chains with the daisies. He was devoted to his granddaughter and always made sure that she was attired in beautiful dresses and the best shoes.

In June 1953, Maddie was staying with her grandfather as the schools were closed to celebrate the Queen's Coronation. True to British weather, it was pouring with rain. Nevertheless, the London crowds refused to be dispirited by the inclement conditions. Many of the well-wishers had spent the previous night huddled on the crowded pavements, excited to witness the special occasion. For the first time, the ordinary people of Britain could watch the monarch's coronation in their own homes. Sales of television sets had skyrocketed after it was announced earlier in the year that the crowning of the Queen would be televised. People across the country planned parties in the decorated streets of their towns and cities. In London, the roads were packed with people waiting to witness the processions.

On June 2nd, 1953, Maddie sat with her grandfather, watching the coronation of Queen Elizabeth II on television. Maddie knew how much her grandfather loved the royal family; therefore, she was not surprised to see tears streaming down his face. Maddie perched herself on his knee and flung her arms around his neck to comfort him. Later, her mother explained to Maddie that her grandfather's tears were tears of happiness and a sign of Jimmie's love and respect for the royal family.

While Maddie was pleased to spend time on her own or meet up with her school friends, she often cycled into town and walked along the riverbank to see her friend Ted, the boatman. She adored that kind, elderly man, whose face was brown and crinkled from sitting outside in the sun during the summer months. The many tourists and locals who came to hire his little rowboats always found him sitting outside his shed on an old wooden bench, lazily puffing on his pipe. Ted greeted everyone with a kind word and a smile, doffing his battered peak cap to the ladies, grinning broadly and revealing the empty gaps between his teeth. He would sit with his pipe hanging from the corner of his mouth, holding it firmly between his teeth while sucking on the stem. Maddie loved to sit and watch as he cleaned it and filled it with tobacco from an old tin. Then, gently pushing with his finger to ensure that the shreds filled the bowl of the pipe, he struck a wooden match against the side of the box and lowered the flame onto the weed until it came to life. She watched as the wisps of smoke curled into the air. It was as if nothing else mattered to him except the pleasure derived from inhaling the gloriously addictive fragrance of the tobacco. She would sit and listen to the tales about 'the good old days' and the mischievous escapades he and his school buddies got up to and his life's journey before becoming a boatman.

When Ted was not busy, he allowed Maddie to take one of the rowing boats out onto the river, on the promise that she wouldn't tip it over and drown herself! It took her a while to master the oars, battling to turn the blades in the right direction and prevent the craft from going in circles. Once she eventually mastered the skill, she would glide down the river past the Royal Shakespeare Theatre and Holy Trinity Church, singing very loudly: *'Row, row, row your boat gently down the stream...'* On occasions, she took along a dog she had recently befriended.

Maddie's love for all animals led her to create a sanctuary; for her, it didn't matter that she couldn't speak like her friends. Her mother, Daisy, was never surprised to find an injured bird lying half-dead in a shoebox in their garage, with Maddie trying to pry its mouth open so she could feed it drops of water in hopes of keeping it alive and helping it fly home to its family. Sadly, most ended up dying.

One day, while visiting her friend Brenda, Maddie spotted a beautiful Boxer dog. She called to him, and he trotted over, wagging his little stumpy tail. Maddie thought he was very handsome, with his brindle coat and four white feet. Looking at the tag on his collar, she saw that his name was Socks. Being a very independent dog, he trotted off down the road. Maddie followed because she wanted to know where he lived and hoped that his owners might let her take him for a walk. Following her new friend down the road, she watched as he turned down the short lane next to her primary school. Maddie knew there was a large house at the end of the way because she had once wandered down there.

While Maddie stood, gathering her courage to approach the house, Socks made his way around the back. She walked slowly to the front door and gently tapped the brass knocker, hoping that someone was home. Feeling anxious, she began to chew on one of her nails.

What if she couldn't get her words out? What if they thought she was a simpleton because she couldn't speak properly!

She was about to turn around and leave when a young woman with a warm smile opened the door.

'Hello, my dear. And what can we do for you?'

Maddie struggled to get her words out:

'C-can I t-take your dog for a w-walk please?' She expected the kind lady to frown or show impatience, but she did neither. Then she called out:

'Socks! Where are you?' Then she tutted. 'He must still be getting out somewhere!'

Maddie indicated toward the back of the house.

'H-he went that w-way.'

Turning her attention back to Maddie, the kind lady gestured for her to come inside.

'Why don't you come in, young lady, and you can tell me who you are and where you live.'

Leading Maddie to the kitchen, she offered her a glass of lemonade and a piece of cake she had baked that very morning, waiting for someone to try.

Maddie didn't get to see Brenda as she spent the next few hours with her new friends, Maggie and her husband John, whom Maddie found very handsome. Before she set off, they told her not to leave it too late to visit them again and also said she could take Socks for a walk whenever she liked, since they rarely found the time to do so. Maddie told her mother about her new friends and mentioned that they would like to meet her sometime.

Barbara had told Maddie that she was thirty-two. Maddie also knew that their two children, whom she had not met on her first visit, were adopted. Bonny, the eldest, was three, and Adrian was just a few months old. John had a factory where he made candles for churches, and Maggie stayed at home to care for the children. When she was not playing with her friends, Maddie spent a lot of time with the family, took Socks on walks, and played ball with him in the large garden.

Maddie was pleased when her mother accepted the family's invitation for dinner. She didn't think Daisy had many friends and had never seen her enjoy the company of another woman, as she did with a man!

Maddie was in her first term at senior school when she convinced the local newsagent to give her a job delivering newspapers. She got up at five every morning, dressed quietly, and made her way down the stairs to avoid awakening her mother. She pedalled as fast as her legs could go to ride the couple of miles into town. After arriving at the newsagent, she would wait with the other girls and boys until the owner opened the shop and the papers, magazines, and comics arrived. They marked out their routes and loaded everything into satchels attached to the front of their bikes, and off they would ride.

During the winter, when Maddie's hands grew cold, she would put them in the bag with the papers to warm them. As soon as the papers were delivered, Maddie would ride back home as quickly as she could to eat breakfast before the ride to school. On Saturday mornings, after the deliveries were completed, everyone lined up to receive their six shillings and six pence for the week.

As an adolescent, Maddie spent many hours waiting patiently outside the stage door of the Royal Shakespeare Theatre, collecting autographs as the actors came and went. Sometimes, they would stop to chat and give her a few coins to buy an ice cream or a cool drink. Perhaps they just wanted to get rid of her?

Every Saturday, Maddie and her friends queued outside the cinema, eagerly waiting to hand over their sixpences, after which they would make a mad dash to find seats. Their favourite shows were Laurel and Hardy, Abbott and Costello, and Charlie Chaplin, followed by the Pathé news. These preceded the serial, which always ended with a cliffhanger, enticing them to return the following week. During the intermissions, everyone scrambled up the aisle to the lady with the tray of lollies and ice cream. Tuppence was spent on an ice cream in a tub with a little wooden spoon. At the end of the matinee, everyone was required to stand as the National Anthem was performed.

Mr. Thompson and Daisy shared a symbiotic relationship. They constantly argued, and she often threatened to leave, which prompted him to beg her to stay. She was an excellent cook, took great care of the house, and anticipated Mr. Thompson's needs. She knew she was lucky to live in a comfortable home and was aware that it would not be easy to find another position where her teenage daughter would be welcomed.

Mr. Thompson purchased a large dairy farm. The old farmhouse was demolished, and a grand house was built in its place. At the beginning of 1956, the family, Daisy and Maddie, moved from Shottery to the farm in Alveston. Mr. Thompson had one of the old barns, which overlooked the main house and gardens, converted into a very cosy cottage for Daisy and Maddie.

1957

While Daisy was becoming increasingly unsettled with her life working and living in other people's houses, cooking, cleaning, and attending to their needs daily, Maddie was happier than she had ever been.

Maddie and her friend Rodney, who lived on the farm next door with his family, spent many hours together after school and on weekends. They rode their bikes on outings and usually took a picnic basket prepared by her mother. Rodney balanced it on a small wire frame at the back of his bike seat.

It was the last day of the school term, and the bus had just dropped them off at the bottom of Rodney's driveway. Both of their satchels were heavy, as they had to empty their desks of all their books. Rodney and Maddie sat on the wall to chat before making their way home up their long driveways. The two farms sat side by side, each with a long, meandering driveway. Maddie entered through the back door, which led into the kitchen, and immediately noticed that her mother was in one of her moods. Daisy was slamming cupboard doors and yanking open the fridge door, practically throwing the vegetables onto the kitchen table.

'Hi Mum. I'm home.'

'I can see that,' she retorted. 'Where have you been, Maddie? You know I worry if you're late. You must learn to be punctual.'

Maddie struggled to hold back her tears as she fumbled to get her words out.

'We were just t-talking. I'm s-sorry, mummy. I h-honestly forgot the time. Our s-satchels were heavy, so we sat on the fence for a while.' She could not understand why her mother was so angry. 'W-what's wrong, Mummy? Has Mr Thompson been upsetting you again?'

'It's okay, Maddie. Please, don't cry. I'm sorry I snapped at you. Mr. Thompson phoned about an hour ago and said he was bringing home guests.' Her chest heaved, and she took a deep breath before continuing. 'He thinks I can conjure up a meal out of nothing. The grocer has not delivered what I ordered, and I've not been able to go to town.'

'Can I help, Mummy? I could chop some of the vegetables and set the table. That will save you some time.'

Daisy graciously accepted her offer. Tenderly placing her hand on her daughter's shoulder, she said:

'If we ask Ted nicely, I am sure he'll go to the village to shop for me.' She quickly scribbled a list of items she needed and passed the piece of paper to Maddie, gently ushering her towards the door. 'Hurry, Maddie. You'll find him in the kitchen garden digging some potatoes for tonight's dinner.'

As she ran to find Ted, Maddie let out a sigh of relief, grateful that her mother had brightened considerably.

Daisy frequently asked her daughter to lay the magnificent oak dining table, teaching her how to set the cutlery in the correct order, ensuring they were evenly spaced and not too far apart. Serviettes and side plates were always placed on the left-hand side of the table. Mr. Thompson often invited them to dine with him, as he remarked that it was depressing to eat alone. Maddie would have preferred to eat in the kitchen, as he always chastised her for pushing the meat around the plate, since she preferred the vegetables and potatoes swimming in gravy.

On a particularly cold and windy evening, Daisy and Maddie were snuggled up together on the sofa, reading their books, when Daisy broke the silence.

'Maddie,' she paused, hesitating.

'Yes, Mummy,' Maddie replied.

Daisy took a deep breath.

'How would you like to move to another country to start a new life?'

Maddie was at a loss for words in response to this unexpected proposition.

'Why, w-why would we go and live in another country, where would we go?' she stammered. 'Has Mr Thompson asked us to leave? Did you have another quarrel?'

Daisy shook her head.

'No, it is nothing like that...'

Maddie interrupted her.

'Aren't you happy here, Mummy? Is that why you want to leave?'

Daisy shrugged her shoulders in response. Maddie waited for her mother to share her thoughts, but her question was met with silence as Daisy sat watching the fire. She knew her mother well enough not to badger her, so she picked up The Colin Girls' Annual, which she had been browsing through, tucked her legs underneath herself, and continued to read. They sat side by side in silence, listening to the crackling logs, while Daisy watched the bright orange and yellow flames dancing in the fireplace. Now and again, Maddie glanced at her mother, wondering whether she would raise the subject again. Instead, Daisy barely moved, lost in deep thought, her eyebrows knit together in a furrowed brow.

Suddenly, Daisy turned toward her daughter and clutched her hand.

'I want us to have a place of our own and a proper job. Not one where we spend most of our time in someone else's house, seeing to their every whim. I have something to show you that I received from the Australian Consulate in London.'

Maddie stared at her mother in disbelief.

'AUSTRALIA!' She could hardly speak as she stumbled over every word. 'T-that is over the other s-side of the world. I might not be very good at geography, but I do know where it is. What about granddad? We will never see him again.' Maddie's eyes flashed. 'I'm not going. I won't leave him. And what about all my friends?' She started biting her lower lip as she tried hard to hold back her tears and refused to look at her mother.

Daisy stood up from the couch and wandered over to the little dining table in the corner of the sitting room. She retrieved her handbag from the chair and began rummaging inside. Eventually, she took out a large brown envelope and withdrew several sheets of paper before returning to where Maddie was hunched over on the couch.

'If you sit closer, I'll explain and show you what I have been sent, and then you will understand.'

Her mother explained that she had heard the Australian government was inviting people to travel there and felt this would be an excellent opportunity for them. She told Maddie that it would be an adventure: a fresh start. She went on to explain that Australia sought new and healthy citizens to migrate, specifically those who wished to become valuable members of Australian society. The Commonwealth Government offered to cover most of the travel costs. In return, new migrants would be expected to stay in Australia for at least two years and accept any jobs provided by the government.

Dismay and confusion consumed Maddie. She did not want to leave her beloved grandfather to travel thousands of miles to the other end of the world. Daisy acknowledged that it would be a massive change in their lives and that it would not be easy for her daughter. Even so, she was determined to embark on this new adventure. Her mind was made up.

'It's an opportunity for us to make a new life for ourselves, Maddie. We must give it a try, and if we don't like it, we can always return in a couple of years.'

Maddie scowled at her.

'Mother, I'm going to bed. I'm tired. Goodnight.'

'Don't forget to brush your teeth. I'll be up shortly,' replied Daisy.

After putting on her pyjamas, brushing her teeth, and drawing her bedroom curtains, Maddie snuggled into bed and stared at the ceiling. She was deep in thought, recollecting all the wonderful times she had spent with her adored grandfather. She cherished their relationship, and to her, he was the most wonderful person in the world. As his only grandchild, she knew he would be devastated if they had to live far away from each other. Maddie couldn't bear the thought of never seeing him again! She wept tears she had been holding back, remembering the times he had cared for her and how he would always let her cuddle up on his knee before bedtime. Jimmie would come to her room to tuck her in with his strong, beautifully manicured hands that reminded her of crispy chicken skin, wrinkled and brown from working in the garden. She shared his love of animals and affinity for humans, which provided her with a sanctuary —something her flighty mother was unable to give. Maddie was still staring at the ceiling, sleep eluding her as she reflected on all the wonderful memories of the times spent with her grandfather. Eventually, she drifted off into a deep sleep.

Daisy woke up early and made her way to the kitchen, where she brewed herself a cup of tea and took it back to her bed. Mr. Thompson, who often travelled abroad, was away in America. As it was Sunday, Daisy could enjoy a lazy day. She propped herself up on the pillows and got comfortable. She needed time to quietly read and absorb the information that had been sent from the immigration department. Daisy knew that the 'Ten Pound Pom Scheme' had been designed to substantially increase the population of Australia and supply workers for the country's booming industries. In return for subsidising the travel cost via ship, adult migrants were charged only £10 for the fare. Children travelled for free. The applicants had to be under the age of 45 and in good health. Daisy, at forty-three, just scraped in. The government promised employment opportunities, housing, and a generally brighter lifestyle. However, upon arrival, those who had not been sponsored were placed in basic hostels, as employment opportunities were not always readily available. They would be obliged to remain in Australia for two years, and if they chose to return before then, they were required to refund the cost of £120 for the assisted passage — an amount that most could not afford.

Later that morning, after completing the application forms, Daisy drove into town and posted them, along with a letter to a friend, Bernard, with whom she had shared a brief relationship before he left for Australia two years earlier. She hoped he might sponsor her. Bernard was the manager of a prestigious hotel in Perth and also owned a small café in Fremantle. Now, all she had to do was wait.

Daisy received a response within days, expressing that he looked forward to seeing her again and assuring her that he had a position for her at his café. He also hoped they could pick up where they had left off before he departed to live in Australia.

Meanwhile, Daisy continued to place bets on the Football Pools, which involved predicting the outcomes of high-level association football matches scheduled for the upcoming weeks. In 1957, Littlewoods began sending collectors door to door to collect everyone's money and, if they had been fortunate with their predictions, deliver their winnings. A couple of weeks later, a letter arrived announcing that Daisy had won £77. It was pure luck, as she knew nothing about the game of football. She had never possessed such a large sum of money, and she knew exactly how to spend it. Having accumulated two weeks of annual leave, she requested time off. She had not yet informed

Mr. Thomson of her migration plans, believing it best to wait until she was sure they had been accepted.

Two weeks later, Daisy and Maddie were packed and waiting for the coach to take them to the port of Dover and across the sea to Calais. It was very wet and gusty aboard the ferry transporting them across the English Channel to France. Conditions worsened halfway across when one of the stabilisers broke down. Many passengers began to panic; parents clutched their children as the ferry rolled from side to side, causing unsecured items to slide across the floor. Glasses belonging to the passengers smashed to the ground. The turbulence created havoc on board as the crew handed out bowls to those in need.

Daisy and Maddie sat with a finger in each ear, eyes tightly closed to avoid seeing or hearing those who were spewing their breakfast. The containers, now full of vomit, slid back and forth. The mess and stench were horrible. It didn't settle down until they were across the Channel and nearing the French harbour of Calais. The passengers were then transported by bus to the train station, where they had to wait for several hours before boarding the train to their final destination.

Upon arrival, Daisy and Maddie roamed the city of Paris, known as the centre of culture and art. Paris was full of life as the world's fashion capital and the hub of European social life. It was an all-encompassing city offering something for every visitor. The Eiffel Tower and the Arc de Triomphe were must-see attractions for them, along with the Louvre, where they saw some of the world's most famous paintings, including the Mona Lisa, a portrait of Lisa Gherardini, the wife of Francesco del Giocondo. It was, and still is, the best-known, most visited, and parodied work of art in the world.

They had to wait for three hours until they boarded the train for their next destination, so Daisy suggested they go to a cinema. Maddie was bewildered.

'Why? I wouldn't be able to understand a word of what they are saying?'

'Not to watch a movie, Maddie, but to have a nap before continuing our journey to Port Bou. It's a long way and we won't arrive until late tonight.'

Once in the picture house, they soon fell soundly asleep. They were still in the land of nod when Daisy was awakened by one of the staff, who was urgently shaking her shoulders.

'He Toi. Allez image terminee.' He pointed to the exit. 'Le film a fini... vous devez partir maintenant.'

Daisy, fluent in French, realised that the movie had ended, and they needed to leave.

'Merci, merci, Monsieur. Merci.'

They were now wide awake and quickly made their way to the exit. Daisy glanced at her watch.

'Quick, quickly, Maddie, we must hurry, or else we will miss the train. Portbou was a sleepy little village in the Costa Brava, on the border of Spain and France. Like any other border village, it had a slightly more colourful history due to the presence of criminals and smugglers. Initially, the valley belonged to the monastery of Saint-Quirze-de-Prades. During the 18th century, the valley was incorporated into the population of what was then called Sant Miquel de Colera. In addition to the smugglers and criminals, there were also farmers, shepherds, and fishermen.

The 'Bonita Buhardilla, ' a small, family-owned guesthouse, was situated on the corner of a quirky little street. Next door, there was a small shop that sold many craft items made by the locals: wicker baskets spilling onto the narrow pavement, brightly coloured rugs, hats, postcards hanging on wire stands, and buckets and spades for the children.

It wasn't long before Maddie met Louis, a waiter at the nearby restaurant. When he wasn't working, they spent every moment together, and in no time, Maddie fell in love. They swam in the little coves, walked along the sand hand-in-hand, and gathered shells as they went. He spoke a bit of pidgin English that he had picked up from the many tourists, so they communicated either through words or by using hand gestures and body language.

Meanwhile, unsurprisingly, Daisy was having a discreet rendezvous, or, more to the point, a passionate encounter, with the chief of the Gendarmerie, Juan. Occasionally, when Louis was at work, Maddie would join them at one of the small beaches, where she would climb over the rocks and explore the nearby caves. When not swimming in the crystal-blue waters, Daisy and Juan lay together on the beach in the secluded cove, out of sight of prying eyes.

One afternoon, a week after their arrival, as they were all lying on the beach soaking up the sun, a small rowboat made its way towards the little cove. As it got closer, Maddie recognised the occupant as one of the local Guardia. He jumped out of the craft, grabbing hold of the rope attached to the bow, and pulled it up onto the sand. Juan jumped to his feet.

'Hey! Jose, welcome; come and join us.' Daisy welcomed him. 'Nice to see you again, Jose. This is my daughter, Maddie.'

After sitting and talking for a while, Daisy suggested:

'Jose, why don't you take Maddie out in the boat for a while and get to know one another?'

Maddie felt quite happy playing around the rocks and collecting shells, but she knew it would be considered rude if she didn't go. Jose was already making his way down to the boat, beckoning for Maddie to follow him. It wasn't until a giant octopus swam alongside the boat, squirting out a jet of black ink through its siphon, that she burst out laughing and began to relax and enjoy the excursion around the bay.

The day before they were due to return to England, Daisy told her daughter that she and Juan were in love. That when she and Maddie were settled in Australia, Juan planned to follow, and they would get married.

Maddie, while surprised by her mother's declaration, knew how easily she fell in and out of love with her suitors. However, this time Daisy sounded serious. She was aware of the time they had spent together, and it was the first time in ages that she had noticed her mother look so happy and relaxed.

That afternoon, Juan drove them to the cove in his fancy Pegaso sports car. When they arrived, he removed a picnic basket that he said had been prepared by his mother. Daisy carried it, while Juan and Maddie lugged rugs and a couple of sun umbrellas. José was already moored up and lying on the beach, waiting. He said it was the last day, so it had to be special, and there were things to discuss and hopefully celebrate.

While the mother and daughter spread the rugs on the sand, Juan and Jose unpacked the basket, which contained a feast of local meats, chorizos, thinly sliced Parma ham, small rolls of bread shaped like logs, local fruits, and a bottle of red wine with four glasses.

After everyone finished eating, Jose and Juan repacked the basket and returned it to the car. While they waited for them to finish, Daisy and Maddie sat in silence, each with their thoughts.

'Maddie.'

'Yes, mummy.'

Daisy fidgeted with her hands for several seconds.

'*What now!*' Maddie wondered.

'Darling, Jose wants to marry you.'

For a moment, Maddie was speechless, and then she started giggling, finding the suggestion preposterous. Daisy looked at her daughter, shrugged her shoulders, and suggested:

'You could become engaged now, and when he and Juan come to live in Australia, you could continue to see one another until you turn seventeen and are old enough to marry.'

'Mum... that's not funny.' Maddie looked at her mother and was appalled to realise that she was deadly serious. She was not larking around. 'What do you mean... marry me? He's years older than me; he's practically bald, old and overweight! You cannot be serious!' Maddie replied.

Not waiting for a response, Maddie grabbed her sandals, which she had taken off while paddling in the water. Without a backwards glance, she stormed off, climbed over the rocks, and headed back to the hotel. It was quite a while before Juan and her mother returned, by which time she had regained her composure. Neither mentioned the conversation again.

When they returned home, a letter from the immigration department was waiting, informing her mother that their application had been successful. They were instructed that they would need to sail from Tilbury in six weeks. It was dated 12th October, three days after they had left for Spain.

When Daisy mustered the courage to tell Mr. Thompson, he was furious. He told her that she should have informed him weeks earlier so that he could find a replacement. He argued that she was going to a primitive country filled with savages and uncouth people who lived in tin houses. In a state of desperation, he even asked Daisy to marry him so that she would stay on as his housekeeper.

Needless to say, Daisy declined his proposal!

Australia
1957 – 1960

Jimmie insisted on driving Daisy and his granddaughter to Tilbury docks, where they were to board the SS Arcadia for their journey to Australia. Quite understandably, he feared it would be the last time he would see them. Daisy glanced at her father but didn't know how to break the silence. Barely a word had been exchanged. Although Maddie was looking forward to the voyage ahead, the prospect of adventure was dulled by the sadness of never being able to see her beloved grandfather again.

On arrival, they were directed to the terminal and then ushered into a large shed where they joined the long queue of passengers waiting to be processed before embarking. Those who were not sailing went to the quayside to wave goodbye to family and friends, wishing them 'Bon voyage' on their travels across the oceans. With a heavy heart, Jimmie embraced his daughter and granddaughter. As Maddie felt the comfort of his arms hugging her tightly, neither spoke lest their tears flowed.

'I love you both more than you will ever know, my darling girls, and will always be here if you ever need me.' Maddie flung her arms around his waist and clung tightly, unwilling to let go. Gently prising himself apart from Maddie, Jimmie, his shoulders hunched, turned and strode out of the terminal without a backwards glance. Maddie vowed that one day she would return to England.

Once onboard the massive liner, Daisy and Maddie were shown to their accommodation, where they unpacked the two cases holding everything needed for the trip. Their compact cabin featured two single beds, a chest of drawers, and hanging space for their clothes. The rest of their luggage, including a large metal trunk and several tea chests containing all their possessions, had been collected a week before their departure and sent to the docks. There were restrictions on the amount they could take to their new home, forcing them to leave many belongings behind. After unpacking and organising everything, they left their suitcases for the steward to store for the duration of the journey.

Once everyone was on board, the Tannoy speakers boomed a message asking those not sailing on the ship to disembark immediately. Daisy and Maddie made their way up to the top deck and joined many other passengers, vying for space along the railings and scanning the crowds below for their loved ones. Maddie squeezed through the passengers, climbed onto the bars, and waved frantically, hoping that her grandfather might have been waiting to bid them farewell.

The SS Arcadia drifted away from the harbour as the brightly coloured streamers winged their way down towards the dock, everyone strained to catch hold of the ends before they floated to the ground. Many landed in the harbour, leaving a colourful patina of water. Thirty-nine days and eleven thousand miles at sea were ahead until they reached their destination.

The ship boasted four upper decks, a large swimming pool, playing courts for tennis and quoits on a games deck, as well as a large dining area, two bars, a grand hall, a writing room and a cinema. On most nights, dinner dances were offered for entertainment and variety shows were periodically staged. Daisy was amazed by the choice and quantity of food served to them. The post-war rations of London were replaced with sumptuous banquets and many exotic tropical fruits.

The SS Arcadia sailed through the recently opened Suez Canal. In 1956, an international crisis involving Britain, France, Egypt, and Israel enveloped the canal. Egypt seized it in July of that same year and kept it closed until March 1957, when political negotiations resulted in Egyptian control of the canal management.

At the first stop, Port Said, Maddie was watching from the ship as local youths in 'bum boats' were diving for the coins thrown by passengers. Then she and Daisy made their way ashore and ventured through the town where they were besieged by locals, all with something to sell or show, such as fez hats, fly-switches and postcards. There was also the Gully-Gully man, an itinerant conjurer with limited tricks. He followed them, chattering in different languages, hoping to gain their attention.

Departing Port Said, the ship sailed through the canal and on to the Yemeni port of Aden. Aden appeared as a parched rock with no trace of green in sight. Some braver passengers took a taxi from the city to nearby villages, where crowds of poor children begging for alms surrounded them. The heat was thick and sticky, yet bearable. It was also a place where passengers could purchase affordable consumer goods from around the world, or items made by the local tourist industry, such as sand-stuffed rag dolls or leather wallets featuring ancient Egyptian motifs. Another day of blazing heat followed.

After some weeks at sea, the ship docked in Bombay, a city of both Eastern and Western architecture. Dense crowds and people were scurrying everywhere. Snake charmers paraded with half-dead snakes. Maddie found it relieving to return to the ship.

Colombo, a beautiful harbour with a smell of spices, was the last stop before reaching Australia. There were celebrations when the ship crossed the Equator, accompanied by the obligatory mock ceremony performed by the crew. Maddie joined the fun, taking her turn on the slippery pole stretched across the pool. Contestants tried to push the other person off the pole into the water. Then everyone was given a certificate stating that, as a daughter of Neptune, they had been granted the Freedom of the Seas. The origins of this ceremony traced back to ancient times when mariners were very superstitious and made obsequious pleas to the God Neptune, the ruler of the seas, to bring them home safely.

After Colombo, the ship enjoyed a clear run to Fremantle, the port of Western Australia. By this time, the passengers had come to know each other quite well, with initial shyness and inhibitions dispelled, and many lasting friendships had formed. The day before reaching their destination, all cases were returned to the cabins and repacked. Labels were attached to them, and later, the suitcases were placed outside the cabin doors for collection.

Daisy and Maddie were among the first up on deck. They were far too excited to eat breakfast.

Venturing out on deck, they stepped into the intense sunshine and were amazed to see such a small area of land, just a stretch of beach with no trees in sight. Someone mentioned that they thought it was called Rottnest Island. They didn't have to wait long before rounding the island from the north to see the coast again, gazing through the heat haze at the houses and pine trees.

Everyone cheered as the ship sailed past the end of the island. A few minutes later, the port of Fremantle came into view.

'So this is Australia!' Daisy's heart sank, shocked by the town's drab appearance. Tanks, cranes, gantries, and various painted signs filled the area. Behind the Customs sheds stood three enormous storehouses: Dalgety's and Elder Smith.

After the Arcadia docked at the pier, passengers waited anxiously for the loudspeaker to announce their disembarkation. Looking down at the dock, they saw a group of men gathered on the quayside, all wearing shorts and blue singlets and carrying Gladstone bags. One of the stewards told the passengers that they were 'wharfies' and provided a brief history of Fremantle, stating that until recent years, the town had been considered Australia's roughest port town.

An incredible amount of activity unfolded, with immigration officials, customs officers, employment officers, photographers, and baggage agents all hustling to perform their duties, not to mention the scores of relatives awaiting them. Once down the gangway, everyone was guided toward one of the large sheds, where they were sorted into groups, such as sponsors, hostels, or employers, and then directed to another area for processing by State Immigration officers. A liaison officer assisted the passengers in sorting their luggage. Everything they possessed in the hold was to be forwarded later. Those without savings were sent to be housed in Nissen huts, former Army barracks. Those who hadn't been sponsored were placed in basic migrant hostels and, disappointingly, found that the expected job opportunities were not always available.

When they had embarked at Tilbury, everyone was assisted with their cases. However, in Fremantle, they were left to struggle on their own. Maddie began to drag her luggage when a strapping young man approached them and hoisted Maddie's case onto his shoulders. He then seized Daisy's case and ushered them as far as the Customs area – the last stop before exiting the terminal. Daisy thanked him and apologised profusely since she had no local currency and could not tip him. Instead, she offered him some English coins, but he just smiled…

'A pleasure, Mam. I hope everything works out for you and the young'un.' When he was out of earshot, Daisy voiced what Maddie was thinking:

'If all Aussie men are like him, I will be very happy here!'

At last, they exited the customs and were greeted by the Fremantle Port Authority hostesses dressed in immaculate red and white uniforms. Their role was to assist both passengers and visitors alike. Daisy anxiously looked around the large shed, hoping that Bernard hadn't forgotten them. She was about to seek assistance from a hostess when she spied Bernard entering the large double doors into the terminus. Daisy grabbed hold of her daughter's hand and started pulling her along.

'Maddie, hurry up,' she implored.

By the time Maddie had caught up with her mother, Daisy and Bernard had already greeted one another. Daisy introduced her daughter, and they all exited the terminus into the glorious spring sunshine. Bernard had taken the large suitcase from Maddie and was now leading them the short distance along the pier towards his parked car.

While making their way into Fremantle, Bernard provided them with a brief history, confirming that it had once been Australia's roughest port town but had reinvented itself since the early 1950s with the arrival of European immigrants. They passed buildings constructed to accommodate the influx of newcomers.

Driving out of the harbour, Bernard pointed out many well-preserved convict-built colonial-era buildings of architectural heritage, along with an old jetty. Maddie was intrigued by the exterior of a small store, which featured a large sign: *"The First and Last Shop in Australia."* The windows displayed packets of Cadbury's and Fry's, kangaroo pelts, Aboriginal weapons from the Northwest, and some trifling souvenirs made of mulga, a hardwood found in small trees or shrubs in the dry regions of Australia.

It was nearing midday, and their stomachs were rumbling, having skipped breakfast. Bernard suggested they visit his little teashop for brunch. After parking the car in a side street, they walked the short distance to the shopping precinct, which was bustling with shoppers and workers on their lunch breaks. Although the café had only a small frontage, it stood out from all the other buildings with its bright red and white chequered gingham curtains hanging in the window. As Bernard opened the door, a tinkling sound came from the overhead brass bell. He stood to one side and motioned for Daisy and Maddie to enter the tea shop. As soon as they entered the small room, Maddie pointed out the eight small round tables, each adorned with a large red and white chequered cloth and fresh flowers.

'Look, Mummy, it is beautiful, just like a small English teashop'.

Agreeing, Daisy replied, 'It is, darling. What a lovely place! And to think that I will be working here.'

Bernard went to the long counter on the other side of the room, where sandwiches, cakes, and scones were arranged under glass domes. A heated server displayed an excellent selection of homemade pasties, meat pies, and sausage rolls. He assured them that the delicacies were freshly baked the same day. Daisy, always careful to maintain her slender figure, chose a chicken and salad sandwich, while Maddie's eyes were drawn to the meat pies. Bernard directed them towards a table.

'Sit and relax for a while. Sylvia will bring your food shortly. I've asked her to brew a large pot of tea to wash it all down.'

Before leaving the café, Bernard introduced Daisy to the staff, who had been informed that she would soon join them. After chatting briefly, the trio exited the shop and returned to the car. Twenty minutes later, they arrived at their new home in Bicton.

While Bernard showed Daisy around the house, Maddie went outside onto the veranda at the back of the house, which was built on stilts. As it was elevated, she could see through the tops of the trees and caught a glimpse of the Swan River in the distance. She ran down the wooden steps that led to an area of flowering bushes and gum trees adorned with pretty red flowers. A flock of noisy pink and grey birds were perching on the branches. She strolled around the corner of the house, joining a short pathway that led from the back door, and came across an old, corrugated shed that she assumed was used for storing garden tools or something similar. She pushed at the rickety door suspended on a single hinge, allowing just enough room to peek through.

Inside, there was a four-foot drum against the back wall, with a wide plank on top extending to the sides of the shed. In the centre of it, over the top of the drum, was a large hole, alongside squares of newspaper. Slowly pushing the door open until she could squeeze inside, she then looked down into the hole and discovered a deep drop. Maddie wrinkled her nose at the disgusting smell.

'Ugh!'

She made a quick retreat back to the house. When she shared what she had seen, Bernard laughed and told her that this was their toilet, usually called a 'dunny' or 'longdrop'. He added that they would all be using it, as they lived in an unsewered area. Maddie asked why it was such a long way from the house, and he explained that it was due to the smell. When the hole filled up, it would be moved to another area in the backyard.

Early one morning, when Maddie was perched on the edge of the toilet seat, trying to ignore the creepy crawlies running around her feet, she heard a scraping noise that seemed to be coming from behind her. She was too scared to turn and see what had made the noise, but eventually, plucking up courage, she turned and looked towards the back wall, where she saw a grey, scaly head poking through a hole, staring at her, all the while flicking a black tongue in and out of its mouth. She froze, too scared to move in case it moved. The creature squeezed its long, stubby body further into the dunny until it almost touched her feet. Maddie screamed! Shaking in terror, she slowly edged herself off the seat while frantically tugging at her pants. Then, she kicked open the rickety door, which nearly came off its hinges. She stumbled out of the shack and ran back to the house as fast as she could, shouting as she went.

'Th-th- th-there's a b-b-b-baby c-c-c-c- crocodile in th- th-the toilet!' Bernard and Daisy rushed outside to see what all the commotion was about. Her mother feared the worst, as she knew that Australia was inundated with snakes, spiders, and many other venomous creatures. After Maddie had calmed down, Bernard reassured her that it was not a crocodile but a harmless Bobtail Goanna that seemed aggressive because it hissed with its mouth open, displaying a blue tongue.

Although there were only a few months until the end of the term and the start of the summer holidays, Daisy felt it essential to enrol her daughter in the local high school. Maddie's first day was horrendous as she encountered the boys ogling her in the skirt and twin set that her mother had laid out for her to wear, accentuating her pert bosom and hourglass figure. The girls were fascinated by her very proper English pronunciation. On the other hand, Daisy soon became unhappy working at the café —she hadn't expected to serve customers or help in the kitchen. Bernard insisted it was part of her job and told her that, being a small enterprise, they all had to work together. Daisy needed to find a job quickly to enable them to stay. Every day, she scanned the newspapers, hoping something suitable would come up.

It wasn't long before Daisy and Bernard realised that they were too set in their ways. Therefore, they decided it would be better for Daisy and her daughter to move into their own home. Bernard took them to see a block of four flats on the outskirts of the city. One had recently been vacated and, although not large, it was fully furnished and comfortable. It was located at the front of the building and contained one bedroom, a bed-sitting room, a small kitchen, a bathroom, and an enclosed sleep-out. They secured tenancy and moved in the following week.

Daisy applied for several secretarial positions, and it was not long before she secured a role with an ear, nose, and throat specialist of Russian descent, Dr. Avrum Einihovici. He and his wife arrived in Australia five years ago. He was a kind gentleman, small in stature, with a big heart. Now earning a decent wage, Daisy enrolled her daughter at the City Commercial College in Perth.

Maddie soon began to enjoy tapping away on typewriters, such as the Olivetti and Imperial, her hands concealed by a tin cover so she could not see the keys. When the teacher was not looking, most students would peek underneath. Maddie became friends with Rita, who lived in the Northbridge area, where many Italians had settled into a small commune since arriving in the country. They then teamed up with Mitzi from Malaysia. The three of them became inseparable, and on many occasions, rather than going to college, they went to the pictures. Sometimes they would watch the same movie twice. On other occasions, they would visit a local café, where they spent their time until the college closed at four o'clock. They enjoyed their truant escapades until Rita's mother phoned the college one afternoon asking to speak to her daughter. She became concerned when informed that neither Rita nor her friends had been seen since their lunch break. That soon put an end to their little adventures. Despite missing some lessons, each achieved excellent results in all subjects.

At the end of the year, the college organised interviews for all students who had received diplomas. Maddie was referred to a large trustee company that managed wills and deceased estates. She was recruited to start work six weeks later, after the summer holidays, as the college deemed it sensible for the girls to enjoy a break before commencing their working lives. Maddie was elated at the thought of six weeks free from college and work. Little did she know that her mother had other plans, informing her daughter that one of the surgery's patients was looking for someone to live with him for a few weeks as a home helper because his wife was imminently due to give birth to their third child. He needed assistance with housework, cooking, and caring for the children while his wife was in the hospital and for a short time after her confinement.

Although she was barely fifteen, Maddie had considerable experience caring for children from babysitting before going to Australia. But cooking and housework!

Maddie assisted the family for nearly a month, leaving her only a few days of rest before commencing her new job.

Midway through January, Maddie began work in the filing department, earning seven pounds and six shillings a week. Within a few weeks, she was transferred to the rent department at the front desk. Occasionally, she was asked to cover for a staff member on the switchboard—a task she dreaded. She always feared cutting someone off or leaving them in mid-air, waiting to be connected as she pulled and pushed plugs attached to long black cables into the appropriate sockets on the switchboard. Four or five lights often glared simultaneously, accompanied by a constant buzzing that alerted her to an incoming call. A couple of times, Maddie disconnected the wrong plug, thus cutting off a caller. Sometimes, if she feared she might stammer, she sat paralysed with anxiety while lights flashed and buzzers alerted her to calls.

Not long after moving to their flat, Maddie met Kay, who lived nearby at the end of a lane between two streets. She had two younger brothers, Scott and Vernon. Her parents loved Maddie and included her in their family outings. On Saturday evenings, Maddie and Kay would go to the Embassy or the Canterbury Court Ballroom. They loved dressing up and were always elegantly attired in fashionable, below-the-knee dresses, gloves, and nylons with seams down the back of the legs, held up by suspenders. They would catch the bus at the top of the road, alighting at Forest Place square, where they walked the remainder of the way through the streets of Perth, never concerned about their safety.

Catching the bus home, Kay and Maddie were dropped off at the shopping centre, a short walk from home. One night, as they were passing the shops, they saw two youths in the distance acting rather strangely. They then heard the sound of glass shattering, and as they moved closer, they realised that they had witnessed a smash-and-grab robbery. When the young men saw the girls, they fled, but not before Maddie and Kay had a good look at their faces. When Kay told her mother about the incident, she advised them to report the theft to the police, as their witness statements could assist in apprehending the culprits. Maddie and Kay were asked to attend the police station to provide a description of the youths and examine a book of mug shots. After going through page after page, the girls felt confused by the many images presented. They never did hear if the thieves had been caught!

Maddie and Kay loved nights at the Embassy, the largest ballroom in Perth. A majestic archway framed a stage at one end of the vast room. A long mezzanine encircled the perimeter, with luxurious logues situated below. A large glitter ball reflected colourful beams around the ballroom, illuminating the centre of the ceiling high above the dance floor as they danced. Eligible young men and women, all dressed in their finest attire, stepped onto the dance floor, many hoping to find romance. The last dance of the night was usually a waltz. The men often chose someone they had admired and danced with them during the evening. Then they would bravely muster up the courage to ask if they could escort the young lady home. During one of their visits, they met Fred and Jack, who were members of the Special Air Service Regiment—a special mission unit with unique capabilities within the Australian Defence Force. Operating under the motto 'Who Dares Wins', SASR is a direct command unit of the Special Operations Command with a demanding role. Fred, an Air Commando, was twenty-two years old. He was soon smitten with Maddie. Each week, he asked Maddie for as many dances as she would allow. At the end of the evening, he would offer the girls a lift home – by now, Kay had lost interest in Jack.

Fred would collect the girls in his 1957 Norton Manxman, which was his pride and joy, and escort them to the dances. Always the perfect gentleman, he was attentive and enjoyable to be with, and Maddie liked him very much. Fred respected Maddie's values, and although he hoped to develop their relationship further, he never pressured her.

Nearing the end of 1959, Maddie's mother joined an introduction agency, and after a few unsuccessful encounters, she met Charles. He revealed that his wife, Angela, had died a couple of years prior. Some alluded to whispers of suspicious circumstances surrounding her death. However, within months, Charles moved into the flat with Daisy, leaving his two children—Robert, who was thirteen, and his eleven-year-old daughter, Lilly—with his mother, Hera.

Robert and Lilly's paternal grandmother was a buxom Maori woman who had been married to a New Zealander. She took no nonsense and declared that she was a Maori Princess. Before long, Hera said she could no longer look after the children and insisted that Charles, being their father, had to accept the responsibilities. Consequently, Charles sent his children to live with his late wife's sister and her husband, who lived on the other side of Perth. They loved their niece and nephew and were willing to assume parental responsibility, providing a home, stability, and love that the children craved, which their father had been unable to give.

During the school holidays, Robert and Lilly stayed with their grandmother, and their father occasionally took them out for the day. Hera disliked Daisy and blamed her for her son's abandonment of his children. One day, Maddie attempted to see Lilly at her grandmother's home to suggest an outing to the cinema together. When Hera saw Maddie at the front door, she grabbed the straw broom leaning against the wall and chased her down the road, shouting obscenities. Naturally, it was a long time before Maddie ventured there again.

After contributing towards her keep, Maddie saved what she could from the three pounds and seven shillings remaining from her weekly wage to realise her goal—a return trip to England to visit Jimmie, her grandfather. She had been employed for a year and saved enough for her fare and spending.

As the year drew to a close, Maddie arrived home from work to find a letter addressed to her. She immediately recognised the large, bold handwriting of Mr. Thompson, her mother's former employer. She'd written to him some time earlier, explaining that she'd been saving to go 'home' and would like to visit him. Maddie was not expecting such a prompt reply, and when she ripped open the envelope, she was delighted to read his message. She was excited and anxious for her mother to return home so that she could share the news with her.

Daisy was amazed when she learned that Mr. Thompson had offered to escort Maddie on a *world trip*, all expenses paid. In his letter, he informed her that he had business interests in Australia and had been intending to visit for some time, but had postponed it until now. He advised Maddie to come over as soon as she could, allowing enough time to spend with her grandfather and other family members before joining him. Maddie had already saved money for her fare to England, leaving some for her pocket money.

Maddie handed in her notice at work, agreeing to stay until the end of the month. Daisy accompanied her daughter into town to book a passage to England. She also wrote a note for Maddie to give to Mr. Thompson, allowing him to take Maddie with him and entrusting her to his care and supervision.

'*This is to state that I give my consent to Mr. P.G. Thompson of Stratford-on-Avon, England, to take my daughter travelling with him, wherever he decides to go…*'

In February 1960, a month after her sixteenth birthday, Maddie set out on the adventure of a lifetime.

Globetrotting England - 1960

Maddie boarded the SS Arcadia – the ship she and her mother had journeyed on two years before. After being shown to her cabin by a young bellboy, Maddie made her way to one of the upper decks and joined her fellow passengers who were already searching the faces below for their loved ones. Her mother, Charles, Kay, and her family were somewhere amongst the crowd. Over the din of voices, Maddie thought she heard someone shouting her name, and, searching the crowd below, she spotted the bright yellow scarf her mother was wearing. Next to her, Kay was frantically waving her arms about in the air and shouting out, but because of the racket below, Maddie couldn't hear what she was saying.

Fred had informed her that the President of France, Sir Charles De Gaulle, was departing on the same ship and that he and his platoon would be at the port with the Premier, Sir David Brand, to give a fitting send-off. Maddie could hear the Army Band approaching, accompanied by Sir David Brand and members of the SAS Special Forces. Scanning the platoon, she saw Fred looking very smart and handsome in his military uniform. She waved and blew him a kiss, but even if he had seen her, he would not have been able to respond. Before long, a voice boomed over the Tannoy speakers, asking all visitors to 'please vacate the ship' as they would soon be setting sail. Maddie could hardly believe that she would soon be crossing the ocean back home to England.

She felt the ship vibrating as the engines roared to life. Within minutes, the vessel began to drift away from its moorings. As Maddie waved goodbye to her mother, Kay, and the rest of the family, a kind gentleman handed her a handful of streamers and told her to hold on to the end and throw them among the crowd. Maddie watched as the paper ribbons unfurled, with onlookers reaching out to catch them as they floated through the air, marking a symbolic connection between the ship and the shore. As they drifted away, the colourful streamers broke apart and descended onto the water, severing their last link to the shore.

When Maddie returned to her cabin, she was happy to see that her roommate, a woman in her thirties, had arrived. Introducing herself as Hazel, she told Maddie that she would only be travelling as far as Colombo. The room was small but adequate, with two bunk beds and several small chests of drawers. After putting her belongings away, Maddie sat on the edge of the bed and wrote the first entry in her diary. She then retrieved the Circa Box Brownie, which her mother had bought her for her sixteenth birthday and left the cabin to go to one of the lounges. Among the crew, many familiar faces remembered her from two years ago.

Before long, Maddie had made friends with a group of young people, and from then on, they included her in many of their activities. Some of the older ones protected her, ensuring she was safe. Mark from Ceylon was in the air force, travelling with two very pretty Ceylonese girls, Jacinda and Mandi. Maddie thought they were beautiful and exotic in their vibrantly coloured sarees. There were two Australians, Tim and Geoff, both professional tennis players. A couple of days later, two other guys joined the group.

Daily newsletters, port-of-call booklets, and decorative menus were provided. Balls, parties, and sporting competitions were organised. 'Stopovers' were necessary for refuelling, restocking with fresh food, and replenishing water supplies. Their first port of call was Colombo, which eventually became known as Sri Lanka, and then on to Aden. Maddie's new friends insisted that she stay with them when going ashore, assuring her it would not be wise to go alone.

Disembarking at the Port of Aden and walking along the main street leading to the markets, everyone gagged – the smell was unbearable. Maddie looked in despair as they passed disabled people with missing arms or legs, or their limbs strapped to low trollies, the wheels wobbling precariously when they scooted along the road. Stray dogs suffering from mange and other afflictions, and skinny cattle slowly ambling along carrying heavy loads. A couple of camels strolled by, pulling carts loaded with furniture and large bundles all tied up with rope. Further on, chickens were squashed into cages, piled on top of each other. What saddened Maddie the most was the children with their bare feet, filthy clothes hanging loosely on their underfed bodies and eyes that looked exceptionally large for their sallow faces. So sad and full of despair. Young and old, with outstretched hands cupped, ready to snatch at anything offered to them. Anxious to move on, they hurried further down the road until they reached some small shops selling clothes and beautiful, intricate filigree. On the other side of the road were wicker baskets of all shapes and sizes, hanging among various implements, including scythes, wooden ladders, and tools, all jumbled together. Before going onshore, they had been warned not to buy anything like stuffed camels or pouffes. They were told those were filled with dirty hospital bandages and would be thrown overboard. Maddie jumped when a dishevelled little man sidled up and tugged at her camera. Mark went to shove him out of the way, but stopped when the ragamuffin raised his hands as if in prayer. Then, lowering them, he pointed towards Maddie's camera. Nobody moved, wondering what he was going to do next and was taken by surprise when he moved closer to Maddie and put his arm around her waist. Then, with his skeletal finger, he again pointed at her camera. Tim was getting ready to send him on his way, but Glen, realising what the guy was trying to tell them, grabbed Tim's shirt.

'You jerk… he wants Mark to take a photo of him with Maddie. He surely means no harm.'

The two girls stood well back, their hands covering their mouths, trying not to show how disgusted they were.

Jacinda was horrified. 'Maddie, look! He's scratching himself… he's got fleas! Don't listen to Glen. He's a dirty little man, and he smells. Come on, let's get out of here!' Maddie laughed:

'Hurry up, Mark! Take the photo otherwise, I will be infested with bugs.'

Mark was laughing as well, so much so that he worried he might drop the camera. He quickly snapped the photo before the little man scuttled off into the crowd.

Geoff winked at Mark. 'That will be something to show your children one day, Maddie!'

Maddie lagged at the back of the group when she became aware of a shifty-looking, shoeless man dressed in a filthy white robe with a bandana coiled around his head. The man was observing her. She wasn't particularly worried, especially after surviving the last incident, but when she noticed that the others were nearly out of sight, she quickened her pace. Glancing back to see if the scruffy man had disappeared, she found he was still following, weaving in and out of the many tourists, locals, and animals. Then, suddenly, he grabbed her arm and pulled her along the road. She panicked and, letting out a muffled scream, tried to pry herself free from his grip.

Hearing the commotion, Geoff looked ahead and quickly realised what was happening, shouting out to the others. Tim sprang into action and, reaching them, grabbed Maddie, dragging her away from her captor as the man sped off without a backwards glance.

Maddie had enough drama for one day! When they returned to the ship, Tim mentioned the incident to his steward, who told him that Maddie was a fortunate young lady, as it was well known that wealthy Arabs paid good money for someone to seize a lovely young white girl for them!

Most mornings, Maddie made her way down to the ship's bakery, where the staff were busy cooking hundreds of loaves and buns for the day. They were accustomed to her joining them as she chatted and munched on hot rolls fresh from the large ovens. There were days when they never saw land, and many passengers grew restless and bored, but not Maddie. There was always something to keep her occupied – deck games, swimming, playing cards with her friends, and enjoying evening entertainment and dancing. She also had a couple of admirers – Ben, one of the stewards, and Edward, a member of the ship's band, both in their early twenties. Maddie enjoyed the attention but made it clear that she was not 'that sort of girl'.

'Neptune's Journey', or the crossing of the Equator, has been a feature of immigrant voyages since the 1800s. However, it became increasingly elaborate in the twentieth century. The ceremony was equally entertaining during Maddie's second voyage.

When the ship docked at Southampton, Mr. Thompson waited for Maddie in the customs area. She was surprised to see that he was using a walking stick and that his hair had completely turned white. He assisted Maddie with one of the cases as they made their way out of the terminal to his car. The two-hour drive to his home passed quickly as Mr. T updated Maddie on all the changes at the farm since her departure two years ago. He was not impressed with her Aussie accent and could not understand how quickly she had lost her cultured English voice! When they arrived, he introduced her to his new housekeeper, Mrs. Clarke, a kind lady to whom Maddie immediately warmed. She had two children—David was ten, and Susan was eight. The house was just as Maddie remembered it, especially the lovely sitting room where she had spent many hours playing chess with Mr. Thompson. Mrs. Clarke helped Maddie with her suitcases as they climbed the splendid, curving staircase to the bedrooms.

That night, Maddie slept soundly, waking just after nine when Mrs. Clarke brought her a cup of tea, informing her not to expect it every morning!

Although anxious to see her grandfather Jimmie, she knew it would be rude to leave so soon. She contacted several of her girlfriends and her special friend, Rodney, who lived with his family on the neighbouring farm. As Mr. T was often away on business, Maddie spent the evenings with Mrs. Clarke and her two children, watching television or going into town to see the latest movie. One day, Maddie and David were playing croquet on the extensive lawn when one of the farmhands drove up from the farm and asked them to gather the cattle because Norman, whose job it was, had not arrived for work. As they made their way across the field, they were pleased to see that the cows were already ambling toward the enclosure. Just as Maddie had shooed the last of them in and shut the gate, she heard David calling out to her and pointing to a cow lying on the ground. Maddie went over. The animal was struggling to get onto her feet and then started cocking her tail and kicking from side to side. Maddie immediately realised that the cow was ready to give birth to her calf. They ran down to the farmhouse to tell Alfred, the farm manager. He instructed them to jump in the truck; once the calf was born, he'd put it in the truck's bed and the mother would follow behind. When they arrived, the cow was already straining to push her baby out, and after what seemed like an eternity, its little hooves appeared. Explaining to Maddie that the calf was coming out the wrong way, he said they needed to act quickly to save the lives of the mother and her unborn baby. With Maddie's help, Alfred gently rocked the calf's legs, swaying the feet from side to side as he slowly edged it onto the ground. David and Maddie looked at one another in awe as the calf lay on the ground coated in slime and blood. Alfred immediately cleared the mucus from its mouth and nose, then pinched off the umbilical cord.

Two weeks later, Maddie lugged her suitcase down the long driveway. Sitting on the wall and swinging her legs, she waited for her grandfather to come. She knew she was early but was so anxious to see him again and longed for one of his bear hugs. Maddie watched as several cars went by until she saw his sleek Bentley coming along the road and stopping at the end of the driveway.

At last, she was back in the arms of her beloved Jimmie.

Over the following weeks, Maddie spent every moment with her grandfather. He was very proud to be the Master of the local Hunt. Maddie thought he looked so grand in the traditional red coat of a huntsman. She was never happier than when they were together, mucking out the stables, grooming the two horses, and, most of all, riding beside him across the Wiltshire Downs. He was a proud gentleman who was admired, respected, and sought for advice.

Maddie wanted to meet her father because the only memory she had of him was a photograph of them together when she was about five years old. Besides that, she had nothing. Before leaving Australia, Daisy gave her the address of his bank in London, as that was the only way to get in contact with him. Maddie wrote, asking if she could meet him and was delighted when a letter with a London postmark arrived a few days later. It was a brief note suggesting that she visit him in London the following week and providing her with details of where and when to meet him. Jimmy was not at all happy.

'I understand that you want to see your father, but I'm angry that he is not taking the time to come here to see you. You are only sixteen, and London is a big place. How will you know where to find the hotel or which train to catch? No, write and tell him to come and see you here.'

Maddie desperately wanted to see her father and, if possible, learn more about her childhood and the brief time she had spent with him.

'B-but I have to go. He's my father.' Jimmy wrapped his arms around her, drawing her gently against his chest.

'Okay, little one, if your heart is set on going, go if you must! I am worried for you, and I don't want to see you hurt. If you get stuck, call me and we will come to get you.' Maddie reached up and kissed his cheek...

'I promise. P-please, do not worry. Everything will be okay.'

On the day Jimmy drove Maddie to the Swindon railway station, he spoke to the station guard before departing, requesting that he ensure she transferred safely to the correct train to Covent Garden tube station. The conductor promised Maddie that he would let her know when they arrived at the station. An hour later, Maddie made her way out of the underground and onto the busy road. She had never been to London before and was in awe of everything. Huge, bright red double-decker buses went in all directions. Large, black taxis whizzed across the streets. Everyone looked so grim and harried that she could not bring herself to stop someone to ask for directions. She was frightened of embarrassing herself in case she couldn't speak clearly. Finally, Maddie braced herself and asked a kindly looking gentleman how far it was to the Strand Palace Hotel. He pointed Maddie in the right direction, saying it was less than a ten-minute walk away. Half an hour early, she stopped at a café to buy a cold drink. She felt extremely nervous as she entered the hotel, taking in the grandeur surrounding her. What if he didn't like her? Would she recognise him from the photos her mother had given her, or worse still, would he recognise her? Readying herself, she strolled up the steps to where a footman, dressed in an impressive scarlet tailcoat and immaculate gold-trimmed waistcoat, was waiting to greet her. He then accompanied her into the stately foyer and asked the concierge to escort her to the restaurant. After shyly thanking him, she followed the young man to the lavishly decorated dining room. Feeling uncomfortable in such a lavish place, she gingerly entered the brasserie, where her eyes searched the room, hoping to recognise her father. She then noticed a tall man moving between the tables and coming towards her. Maddie glanced up at him nervously as he slid his arm over her shoulder and guided her towards a table over the far side of the room. Studying her father's face, she hoped to see similar features, especially as everyone had always said she looked like her mother; she desperately needed to see some of her father in herself. She had often wondered why she had a Grecian nose. Her mother's and her grandparents' noses were larger and broader. While scrutinising his cornflower blue eyes and elegant nose, she knew her father was part of her. She was so nervous that her stammer was more prominent than usual. When she saw his shocked response, Maddie realised that her mother had never told him.

Absorbed in thought, Maddie made her way back to the railway station, unaware of her surroundings. As promised, she called her grandfather to inform him of the train's departure time. Afterwards, she went to the platform and sat on an empty bench to wait for the train's arrival. When it was time to board the carriage for her return journey to Swindon, she huddled in the corner by the window, closing her eyes tightly and squeezing them shut to stop the tears streaming down her cheeks.

Nothing had been as she expected. She wished she had never gone to meet him. She tried hard to recollect what they had talked about, but so much of their meeting was a blur. He asked many questions about her mother: Was she happy? Had she married? Did she bring any photos? After finishing their meal, Jacque told her he had an important meeting with a client and would soon have to leave her. They left the restaurant walking side by side through the foyer and down the steps onto the street, neither saying a word. Hailing a taxi, he turned to Maddie and hugged her, followed by a kiss on the cheek. Then he was gone without any mention of meeting her again. Maddie slowly made her way in the opposite direction, her head bowed low so the passersby could not see her tears. She had never felt so unloved and alone. Absorbed in thought, Maddie made her way back to the railway station, unaware of her surroundings. As promised, she called her grandfather to inform him of the train's departure time. Afterwards, she went to the platform and sat on an empty bench to wait for the train's arrival. When it was time to board the carriage for her return journey to Swindon, she huddled in the corner by the window, closing her eyes tightly and squeezing them shut to stop the tears streaming down her cheeks.

Three months later, Maddie went to stay with her great-aunt Violet in Dumfries, Scotland. Violet was her grandmother's sister. Maddie loved her time there, visiting various relatives scattered around Kirkcudbrightshire and Dumfries. Most were connected to the Smiths, her grandmother Jeanie's side of the family. Maddie learnt a lot about her mother's childhood and her numerous relatives. She stayed for a month, made friends, and enjoyed many adventures. Violet asked after her grandfather, but he was never mentioned again, which puzzled Maddie.

It was around the time when Princess Margaret married Anthony Armstrong-Jones, who was described as a Bohemian-style photographer with a 'sense of mischief.' At that same time, the Beatles were experiencing widespread success. Their music dominated the charts and became the soundtrack of a generation, regarded as one of the most influential bands of all time. It was the beginning of Beatlemania.

Maddie spent the last two months with her grandfather and Trix, Jimmie's companion and best friend. As before, Maddie and her grandfather spent many hours together grooming the horses, mucking out the stalls, and cantering side by side across the Wiltshire downs. With Trix joining them, they attended the Point-to-Point, gymkhanas, and horse sales. Whenever anyone wanted to buy a horse, they always consulted Jimmie.

The time came for Maddie to leave her darling Jimmie, not knowing when or if she would ever see him again. She was torn between staying in England with her grandfather, who had desperately wanted her there, but she knew her mother would never agree. She realised that if she were ever to return, he might no longer be there to greet her!

Homeward bound

A week later, Mr Thompson and Maddie boarded the Boeing 707. It was known as the Golden Age of flying, but taking to the air in those days had downsides. It was much more dangerous and far more expensive. There was the smoke from all those cigars, cigarettes and pipes, but the champagne flowed endlessly. They had nicely folded napkins, as well as smoked salmon and lobster. Maddie felt extremely grown-up and knew she could easily get used to living a life of luxury! Their first destination was New York. They landed at the airport in the early evening. A chauffeur greeted them and took them to the Manhattan Hotel in the heart of Times Square. When they were shown to their rooms, Mr Thompson said he wanted to rest until it was time for the evening meal. Maddie, lost in thought, was overwhelmed by the size and opulence of her room, which overlooked Times Square. She had never been in such a lavish place. The ringing of the phone interrupted her train of thought. She hesitated, wondering if she should pick it up.

'Y-yes, hello.' It was Mr T. 'Maddie. What do you think of your room?' Maddie attempted to sound sophisticated and calm; instead, she blurted out.

'Wow! It's fantastic. There is a large bowl of fruit, and you should see the beautiful orchid, it's...' Mr Thompson interrupted.

'You must pin that to your dress when you come to dinner this evening. I suggest you rest, and I will see you in the lounge at seven o'clock sharp.' He'd hung up before Maddie could reply.

Before leaving, Jimmie had given Maddie money to buy some nice clothes for the trip. That evening, she was going to wear the beautiful pink satin cocktail dress. She also had two very chic suits, a petticoat, stockings, elbow-length evening gloves, and smart shoes. She'd never had so much money to spend on herself.

The following morning, Mr. T had a business meeting, allowing Maddie to do as she wished but cautioning her not to get lost. Bewildered by the city's size, she decided against venturing far. Instead, she spent most of the morning in and around the hotel, chatting with other patrons and the staff, who were fascinated by her Australian accent.

They enjoyed the city's sights most evenings and dined at exclusive restaurants. They also went to the cinema to see "Oklahoma" and "South Pacific," both of which were shown in CinemaScope. A week later, they boarded a plane to Albuquerque, where they stayed for two days. After that, they took a Greyhound bus and travelled through New Mexico, passing by mountains and rock formations that stretched for miles. They journeyed across Arizona through Navajo country, alongside the Painted Desert, which extended from Grand Canyon National Park to Petrified Forest National Park, passing many small towns. Most were little more than trading posts, while others were ghost towns. There were Native Americans who made their living through these trading posts. Finally, upon arriving at the Grand Canyon, they checked into the New Canyon Lodge on the hill above the canyon. The receptionist advised them that if they rose early in the morning, they would see one of the most inspiring sunrises in the world. That evening, they were entertained by the Navajo troupe Pollen Trail Dancers. They performed authentic dances traditionally featured at powwows, including storytelling performances such as the "Bow" and "Arrow Dance," which told the story of Navajo hunting days, and the "Basket Dance," which demonstrated the importance of baskets and basket-weaving in Navajo life. Maddie sat in awe, wishing it could last much longer.

From there, they flew to San Francisco, where they stayed at the Hyatt Regency San Francisco Hotel. Although Maddie was accustomed to such luxury, she was stunned when, on their first evening, they dined in the revolving Equinox Restaurant located at the top of the hotel. She couldn't take her eyes off the incredible view as they rotated a full 360 degrees, taking in the city and the bay. The following afternoon, they boarded the tramcar, which took them over Nob Hill and through Chinatown. Finally, they stopped at Fisherman's Wharf before returning to take a cab back to Chinatown for a meal.

The next stop was Hawaii. In 1959, it became the 50th state of the United States. They stayed at the Reef Hawaii Beach Hotel in Honolulu, just meters from the famous Waikiki Beach. Maddie rented a small surfboard, hoping to catch some waves, but after falling off a few times, she gave up and decided to stick to body surfing. They visited several historic sites and the International Marketplace, dining at one of the many restaurants where beautiful young ladies entertained them by dancing the hula in ankle-length grass skirts. One evening, they met a young South African who introduced himself as Robert Vorster. He told them that he was on a business trip with his father. Before they parted, he asked Maddie if she would do him the honour of dining with him the following evening. Maddie was unsure if Mr. T would agree, but surprisingly, he didn't object.

Their last destination before flying to Perth was a week in Fiji. As always, Mr T had a limousine waiting to take them to the hotel at Korolevu Beach. It was a magnificent bure-type building, adorned with bamboo, tapa, and tiki décor. All the settings were in bamboo – the bar, the stools, the chairs and the tables. It was as though the sunshine had settled on everything –inside and out. Maddie loved that it was so different from the glamorous hotels they had stayed at.

When they checked in, the receptionist beckoned to the young Fijian porter, whom Maddie came to know as Taito. They followed him as he led them outside to a vast tropical area where many thatched-roof bures (bungalows) were surrounded by extremely tall coconut palms. Maddie looked around in awe as she absorbed it all. Then, turning to gaze past the bures, she could see the sea and the lagoon, partially hidden among many more coconut palms, their slightly curved stems dancing and gently swaying in the breeze. She quickly caught up with the two men, and after Taito had shown Mr. T to his bure, he took Maddie up another small pathway leading to the bright red door of her hut. After he left, Maddie looked around the room in amazement. The beautiful woven-bamboo ceiling, the polished mahogany flooring, and the large gauze-draped canopy bed with an enormous mosquito net attached to the head of it... There was a bathroom, large overhead fans, and a phone.

One of the Fijian waiters, Albert, took a fancy to Maddie. He also played a traditional drum called the Lali in the band that entertained the guests during the evenings. When he wasn't working, he would join Maddie at the lagoon, where they would swim together. She was most impressed watching him skim up the palm trees like a monkey, pluck a coconut, and throw it down to the ground. It was all part of the entertainment!

Maddie was sorry to leave and could have happily stayed on the magical island. A limousine arrived to take them to the airport, where they boarded a plane that would take them to Queensland, spending three days there before flying on to Perth.

Perth
October 1960

The air hostesses had just finished clearing their lunch trays when the flight captain informed all passengers to ensure their seatbelts were fastened and their trays were upright, as they would soon be landing at Perth Airport. Maddie was sitting with her nose against the window as the plane bumped along the landing strip, eventually coming to a halt. Having travelled first class for the entire trip home, they benefited from being among the first to disembark. After showing their passports, they collected their luggage from the baggage area and making their way through the exit door into arrivals, Maddie heard her name being called.

'Maddie, Maddie!' The next thing she knew, Kay was throwing her arms around her friend's neck as they clung to each other.

'I didn't think you'd come back! I cannot believe it! I can't wait to hear about all your wonderful adventures.' Giving her another hug, Maddie told her friend. 'It's wonderful to be back. I've missed you all and there is so much to tell and many photos to share.'

Then, turning to her mother, Maddie hugged and kissed her, expressing her happiness to be home. After all the introductions were complete, Mr. T informed Daisy that he had a reservation at one of the hotels in the city. Charles offered to drive him there, but he politely declined, stating he would take a taxi. Daisy promised to get in touch when he had a chance to rest and hoped he would join them for a meal. He told her that he wanted to look around the city first and that he would contact them in a few days.

As he had not yet been in contact, Charles suggested they call the hotel to ensure everything was alright. Daisy advised him to wait a while, as she knew he would ring when he was ready. She was aware that Mr. T liked to do things his way and was much happier when surrounded by luxury and like-minded people. He was used to living in luxurious surroundings, not in a small flat and taking meals in the kitchen.

The following day, Daisy arrived home from work and was making her way up the pathway when she heard the phone ringing. Quickening her pace, she fumbled in her handbag for the key and unlocking the door, rushed inside. Dumping her bag on a chair, she reached for the phone just as it rang off.

'*Blast…Oh, well, if it's important, they'll ring back.*' She was about to walk into the kitchen when it began ringing again. Before Daisy had time to say hello, Mr T's voice barked down the phone.

'Hello… Is that you, Daisy? It's Mr Thompson.'

'Yes,' she replied. 'I'm so pleased to hear from you at last. I hope that…'

He interrupted her rudely, saying. 'I've called to tell you that I am flying home tomorrow,'

Daisy was dumbfounded. 'Tomorrow! But why? Charles was going to show you around, and I wanted you to join us for a meal. It's the least we can do after your kindness to Maddie. She never stops talking about how kind you were and all the wonderful places you took her. She will be dis….' Cutting her off, he went on to tell her.

'I have completed all business transactions, which, as you know, is the main reason for my visit.' Then, hesitating, he said.

'Whatever made you come to this backwards and barbaric country?'

Daisy was puzzled as to why? 'I don't understand.'

'Well, if you must know, I was very nearly crushed by one of your trains. Your railway crossings are diabolical. There are no barriers, nor lights, just a wooden sign indicating a railway crossing.'

'But…' Daisy realised she was not about to get a word in.

'Yesterday, I was halfway across when a train came hurtling towards me with no warning. No lights, just flimsy barriers that are no good to a man or a beast. I would have been killed if I had not reacted as quickly as I did!' Daisy had never heard him so angry.

'Are you aware just how dangerous they are? I repeat… Australia is barbaric, and the people are uncouth! I will never return. Never!'

Once he had calmed down, Daisy expressed her regret but was pleased that he had escaped unscathed. Then, tactfully changing the subject, she pointed out how unhappy Maddie would be if he left before she could say goodbye.

Maddie was disappointed, knowing she would not get to see him, especially since she had bought him a small gift as a gesture of appreciation for his kindness. It had been an adventure of a lifetime. The next morning, she asked her mother to phone the hotel to see if he was still there. If so, she wanted to go and see him, but he had already checked out.

Not long after Maddie returned home, Fred came to see her. It was as though she had never been away. He took her dancing, driving in the countryside, and to the movies, always acting like a true gentleman – never asking more of her than what she was prepared to give. Maddie still harboured bad memories of being fondled all those years ago, which left her anxious whenever she thought Fred was becoming more affectionate and his kisses more passionate. Although Maddie had missed him very much, she started seeing him. At that time, she didn't know that many years later, she would look back with regret.

A friend of her mother, Don, had just started a new business transporting goods interstate. He asked Maddie if she would be interested in working for him, telling her she would be responsible for delivering the assignments in and out of the warehouse, answering the phone, and serving as a general dogsbody. Maddie didn't hesitate to accept his offer. She had been working in Charles' tobacco shop in Perth until she could find something more suitable.

The interstate drivers collected their consignments from Perth, travelled North-East to Coolgardie over four hundred miles, and then headed down to Norsman, the start of the Nullarbor Plain, taking them to South Australia, Victoria and New South Wales. The distance from Perth to Adelaide was vast, about 3200 miles. They would then reload for delivery in Perth and head straight back. Most drivers who drove interstate were on 'uppers and downers' – uppers to keep them awake, and downers to help them sleep. When unloaded into the warehouse, local contractors would be present, ready to collect their consignments and deliver them in and around the Perth area. Many items had 'fallen off the back of a truck!' – stockings, petticoats, chocolates, perfume and many more. The drivers took those home to their wives and girlfriends. There was always something for Maddie.

One morning, Maddie found a young man sitting at her desk when she arrived at work. She smiled.

'Hello, I'm Maddie. Can I help you?' He grinned, eyeing her appreciatively.

'G'day. I'm Alan, but my friends call me Snow."

Hesitating for a moment, she watched as his eyes travelled over her body, making her feel extremely uncomfortable. 'Oh.' She said.

'I'm doing contract work for the company and waiting for a load to be cleared. After that, I'm on my way. In the meantime, maybe we can get to know each other?'

Just as Maddie was about to reply, Don shouted from the loading bay.

'Stop buggering around Snow, your consignment's loaded and ready for the off.' Get yourself down here quick smart.'

'Okay, hold your horses, mate! I'm on the way.' Then, turning to leave, Alan smiled at Maddie.

I handle all the local deliveries, so I'll be in and out of the place most days. I'll see you later.

Maddie nodded. Although he seemed friendly, she was not attracted to him. Her grandfather would have called him a 'rough diamond'. He wasn't bad looking, quite tall, and appeared pretty fit.

He visited her office while dropping off goods or waiting for his lorry to be loaded. He was twenty-five and mentioned that he had been married to Elaine for two years, but they had recently separated. They had been struggling financially as he couldn't find work, so he took a job on a cattle station in the Northern Territory, telling Maddie that while he was away, she had met someone and moved out of their marital home. When he returned, he moved into a boarding house.

Christmas was just a week away, and business was hectic. Everyone wanted their deliveries before the warehouse closed for the festivities. Maddie was the last to leave the office, feeling happy that she would have a few days off. Locking the front door, she turned to walk down the road toward home when she noticed

Alan's old 1950s Ford Prefect parked on the opposite side. Poking his head out of the window, he shouted, asking if Maddie would like a lift.

Before dropping her off at the flat, he asked if she would go out with him on Christmas Eve, mentioning that he was going to a party at his aunt's. It had not been long since Maddie had broken up with Fred, and not wanting to spend the evening alone at home, she accepted. They agreed that she would wait for him at the bus stop on the main road at seven o'clock. Maddie was apprehensive about him picking her up at home because she felt her mother would disapprove, as although he was separated, he was still married to Elaine. Ando, at twenty-five, he was eight years older.

Anxious not to be late, Maddie arrived fifteen minutes early. She sat on the bus stop seat, waiting patiently. Vehicle after vehicle drove by. Half an hour passed, then an hour, and still no sign of Alan. She was ready to head home when his Ford Prefect pulled alongside the curb. Leaning over and pushing the passenger side door open, he beckoned her to get in.

'Hop in. Sorry I'm late, luv, but I stayed and had a few drinks with the guys for Christmas.' He looked a bit sheepish, but his words were more a statement of fact than an apology. He grinned and added: 'Once you get into a round of drinks, it's not easy to leave.'

Getting into the car she was taken aback by the pungent stench of alcohol. As she settled in, he reached over to retrieve two empty cans from the floor, tossing them over the back.

'Hi.' Maddie didn't know what to say and felt miffed that he didn't seem concerned she had been waiting for over an hour.

'Okay, let's go. Everyone will be there by now, and as you're the girl I'm going to marry, I want them to meet you.' Maddie laughed nervously, feeling uncomfortable, and began to think she would have been much happier if she had gone home instead of waiting so long for him to show up.

'Don't be silly! We hardly know each other … Anyway, you're already married.' Then quickly changing the subject. 'Where do they live? Are they expecting us?'

Grinning, he replied' "We'll see. No, it's not far from here, and yes, they are expecting us and looking forward to meeting you.'

From the moment they arrived, Maddie felt uneasy, as she could see they had been celebrating for quite some time. She felt out of place and wished she hadn't come. Despite saying she didn't drink, they kept insisting until she took a glass, held onto it, but without drinking. They also continued commenting on her posh accent, asking if she always spoke like that, which made her more conscious of her stammer, even though no one commented. Maddie couldn't hide her embarrassment when she saw Alan's cousin sitting on his knee, her arms around his neck and rubbing against him. Maddie had never seen such behaviour. As the night progressed, their voices grew louder and the jokes became more vulgar.

It was after midnight when they left the house strewn with empty beer bottles, cans and ashtrays overflowing with cigarette butts. Everyone was very drunk, including Alan. The drive home was hairy as his driving was erratic, to say the least. Maddie was relieved when he pulled the car outside the flat and stopped. And then he leant over to try and kiss Maddie, but she quickly got out – the stench of beer was too much. She turned and smiled, always polite and not wanting to hurt his feelings.

'Thank you for a lovely evening. It was very nice meeting your family. I'll see you next week when we're back at work. Goodnight.'

Before Alan could reply, Maddie had walked up the path and entered the building.

On Boxing Day morning, Alan called Maddie and asked if she would go for a drive with him. As she hesitated, he seized the opportunity to say he would come and pick her up from her house. Maddie started to protest, saying she wasn't sure what her mother had planned, but he wouldn't take no for an answer. He continued to call most nights, always wanting to know where she had been and with whom. Maddie was beginning to feel trapped. She hadn't seen Kay for weeks and missed their time together— the roller skating and the weekly dances. She missed all the fun things she used to do before Alan had come into her life. He was extremely jealous. If a guy wolf-whistled or even turned to give her a second look, he'd walk toward them, clenching his fists, and tell them.

'Keep your eyes to yourself, mate, or I'll punch your lights out'

Don sold the transport company, and since they were bringing their staff, the employees were no longer needed. Alan told Daisy that he could no longer afford to stay at the boarding house and asked if he could stay with them until he found a decent job and somewhere he could afford. Daisy told him that he was welcome to use the sleepout. He moved in the following day.

Maddie found employment at a bakery in Cottesloe, icing cakes, making sandwiches, and serving customers. It was sometimes heavy work, especially when she had to carry large bags of sugar and flour from the storeroom. The boss was very kind, and Maddie got along well with the rest of the staff. Alan was desperately looking for work for his truck, but in the end had to sell it because he needed the cash to pay bills. He had applied for several positions up north where he knew he could make good money.

Leaving the bakery on a particularly wet and blustery evening, Maddie struggled with her umbrella as the wind threatened to turn it inside out. She made her way up the road, hoping to catch the 5:45 p.m. bus when Alan drove up alongside. Grappling to collapse the umbrella, she quickly got into the car.

'Phew, that was good timing! I may have missed the bus, and it's another twenty minutes till the next.' Alan smiled. 'I got off work early, so I thought you might appreciate a lift home as it's such a dreadful night.'

He fell silent for a moment before turning to look at Maddie.

'I've got some good news. The Pastoral Agency phoned this morning saying that they had a situation that might be of interest. I didn't waste any time getting in to see them, and after being put through the third degree, they said the job was mine.'

Maddie was unsurprised by the news, as he had recently told her he wanted to return to the North, where he could earn much more. Rather than being disappointed that he would be away, she felt happy, as perhaps she could make the break, especially since they were always arguing about how much time he spent drinking with her mother and Charles.

'That is great news. When are you leaving?' He looked at her in surprise, as he had expected her to be unhappy that he would be away for so long. He replied.

'In two days' time. Sunday afternoon! They're flying me up in their private plane. It's a large sheep station. Yardie Creek, in the Gascoyne area near Exmouth Station.'

They both sat in silence, and nothing more was said. Then, just before turning down the road home, he pulled over to the curb and turned off the ignition. Maddie felt puzzled.

'Why have you stopped?' Alan leant over and took Maddie in his arms:

'Will you marry me? I don't want you to find someone else while I'm away. You're my gal, Maddie!' Then, digging into his trouser pocket, he pulled out a little box, opened the lid, and produced a ring. 'It's not a diamond, but I will get you a decent one when I return.'

Taken by surprise, she didn't know what to say. Moments ago, she had felt happy and carefree after being told that he would be working away, giving her the chance to move on with her life. Now, here he was asking her to spend the rest of her life with him!

'Alan, I'm only seventeen. I don't want to get married yet, and even if I did, you're forgetting that you're still married to Elaine!'

'I've already asked Elaine for a divorce, and once that's finalised, we can be married. Nothing is stopping us from being engaged. I want everyone to know that you are promised to me. We can tell your mother this evening.' A cocky grin spread across his face as he added: 'She likes me. She won't stand in our way.' Maddie put her hand on his knee.

'I'm sorry, but I am not ready to marry you or, for that matter, anyone! Surely you understand that!'

Pursing his lips, he turned back in his seat, switched on the ignition, and putting the car into gear, roared off up the road. Not another word was spoken. Since meeting Alan, she had lost contact with all her friends because he was jealous and wanted her to himself.

Alan left for Yardie Creek Sheep Station the following day, seven hundred miles from Perth, just above the Tropic of Capricorn. While on the flight, he wrote Maddie a letter on the back of the flight form and gave it to the air hostess to post for him when she returned to Perth. It was a loving letter full of regrets about leaving her, and he was unsure how long he could endure the separation as he once again asked her to remain faithful to him.

A few weeks later, Maddie came home from work to find a telegram addressed to her pushed under the front door.

'*Carnarvon Hospital. Red back spider bite. yardie.*'

When Daisy arrived home, she contacted the hospital and was informed that they were flying him to the Royal Perth Hospital. The following morning, as Maddie was preparing to go to work, she heard the drone of a plane. Looking up, she recognised it as the Flying Doctor aircraft. Circling several times above the flat, it then disappeared. Later that evening, she received a call from the hospital. It was Alan.

'Hi, honey. They said I could make a quick call to let you know I'm okay. Did you see me waving as we flew over the flat?'

'How? Where did you get bitten? I always thought a person died from a Redback spider bite!'

Alan interrupted her.

'Hey, hang in there and give me a chance. I'd just sat down on one of the most disgusting dunnies, what you call a toilet, sweetheart, when I felt a nip on my backside. It hurt like billy-o!'

'Oh... that sounds awful. Were you aware that it was a spider that bit you?'

'No, not at first, but then all of a sudden, the pain became excruciating and worsened by the minute. I was doubled over with abdominal pain. That's when they called the Flying Doctors to take me to Perth. Anyway, I have to hang up because I'm using the phone in the ward sister's office.'

He'd replaced the receiver before Maddie could ask if he had any idea how long he would be there.

That evening, just as Daisy and Maddie were getting ready to leave for the hospital, they noticed a taxi pull up outside the building. To their surprise, it was Alan. They watched as he retrieved his battered suitcase from the back seat and, after paying the driver, strolled up to the front door. He stayed for supper and afterwards shared tales from his brief time at the station.

Maddie was thankful that since returning home, Alan had found a place of his own. Then one evening, he called to let Maddie know that he was driving over to see her. When he arrived, he asked her to go for a drive with him. He drove them to Kings Park, where they sat overlooking Perth and the Swan River. He then started pleading with Maddie, telling her he loved her and promising to cut down on drinking if only she would agree to marry him. Suddenly, he kissed Maddie hungrily and fumbled with her clothes, telling her how much he loved and needed her. That night, she lost her virginity.

Most Saturdays, Charles and Daisy went to the Fremantle Workers' Club. Occasionally, Alan and Maddie joined them; Maddie loved listening to and dancing with the five-piece band. Alan preferred to sit and talk with their friends. Maddie was never short of a partner. Alan would inform them that she was unavailable if someone asked her to dance more than once. On one occasion, a rather nice-looking young man asked her to dance. Before escorting her back to the table, he introduced himself as a professor at the Western Australian University. He wondered if she would be interested in modelling for his art students. Quite taken aback, yet also flattered, she said she needed time to think about it. When she told Alan what the professor had said, he went ballistic.

'HE WHAT! You're not posing for anyone!'

Maddie was taken aback and couldn't understand why he was so upset.

'Bu...but... It's for students. Wh-what harm is there in that?'

Alan looked the other way, ignoring her. Then, without saying a word, he walked over to where the other man was sitting with his friends. Tapping him on the shoulder, he indicated that he wanted to speak with him away from the table. Maddie watched nervously as Alan stood close to the professor, his face almost touching his, fists clenched at his sides. Moments later, Alan returned to the table, his lips pursed tightly and unyieldingly.

'That dirty bastard wanted you to pose alright... In the NUDE!' He shouted so loudly that everything fell silent. Maddie had no idea that the professor meant she would be standing naked in front of a room full of students, but that did not give Alan the right to verbally attack her in front of so many people. Before she could say anything, Alan had stormed off to the bar for another drink and, on his return, continued to ignore her for the rest of the evening.

Alan told Maddie he would teach her to drive. Initially, she declined, aware that he was not the most patient, but then her mother suggested that once she got her licence, they could buy a little Issetia Bubble car together. Therefore, the sooner she learnt to drive, the better. She almost gave up, as every time she took her foot off the clutch, the car started hopping along the road. Despite Alan shouting at her whenever she missed a gear or went the wrong way, she remained determined and optimistic. Then one day, Alan suggested they drive the thirty kilometres to Yanchep Park, noted for its caves, native bush, and koala colonies. He drove until they were out of the built-up area, and then Maddie took over. She was doing quite well until they arrived at the entrance, and Maddie noticed a man standing next to a shed selling admission tickets. When he proceeded to walk towards the middle of the road, Maddie panicked; her foot slipped on the accelerator, sending the car towards him! Much to Maddie's relief, the man jumped aside just in time, and when they explained that she was still learning to drive, he managed to see the funny side of the situation, saying it was not a good idea to go running old men off the road and not to come back until she had learnt how to stop the car!

After spending time wandering around the park, they had lunch in the cafeteria before deciding it was time to head home. Alan let Maddie drive as she needed much more practice. She was doing okay until Alan yelled at her, causing her to grind the gears. They ended up having a huge argument, with Maddie telling him it would be better if he drove the rest of the way home. She watched as he got out and made his way around the back of the vehicle. Then, manoeuvring the gear stick into drive, she drove off, leaving him to find his way home.

Maddie had always struggled with her periods, so she was not worried when her period was late. However, a couple of weeks later, when nothing had changed, she decided to visit her doctor, who instructed her to provide a urine sample. She took it to the surgery the next day. The following day, she left the surgery in a state of utter shock. She had been so naïve! It had never crossed her mind that when Alan took her virginity, she could end up pregnant! Her head was whirling, and her stomach felt as if it had sunk to her feet. Doctor Warner had been very kind. He said that she would have to return and see the prenatal nurse in a month, and when the time came, she would need to decide if she wanted to keep her baby. Maddie was scared, but she felt she had no other choice. She didn't want to spend the rest of her life with Alan. Yet, she knew that having the baby would dramatically change her life. She didn't want to tell Alan, but she needed to make a decision before it was too late.

Trembling, Maddie knocked gingerly on the door of a shabby council house and waited until a woman in her fifties came and quickly ushered her into a room devoid of everything except for a bed and a small table. There was complete silence as Maddie tried to suppress her emotions.

'Do you have the money?' the woman asked. Maddie handed over the cash and waited until she counted it. Then a tall, thin man in a white gown entered the room, barely acknowledging her, then speaking abruptly:

'How many weeks? When was your last period?' Maddie was trembling, struggling to speak fluently.

'I… I'm so irregular. I don't know. I had a test at the doctor, who said I'm about five weeks.'

He then told the woman to take her to the bathroom to empty her bladder, and then to remove her panties. It was then that Maddie knew she could not go ahead with it. How could she murder her child? And what if she died?

'I-I can't d-do it. I want to go home. I'm going, I'm going NOW!'

Maddie stumbled toward the chair where she had left her clothes, shaking visibly as she struggled to dress. Ignoring her, the man departed the room.

'It's okay, my dear. You are not the first to change your mind. Sit there and relax for a minute, and then you can get someone to come and take you home.' Then, reaching for Maddie's hand, the woman placed the wad of notes Maddie had paid into her palm. Gently closing her fingers over the top, she said. 'When the time comes, you will need this for your baby.'

That evening, Maddie told her mother she was pregnant, but did not mention that she had come very close to having an abortion. She was surprised when her mother showed neither anger nor particular upset.

'Have you told Alan yet? If not, I believe you should. It's his problem also and you will both have to consider the future and what you both want. I think that you should get married.'

'But mummy, we can't. He's already married!'

Married! A fine pickle you've got yourself into. Mark my words, there will be trouble when she finds out, and she will eventually.' Maddie began to cry…

'It's not like that. He was separated before we met. They no longer live together because she went off with another man.'

Her whole world had turned upside down. She needed to tell Alan, but she knew she had to choose the right time. He always went to the local pub for a few pints after work, and by the time he finally got home, he would be worse for wear. She decided to call him in the morning and managed to speak with him before he left for work.

'Alan, I need to talk to you. It's important.'

'Can't it wait? I'm running late for work. I'll come over this evening and we can talk.'

'No. It can't wait. I'm pregnant! What are **we** going to do?'

A broad grin spread across Alan's face as he took Maddie in his arms.

'That's wonderful news! How long have you known? When is it due?'

'The doctor said near the end of December. But what am I going to do, and what is everyone going to think? I am so ashamed.'

He grabbed his car keys off the table and, kissing Maddie, he said:

'This was meant to be, my darling. We will get engaged and get married as soon as Eileen agrees to a divorce. I'll see you this evening. Don't worry; we'll work it out.'

Daisy was delighted that Maddie and Alan were engaged and arranged an evening to celebrate the occasion. Charles ordered a taxi to take them all to a swish Perth hotel. Alan was overawed – he had never been in such a fancy place. After selecting their choices from the à la carte menu, Daisy ordered a nice wine and asked for it to be brought to the table while waiting for their meal to arrive. A few minutes later, the wine waiter arrived, uncorked the bottle, and poured a small amount of wine into Alan's glass. Then he stood to one side and waited for Alan's approval.

Looking up at the waiter, Alan asked.

'What's wrong, mate? Why are you staring at me?'

It was only when Charles leant over and whispered to Alan that he was meant to taste the wine that he picked up the glass and drank it in one gulp.

'I'll need more than that to decide whether I like it! On second thoughts, you'd better bring me a can of beer.'

Daisy, though unimpressed, said nothing. Maddie wished to crawl under the table, while Charles burst out laughing.

In the meantime, Alan had contacted his sister, Rita, who lived in Sydney, and asked if they could stay with her for a couple of weeks until he found a job and a place to live. Maddie was relieved because she didn't want her friends, especially Kay and her family, to know she was having a baby. She didn't have that wonderful feeling of being in love; she didn't feel the happiness she had always dreamt of.

Although only twenty-five, Alan lacked exuberance and spontaneity, drank too much, and was moody! She dared not think of what lay ahead.

Alan

Alan slipped out of his mother's womb three years before the start of the Second World War, when Nazi Germany invaded Poland on September 1st, 1939. His parents, Sidney and Martha, were already struggling to feed and care for his three siblings: Rita, aged 7; Tommy, aged 5; and Barry, who had just turned 3. Martha was still mourning the birth of a little girl who they said had died at birth. Sometime later, it came to light that the midwife who had attended the birth neglected to notice that the newborn, although breathing shallowly, was still alive. By the time someone realised the error, it was too late!

When Martha's father died, her mother came to live with them. Granny Smith was a real character and a canny one at that. None of the family knew when her birthday was or what year she was born, but to them, she had always looked old, with her long, scraggly face, pointed nose, and chin. She spent much of her time sitting in an old rocking chair in the backyard, usually bent over double and fast asleep. She said it was the only way to escape the noise and arguments in the house. She was always dressed in long black dresses and a large floppy felt hat jammed on her long, straggly, grey hair. The children used to laugh and say she looked like a witch.

Unlike the rest of the family, Granny was very careful with her money and kept it stashed where no one could access it. Wads of notes, all neatly folded, were safely hidden inside her brazier. Her eyesight was poor, and she refused to wear glasses. The children took advantage of this when cadging money from her. She would reach down into her bosom and, pulling out the wad of cash, peel off what she thought was a ten-shilling note, and, handing it to them, she would ask if it was the right one. They would assure her it was, then scurry off with a pound or more.

November, five more days until Guy Fawkes. Sidney made an effigy of an old tramp, stuffing an old pair of dungarees and a shirt with straw, and adding more straw into an old sack for the head. Finally, he placed a tattered black hat on top. This was for the village bonfire that the local children had built over the past few weeks. On the morning of November 5th, some local lads were sent to collect the guy. After knocking on the door and receiving no response, they decided to look for it at the back of the house and were relieved to see the guy in a rickety chair outside the back door. They thought it would be easier to carry if the guy were left in the chair. So, with one tugging and the other pushing, they started dragging it along the ground. They had only gone a few feet when suddenly the figure began screaming and waving its arms. The children were so shocked that they let go of the chair and scarpered off, shouting.

'It's alive, it's alive!'

Meanwhile, poor Granny was cursing and yelling for someone to come and help her. The real guy, the one that Sidney had created, was still in the garden shed!

Alan applied for his birth certificate at fifteen, allowing him to enlist in the Army for a three-year term. He was informed that he might be required to serve one year in Korea, but he was fortunate enough to avoid being dispatched there.

When Alan left the Army, he decided to travel north, where he knew he could earn a good living. Eventually, he found work as a boundary rider on Victoria River Downs Station, near Arnhem Land, one of the largest cattle stations in the Northern Territory.

He had been there a couple of weeks when he was sent to repair a fence along one of the boundaries. Still on his horse, he leant over to adjust a steel standard when his horse bucked, throwing him to the ground. He lay there for three days with a broken pelvis and near death. The heat was so intense that he was covered in ants when they found him.

Leaving Victoria River Downs, he joined a team of drovers herding several hundred head of cattle from Marillana to Roy Hill, where they collected another mob of cattle. They continued on to Bulloo Downs, gathered another mob, and picked up unbranded strays. They drove them south to the railhead at Meekatharra. The journey took ten weeks.

During the journey, a continuous watch was kept over the cattle at the night camp, and one horseman would ride around the mob. If the cattle became restless, there would be two riders. They had to be vigilant in case of sudden noises, such as a dingo howl, a bolt of lightning, or sparks from the fire that could start a rush. If that happened, drovers could be trampled to death in the rush, sometimes still in their swags.

They had a camp cook, a roustabout who assisted the cook and cared for the spare horses, a donkey, a lead rider, four wing riders, and a tailer. Tailers were the individuals at the back of the mob who carried stock whips; however, if they used them, they would be in serious trouble, as the cattle had to be in the same condition as when they left, if not better. Their stores consisted of salt beef, which was kept in salt barrels or brine, goat, and mutton if they were lucky enough to find a sheep, kangaroo, emu, bush bustards, potatoes, and onions. Additionally, there were sweet custard, dried apples, apricots, and bread or damper, depending on the camp cook's skill.

Later, Alan joined nine others to take on contract cattle mustering, which involved travelling in an old Army Blitz without a roof, using a plank instead of a seat, and navigating a steering wheel protruding in mid-air. They retrieved it from the USA Base in Exmouth, where it had been burned out. A Polish guy who had been in the underground in Poland during the war and was still being sought by the Germans got it in working order for them.

They were paid five shillings per head for cattle and one shilling for sheep. Sometimes, they received 10,000 head of cattle and 4,000 head of sheep. They usually started their trek at daylight and continued until dark. They would shoe the horses if they arrived at the next camp earlier than expected. Due to the rugged terrain, they were crossing, the horses had to be shod every three to four days.

Driving through the countryside was challenging, as most of the area was bush, with occasional worn tracks compelling them to follow the sun and seek out food. The land was barren, except for small blue gum trees that resembled shrubs. Numerous valleys existed, and at the windmills, the water was often too salty for human consumption, although it was acceptable for the cattle. They placed charcoal in large cans with holes punched all around, followed by a layer of sand, and then more charcoal. Next, they added the salty water, which they filtered through the sand and charcoal to remove the salt. Additionally, they had two mules pulling a cart with wide wheels that carried their tucker and other gear.

They drove the Canning Stock Route, spanning 1,150 miles, the longest historic stock route in the world, an area where droughts could last up to ten years. The Aborigines always welcomed them, giving them tobacco and other items.

Alan returned to Perth in 1957. Shortly after, he met Elaine, a divorcee with a young child, and they married six months later.

Misgivings

Alan sold the truck and his car. Maddie had managed to save a little after returning home to Australia, but she knew they would need more. So, she sold her bike along with her stamp and coin collection. Although their luggage was limited, Alan insisted on taking a huge suitcase that, much to Maddie's surprise, was full of magic tricks. There was so much to learn about the man with whom she was about to spend the rest of her life.

The day had come for Alan and Maddie to leave Perth. Daisy took the morning off work to drive them to the station where they would begin their four-day journey across Australia, travelling 2.700 miles along the Trans-Australian railway. Maddie was saddened to be leaving without saying goodbye to Kay, her best friend, and the family who had been so kind to her, but she knew they would be upset, as they were aware of Alan's family and their reputation. Unfortunately, Maddie did not realise this until it was too late.

As soon as they arrived at the station, Alan disappeared with the two large cases, hoping to find a porter to place them in the designated carriage. Groups of people were scattered along the platform, embracing loved ones and eager to be on their way. Before long, the guard announced that they would leave in five minutes and that all passengers had to board.

Maddie was on the verge of tears as she hugged her mother, not knowing how long it would be before they saw each other again. Daisy embraced her daughter, fully aware that hard times lay ahead, and wondered if she had made the right decision in persuading her to marry Alan.

'Take care of yourself and remember I will be here if you need me. I love you very much, even though I don't always express it. I'm sorry if...'

'I k-know, mummy. Please, don't worry about me.' Maddie giggled, 'If I can travel across the world on my own...'

Daisy took hold of her daughter's hands.

'You are still no more than a child... It will not be easy.' Then, pressing an envelope into her daughter's hand, she added: 'This is for you. Keep it safe and use it wisely.'

Maddie gave her mother another quick hug.

'Thank you, mummy. I love you and will write to you as often as possible. I-I'm so s-s-sorry...' She broke off, unable to find the words to express her fears and admit that she was scared of the future, for herself and her unborn child.

Then, putting on a brave face, she turned and walked towards the train. The guard strode along the platform from one end to the other, ensuring everyone was aboard. After retracing his steps, he slammed shut all the open carriage doors. Once that was completed, he raised the bright red flag, blew his whistle, and watched as the train slowly gathered momentum on its way out of the station.

A young lad showed Maddie and Alan their sleeper compartment, which was spacious enough for two people to move around each other. It contained a bunk bed and a foldaway wash basin in the corner. They left their small overnight case in the room and headed to the seating areas.

After departing from Perth, the train travelled through the Avon Valley toward Kalgoorlie, one of Australia's renowned gold mining towns. Upon arrival, it was dark, and the train briefly stopped to pick up passengers.

They enjoyed a lovely meal in the dining car before proceeding to the lounge area, where the friendly waiter, Roberto, was eager to point out highlights of interest during their journey.

The following morning, while they were having breakfast, they passed a railway settlement. Roberto told them that the three or four dwellings, which clung to the line amid the rolling red dunes, were all that remained of a once-thriving settlement.

The following day, they arrived at the start of the Nullarbor Plain—a journey of 1,041 miles from Western Australia to South Australia. They passed through a desolate ghost town in the treeless expanse, with a population of four and nothing to indicate its presence.

Alan had always been interested in Australia's history and was listening with great interest to a retired engineer who was sharing their table that evening. He told them that he had spent considerable time researching the history of the Trans Australian railway. In 1916, over 3400 workers were employed to build the line. Maintenance crews lived along the line at intervals and were supplied by the weekly Tea and Sugar train, which later serviced railway workers and their families. It took five years for the teams of rail workers to lay the 2.5 million hardwood sleepers, and 140,000 tonnes of rail were needed to complete the 1,693-kilometre job.

Maddie spent a lot of time looking at the scenery as the train swayed, jolted, and shuddered along the line. It was endlessly flat yet mesmerisingly beautiful miles of desolate, barren land with little greenery except for patches of low-lying salt and spinifex bushes. The only signs of life were the countless kangaroos balanced on their tails, watching as the great monster whizzed by. Those that had taken fright would bound away at tremendous speed. Occasionally, a wedge-tailed eagle would swoop down to attack its prey.

Maddie was not looking forward to living with someone she had never met, even if that person was Alan's sister. Her thoughts kept returning to the time before she met Alan, and she wondered how different her life would have been if she had not broken up with Fred. If only she hadn't been so anxious just because he gave her a passionate kiss. Yet, why then did she not protest more when Alan... *Why!* If only her mother had told her things. About life! All she had ever known was that men could be demanding and would want her to do bad things! Why?

When they arrived in Adelaide, they changed trains to continue to Melbourne and Sydney. They met some interesting people, including Tina and Don, a couple who were trapeze artists travelling to join their circus in Melbourne, sailors Benny and Skip, and a young lad named Vernon, who was embarking on an adventure, hoping to make his fortune.

At last, they arrived at Flinders Street Railway Station in Melbourne, where they had just over an hour to alight onto the train to Central Sydney Station. A group of them went to the station diner to pass the time, where they ordered snacks and drinks. They were enjoying each other's company when the guard blew his whistle, warning them it was time to board. Unfortunately, Benny had just ordered a bottle of champagne, which was still uncorked! They had been told that no alcohol was to be taken on board the train, but Benny said there was no way he was leaving it behind.

Quickly stuffing the cork back in the neck of the bottle, Benny tucked it inside his jacket. By now, the station guard was getting impatient, so they all raced to the train before it left without them. Benny was the last to make a quick spurt to the carriage steps, and as he was about to board, there was a loud 'Pop!' followed by a sputtering sound and a thud as the cork catapulted into the side of the train, barely missing the window. Everyone, except Benny, laughed and watched as the champagne belched out of the bottle and drenched his shirt.

That evening, Alan produced a pack of playing cards and amazed everyone with his sleight-of-hand tricks. They were also entertained by someone playing the piano, the guitar, and even an old squeezebox. It was a lot of fun. After it had quietened, the guys played poker while the women sat together and chatted.

On the last day of their trip, a somewhat cocky young guy asked to join their poker school. Begrudgingly, they let him in but soon regretted it when he started winning most of the hands and building up a nice pile of notes in front of him.

Alan had become suspicious, and it didn't take him long to work out that he was a professional card sharp. He was using the oldest trick in the book – the dude was skilfully dealing from the bottom of the pack.

A few minutes later, the young man informed them that he was tired and would be retiring from the game. Alan laid a hand on his arm.

'Hey mate, not so fast. How about another couple of hands, eh?'

The man hesitated for a few seconds and then replied with a snigger.

'As you wish, but don't you think you've lost enough for the evening?'

Alan bristled:

'Let me be the judge of that. Are you in or not?'

The guy sat down and scooped up the pack.

'I'll toss you for the first shuffle'

Alan stared him straight in the eyes, not blinking or moving a muscle.

'I'll do the toss, mate. Heads or tails?'

The guy stared right back at him.

'Tails and if it lands, I shuffle.'

Alan threw the penny high in the air. It came down heads, and he got to shuffle the pack. Listening to the altercation, some other passengers gathered around to watch how Alan outwitted, mystified, and fleeced his opponent of all he had swindled from him and his friends. He was their hero! Especially when he returned the money his friends had lost.

When they arrived at Central Sydney Station, it was overcast. Maddie jumped when the engine driver blasted the train's horn. Peering out the window, Alan spotted Rita standing amongst the crowd and pointed her to Maddie. As soon as they got off the train, Alan told her to go and introduce herself while he rescued their cases.

Making her way over to Rita, Maddie could see the striking resemblance to Alan. Although much shorter and rather tubby, there was no mistaking their facial features.

Her future sister-in-law greeted her warmly.

'You've had a long journey, my dear. We'll get you home as soon as Alan has rescued your cases. Frank will be on his way from work and hankering after his tea, and the kids are excited to meet their uncle. C'mon, it's a good hour drive, so let's get going.'

Rita offered to help Alan with the lighter of the suitcases, but he shrugged her off, explaining that he was best off with one in each hand as they balanced. Maddie picked up her case and they followed Rita out of the station gate and across to a dilapidated 1950s Hillman Minx.

While Rita was chatting with her brother, Maddie gazed out the window, amazed at how different everything looked. When they arrived at the house, Rita left them to see to their suitcases, while she went in to check on the children, hoping they would be asleep and would give them some peace until morning.

Several bikes and toys were scattered over the small front garden, and everything looked tired and neglected. Maddie was already regretting coming. Once inside, Rita took them to the back of the house to the sleepout, where they would spend the night. She invited them to make themselves at home while she made the last-minute preparations for their evening meal.

Alan followed his sister into the kitchen. Maddie stayed in the room feeling lost, lonely and deeply worried about the future. Then she ran a brush through her long wavy hair, straightened her blouse and entered the kitchen, just as Frank arrived.

'Long time no see, mate. How's things?' he said while shaking hands with Alan. Before waiting for a reply, Frank turned to Maddie, who was laying the large kitchen table readying it for their meal.

'Welcome, my dear, but pray tell me, how on earth did you get tangled up with this brother-in-law of mine? You look much too nice for the likes of him!'

Maddie blushed and was thinking of an answer when Alan retorted:

'It's my wonderful personality and good looks. She couldn't resist me!'

Frank laughed and slapped Alan on the back.

'Quite so, mate, quite so.'

Maddie was starting to feel more at ease—Frank and Rita had made them very welcome. She realised that Rita called the shots in their house since Frank was very easy going. As long as his wife was happy, everything was fine. Where his wife was short and plump, he was of slight build and quite tall.

Frank went to bed not long after they had eaten, as he had an early start the next morning. The others stayed on. Rita was reminiscing with Alan about the times spent as a family.

Early the next morning, Rita pushed open their bedroom door, entered and placed two cups of tea on the bedside table.

'Don't expect this every morning, but I thought you might like a sleep in as it was quite late when we all went to bed last night.' She was just about to shut the bedroom door when she paused. The children are all anxious to see you. It would be great if you were up before Lucy and Sarah leave for school. They are beginning to get on my nerves!'

'Thanks for the cuppa, Sis. Maddie will go and see the kids. Just leave me be for a while. I'll see them this evening. I'm going to spend the day looking for work.' He rolled over, facing away from the door, and pulled the bedclothes up around his neck. 'Let me be for a while.'

Maddie put on her dressing gown, picked up her cup, and followed Rita into the kitchen. She was surprised to see four children sitting around the table eating breakfast. Lucy was eight and the eldest, a pretty, chubby little girl with curly, golden, honey-brown hair that she kept flicking away from her eyes. She had the most beautiful smile and appeared quite shy.

Sarah, who was six, was different in every way – with her mop of ash-blonde hair and, although not as pretty as Lucy, she was alluring. She perched herself on Maddie's knee, wanting all attention to herself, hardly drawing breath while chatting nineteen to the dozen and insisting to know why Maddie had not been to see them before and how long she was going to stay.

Michael, who was four, bore a resemblance to his father, with his slight build and dark, wavy hair. What struck Maddie the most was the defiant way he held her gaze with his deep blue eyes. When she spoke to him, he just shrugged his shoulders.

Lastly, there was little Tommy, who had just started walking and was creating havoc everywhere.

When Lucy and Sarah left for school, Maddie returned to their bedroom. Moving around quietly to avoid waking Alan, she dug into one of the suitcases and found some suitable clothes.

The previous night, she'd felt relaxed and hopeful that everything would be okay, but waking up in the morning, all she could think of was how far away they were from her mother and friends. She thought of her beloved grandfather and how disappointed he would be. Maddie had never felt so ashamed.

A New Life

Alan got a job with the Railways, for which he was paid seventeen pounds a week. They informed him that his pay would increase by three pounds upon completion of the training course. They also gave him a train pass.

Before leaving Western Australia, Alan had asked Elaine for a divorce. Shortly after arriving in Sydney, he received a letter from his solicitor advising him that before she agreed, she demanded sixty-three pounds to cover all her costs. Alan knew they had no way of paying it. He had just bought a car on hire purchase, and after paying Rita for their keep, they barely managed from one week to the next.

Summer was on its way, and the days were getting hotter. Maddie was in her fifth month and just starting to expand. She desperately needed some maternity clothes. Alan had quit his job because the raise he'd been promised had not materialised, and they were struggling to pay for their upkeep, let alone buy anything for when the baby arrived.

One afternoon, when Alan was out looking for work, Maddie took the train into Parramatta and went shopping. Walking into a haberdashery, she asked the shop assistant if she could look at the swatches of material. A couple of minutes later, the young lady reappeared with about thirty squares of coloured cloth, each measuring a foot square, all clipped to a board. Feeling embarrassed, but desperate, Maddie explained that she didn't have the money to buy a maternity top, but if she could have some of the samples, she could make one.

Several minutes later, Maddie returned to the train station with a huge smile and a spring in her step. She couldn't believe how kind they had been. After speaking to her manager, the young assistant had told Maddie that he had let her have all of them. She had also explained that it was nearing the end of the season, when new stock would be arriving, along with additional samples.

Over the next few days, Maddie spent time stitching and sewing, creating three multicoloured tops for herself. She was so proud of herself.

Jack and Rita worked at the local Services Club. Jack worked in the bar, while Rita managed the restaurant. Maddie stayed home to do the housework and look after the children when they came home from school. Maddie waited anxiously for the day they could get their place; everything seemed to be going pretty well—until one day…

Most nights, Alan would have a couple of pints at the pub and be home in time for supper. However, there were still times he stayed out much later. Those were the nights when Maddie's stomach would churn with the knowledge that he would be very drunk.

One night, when Alan still hadn't come home after the pubs had closed, Maddie gave up waiting and sobbed into her pillow, wondering if he would ever change. She slept fitfully, waking now and again to look at the clock on the bedside table. Just as the morning light peeked through the curtains, she was awakened by the sound of the opening bedroom door. She knew it could only be Alan. She could smell the stench of alcohol, the mixture of beer and strong liquor. Quickly shutting her eyes, she lay very still. By no means was she going to let him know she was awake.

She felt the sagging of the mattress as he sat on the edge of the bed. Squinting, she saw him struggling to remove his shoes. Then, he swayed while he tugged at his shirt, straining at the buttons as he pulled it over his head. He tumbled back onto the bed, and before passing out, he managed to say:

'I'm tired, I ssshpent the night in the clink. I need t'sleeeep.'

Maddie got dressed and left the room.

The children had left for school, and Rita had gone shopping with a friend, leaving Maddie to clean up the breakfast dishes. She was sweeping the floor when Alan ventured out of the bedroom. She refused to look at him.

'Maddie!'

She ignored him.

'Maddie… I couldn't come home. I was in jail!'

She turned to face him, refusing to believe what he had just said, waiting for the cough and the clearing of the throat that he always did when he was going to tell a lie. It didn't come. Instead, he indicated towards the kitchen table.

'Please come and sit down. Give me a chance to explain.'

Maddie walked over to the sink, filled the kettle, and put it on the stove. Then she pulled out a chair on the opposite side of the table and sat down, waiting to hear what he had to say.

'I didn't go to the pub. I caught the first train home, and that's the truth. When the train pulled into the station, I couldn't find my pass, but I wasn't that worried as they all knew me. I jumped off the train and made my way to the exit, but as I got through the gate, a pimply faced brat, whom I'd never seen before, demanded to see my pass. I told him I couldn't find it. The cocky little bastard then said I would have to pay before I could leave. I ignored him and continued on my way. The next thing I knew, he had grabbed my arm, saying he was taking me to the Station Master's office.'

Maddie interrupted:

'Then what happened?'

Alan's jaw tightened as his hand bunched into a fist.

'I hit him! He fell to the ground like a sack of potatoes. I left before someone came, knowing I would be in trouble. I'd not gone far when a paddy wagon, blue light flashing, pulled up alongside me and one of the cops jumped out, grabbed hold of me and handcuffed my hands behind my back. Then another cop came over and frogmarched me to the back of the wagon, saying I was under arrest for grievous bodily harm. They then opened the door and shoved me in.'

Maddie was too stunned to say anything. He paused while Maddie pulled the kettle off the stove and filled the teapot, leaving it to brew.

'When we arrived at the lockup, they took all the usual details and said they were putting me in a cell to cool off.'

'Why didn't you phone me?'

'I couldn't.'

'Why?' Maddie could not understand why he hadn't been allowed to make one phone call.

'When they found out I was a professional boxer, they charged me with 'assault with a lethal weapon. I was allowed to contact one person, so I phoned my boss, hoping he would come and bail me out. Which, thankfully, he did.'

'Why did you have to be such an idiot? Did you HAVE to hit him? What did it solve?' Alan glared at her.

'What was I supposed to do? Let some snotty-nosed kid make an idiot of me? NO WAY!'

'W-what did…'

Alan glared at her.

'Do you want to hear what happened next, or not?' Maddie ignored him, picked up the teapot and poured them a cuppa. 'They threw me in a cell with a smelly old wino and to make it worse, I was sober.' He started to laugh. 'The best part is yet to come. I couldn't believe my eyes when he pulled up his trouser leg and produced a half-bottle of whisky from the inside of his sock! And when we finished that one, he produced another from the other leg. Bingo! Best night I've ever spent in a cell. When my boss came and they let me out, they said that it was the first time they'd ever locked someone up sober and let them out drunk!'

Maddie couldn't believe what she was hearing – it all seemed so far-fetched to be true!

Before leaving the lockup, Alan was told he had to present himself at the local Court that afternoon. The judge gave him a good dressing down and warned him that he would be banged up for a lot longer if he came before him again.

Maddie was now into her sixth month, and her baby bump was increasing. She craved oranges and ice cream. Rita was getting her to do more around the house, such as cleaning the tops of the cupboards, which she could only reach by climbing onto a kitchen chair, and mucking out the chook run, among many other chores. Maddie never complained; she knew it was difficult for Jack and Rita to have them there.

Alan was now working for the local council, maintaining the roads, and had been given a supervisory position.

One afternoon, when everyone was at work and the children were at school, Maddie heard someone knocking at the door. When she opened it, she came face-to-face with a rather brash, not unattractive young man. Standing behind him was a young girl with short jet-black hair and a pale complexion.

'Hello, can I help you?' Maddie asked.

'G'day, I'm Adrian, and who are you?' Then, without waiting for her to reply, he pushed the door open wider as they both made their way through the small hallway into the kitchen. 'This is my wife Pat. We've come to see Sis. We've travelled down from Queensland and need somewhere to kip for a few days.'

'Hello. Y-yes, I'm M-Maddie. Alan and I arrived a few weeks ago.' Still stumbling on her words, Maddie told him they were all at work.

'No probs, we'll have a cuppa and wait until Sis gets home.' Then he turned to his wife: 'Pat get off your ass and make us a cuppa while I bring the bags in. You never know what goes on in an area like this. Look the other way and they'd be gone!'

Maddie motioned for Pat to enter, taking her through to the kitchen.

'Sit yourself down and I'll put the kettle on.'

Looking at her watch, Maddie realised it would not be long before the others arrived home. Much to her relief, Adrian did most of the talking.

We left Queensland a few days ago and made our way West. Pat is from Melbourne, so we will stop by to see her mother before continuing to Perth. We were making good time when we arrived at Coffs Harbour, stayed the night, and continued to Newcastle the next day.'

Pat had hardly spoken, but here she gave Adrian a withering look:

'At this rate, I don't think we will get to see my mother! On our way to Parramatta this morning, the engine overheated and caught fire. We had no money for food and had to leave the car where it was and hitchhike. They said the car would have been ready one day next week, but you insisted on leaving without it. Now we are well and truly up the creek without a paddle! Or, should I say, a car?'

'Shut up, Pat!' Adrian put his cup down and spread his arms out in exasperation. 'I told you I will sort something out. I'll get a job while we are here, and when I've saved enough for our train fare to Perth, we can be on our way. That's, if you'll stop nagging and give me half a chance.'

After a few minutes of silence, Adrian was again the first to speak, asking Maddie how she had met his brother, what they were doing in Sydney, and how long they were staying.

Much to Maddie's relief, Alan came home early—finally! Soon after, Rita walked in, and upon seeing her younger brother, she demanded to know why they were there. After introducing Pat, he explained that they were on their way home to W.A. and needed somewhere to stay until their car was fixed. Rita told them they could stay for a couple of days, but after that, they would need to find somewhere else, as they were already cramped.

When Jack arrived home, he was unhappy to see Adrian. He told him that they did not have the space and that he and his girlfriend, or wife—whatever she was—would have to find somewhere else to stay. Eventually, Rita convinced her husband to let them stay for the night and then discuss the situation in the morning.

That night, three children shared a room while Tommy slept with his parents. The next morning, Adrian borrowed Frank's paper and scanned the Situations Vacant column, finding nothing. He walked to the station and hopped on the train to Parramatta to search for work. Meanwhile, Pat stayed home and did nothing.

When Adrian was ready to go out again the next day, Pat insisted on going with him. They ended up arguing until Pat eventually relented. Left behind, she moped around the house all day, doing no work. Eventually, Adrian found a job, and a week later, they set off in search of a new place to stay.

One morning, after the guys had gone to work, Maddie went about her daily chores while, as usual, Pat was nowhere to be found. She went to the bathroom to collect the wet towels that everyone had left scattered on the floor, to remove the soggy soap from the bottom of the bath, and to gather the clothes. She was rather surprised to find the door closed, turning the handle, she pushed it open where she was shocked to see Pat lying on the floor with an untwisted coat-hanger attempting to insert it into her vagina!

'PAT! What on earth are you doing?'

Pat looked up in shock, unaware that Maddie had entered the room.

'I... I... Oh, God! Leave me alone. Go AWAY!'

Maddie had no idea what she was doing or why, but she knew it was wrong and dangerous. She turned away and, stumbling out of the bathroom, slammed the door behind her.

They didn't speak to each other for the rest of the day. Maddie, although not wanting to pry, wanted to know why Pat was doing such a dangerous thing.

Later the next day, when everyone else had gone out, Pat entered the kitchen while Maddie was washing the breakfast dishes.

'About yesterday... I need to talk to you.' Pat's eyes held no emotion, and a look of defiance was on her face. 'I am having a baby, Maddie.' She paused and then looked away from her. 'I **don't** want this baby, I'm **too** young and I'm not ready to become a mother. I've tried every other way to get rid of it!'

Suddenly, it dawned on Maddie that Pat had been trying to kill the child she was carrying. She felt sorry for her, remembering how devastated she had felt when she found out that she was pregnant and how she had come so close to having a back-street abortion. But to do it in such a way? It left her shocked.

'Don't dare tell anyone, especially Adrian, or you will regret it. I promise you!' warned Pat.

'I-I swear I will never tell a soul. D-did you get rid of it?'

Turning her back on Maddie, she made her way out of the room and mumbled.

'No... I didn't! I will pack the rest of our belongings, and when Adrian returns, we will leave. I hate this place, and I hope never to see any of you again.'

Two days later, they moved out.

Once again, Alan was out of work. Rita said she would ask the manager at the Services Club if they could find something for him. Luckily, someone had just handed in their notice. Alan was scheduled to start work the following evening as a bartender. He was not impressed. He also told his sister that he would not wear the uniform, which consisted of black trousers, a white shirt, a bow tie and a cummerbund around his waist, saying he would look like a complete prat! Rita warned him that if he wanted the job, he would have to wear it, and he had to make up his mind or forget about it, but she also reminded him that she would be in trouble if he didn't show up and they were left in the lurch.

He reluctantly donned all the gear and headed to the clubhouse. Rita told him to look after a table in the far corner. She explained to him that the gentleman was celebrating a special birthday with his group of friends. Although not happy waiting on tables, Alan knew his sister had gone out of her way to get him the job. Then, about halfway through the evening, Alan complained to Rita that the man was a dickhead and was making a big man of himself to impress his friends. When the guy ordered Alan to take one of the jugs of beer back because, according to him, it was not full enough, that was the last straw for Alan. He'd had enough. Grabbing the jug off the table, he took it to the bar to be topped up. Alan returned a few moments later.

'Sir, your beer!'

He then tipped the entire contents of the jug over the guy's head. Then he slammed the container onto the table, turned round and walked away. Everyone had stopped talking, watching agog as the customer became pale and trembling with anger, after which he started screaming obscenities at Alan.

Alan continued walking out of the dining room, pulling off his tie, jacket, and cumberbund and throwing them on the floor. Then he marched out of the building. No one attempted to stop him. Rita was in the kitchen but hurried into the dining room to see what the commotion was about, just missing Alan as he had disappeared from the front door.

Later that evening, arriving home from work, she was furious.

'What the hell did you think you were doing? YOU, you bloody idiot, you nearly lost me my job last night. For God's sake, grow up and stop acting like a prima donna! Get dressed and find another job because if you don't have one soon, you and she can leave my house.'

Alan was sheepish but on the defensive.

'Sis, I don't take shit from anyone. I was not going to stay there and be treated like a bloody servant. I'm sorry if it embarrassed you, but that's the way it is.' With that, he stormed out of the room and went to bed, leaving Maddie to try to calm Rita down.

A few days later, he secured a position with a large construction company, and before long, he was promoted to supervisor. He got along very well with the owner, who loaned Alan money to buy a used car. It was to the manager's advantage that his workers had transport.

Alan bought a 1950 FJ Holden. It was not the most reliable car, but he bought it anyway. Within a few days, it broke down, so he took it back to the dealer, who changed it for an old Triumph Herald. Maddie hated it because whenever they were out together, it was her job to crank the handle to jump-start it, often taking several turns of the handle as it was very stiff.

Sometime later, the engine blew up. Once again, they were scouring the car yards to find something cheap and roadworthy. They ended up having to take out a loan for £200 to buy a 1958 Austin A55 Cambridge. Alan was still paying off the loan at work.

Meanwhile, Christmas was approaching, with less than a month to go before their baby was due. They had just moved into a little flat in Parramatta. Alan invited one of the guys from work to spend Christmas Day with them. One problem was that Maddie had never cooked more than a few eggs on toast.

Alan suggested that a chicken would be best, assuring her it would be easy. Maddie had made friends with a very kind lady who lived next door, so she asked her for advice. Besides leaving the plastic bag of giblets inside and the lumpy gravy, Madie was proud of her first attempt at serving her first Christmas dinner.

Alan had cut down on his drinking and was looking forward to their baby.

Maddie emerged from a deep sleep, desperately wanting to empty her bladder. As she got out of bed, she felt a massive gush of liquid streaming down her legs, saturating her nightgown and forming a pool of water on the linoleum floor. Her water had broken. It was time to leave for the hospital.

Maddie paddled slowly around to the other side of the bed.

'Alan.' She gently prodded him. 'Alan, wake up.'

Slowly sitting up, stretching his arms and straightening up his back, Alan squinted at Maddie.

'What time is it?'

'It's just after six. It's time to go to the hospital. At least we'll miss most of the early morning traffic.'

She pulled off her nightdress, which was clinging to her body.

'I'm going to the bathroom till you come into the land of the living.'

After a quick shower, Maddie returned to the bedroom, where Alan was dressed and ready to go. She retrieved the overnight bag, which had been sitting on a chair since she'd packed it several weeks ago.

'I've warmed the old girl up, as you know how temperamental she can be in the mornings. I need to get some work done on her. New pads for the brakes and the handbrake need adjusting. It will give me something to do while you're in the hospital,' he said.

Within minutes, they were en route to the hospital.

Morning was breaking, and the roads were quiet, but they knew it wouldn't be long before the early commuters appeared. Maddie's contractions were occurring every three to four minutes, each lasting a minute or more. Although she remained calm, she was terrified that her baby would be born in the car, as the pain in her back intensified and she felt as though her insides were collapsing.

Alan was getting agitated.

'I'm going as fast as I can. Do we turn left or right at the bottom of the hill?

Struggling to speak as she felt another contraction, she attempted to respond:

'D-down the bottom of the hill, then r-right at the lights, a sharp left and then keep going. It's not that far now!'

They reached the crest of the hill, and Alan put his foot on the brake to slow the car down. When nothing happened, he started pumping the brake with his foot, and when that didn't slow the car down, he pulled up the hand brake, but it was limp in his hand.

'Hold on, Maddie! The brakes aren't working, and the bloody hand brake is stuffed.'

Maddie gripped the edge of the seat so hard that her hands were hurting, and her heart was thumping as Alan changed down a gear and then another, and they rapidly picked up speed. Seconds before arriving at the lights, they changed to green, and they coasted over the main road without incident. Giving a huge sigh of relief, realising just how close they had come to having an accident. Five minutes later, Alan was pulling up outside the hospital's emergency entrance.

Their son was born within the hour. Maddie was exhausted and feeling extremely sore, having had several stitches where the skin and vaginal muscle had torn. They whisked her son away, telling Maddie she needed to rest.

While she was being wheeled out of the labour ward, she spotted Alan chatting to another expectant father. As soon as he saw his wife, he walked over to her, and the nurse stopped for a moment as he kissed Maddie and then told her he was off to the pub to wet his son's head and would return later in the evening.

Visiting hours were nearly over when Maddie heard quite a commotion from the nurse's station. She thought it was most likely a problem with one of the patients. Also, Maddie was not surprised that Alan had not turned up. She knew he would have had a session with some of his mates.

Sometime later, one of the nursing staff came into the ward and, making her way over to Maddie's bed, she apologised:

'Maddie, I'm afraid we had to turn your husband away as he was **very** drunk. I'm sorry, love, but we couldn't let him in. We told him to come back in the morning.'

'Thank you for letting me know. I'm not surprised, as he had told me he was going to see his mates and celebrate the birth of his son. He'll be in tomorrow after work.'

The following morning, Rita popped in on the way to work and gave Maddie a lovely bunch of flowers and fruit. Four other mothers were in the ward, watching the door anxiously for their husbands and families to arrive.

Maddie had finished feeding Peter, and he was fast asleep in the little cot beside her bed. When the visitors' bell sounded, Maddie watched as fathers and family trooped in, all anxious to see mother and baby. Maddie had just finished lunch when the nurse brought a basket of flowers and a note from her mother, congratulating them on becoming parents and expressing her pleasure that everything had gone well.

The evening visitors had just started arriving when, much to Maddie's relief, she saw Alan approaching her bed and holding a small bunch of flowers tied together with a piece of old string. After kissing her and taking a peek at Peter, he said he hadn't had time to buy any and had pinched some from the gardens he'd passed on his way to the hospital. Maddie could not help giggling, thinking it was rather romantic… in a crazy way.

Maddie's heart exploded with love for Peter. Someone needed her for the first time in her life— the unconditional love of a child for his mother.

Travelling the Nullarbor, 1961

The day came when Alan wanted to move on again, telling Maddie he wished to return to Perth, expressing his frustrations with the pace of life in Sydney. He noted that Perth, despite being remote from the rest of Australia, was friendlier and sunnier, with everything moving at a much slower pace. Maddie needed little persuasion; she was as eager as her husband to go back, and Peter, at four months old, was a healthy and very calm child, so she was confident that the train journey would not harm him. She was unaware that the plans would soon change...

Adrian called around to see his brother, as Rita had told him about Alan's plans to return to Perth. As Maddie had washing to hang out, she left them to it. Returning inside a while later, she became worried when Alan informed her that there had been a change of plans. Instead of taking the train, he and Adrian decided that taking the car would make more sense. Maddie started to protest, but Alan argued that it would be an advantage for all of them, and they could share the driving and the fuel expenses. Maddie tried reasoning with him, explaining that their son was too young to undertake such an epic journey across hundreds of miles of desolation. The brothers were adamant that it would be safe and much cheaper than taking the train. Maddie agreed reluctantly but insisted on taking Peter to the doctors for a check-up before leaving.

They would be undertaking a journey of 2,400 miles from Sydney to Perth. The 1,500-mile drive from Adelaide to Perth included 1,100 miles of unsealed dirt roads, with very few supply points along the way. Fuel was a scarce commodity, generally only available by driving into the few remote homesteads along the way. Maddie was unsure that their 1948 Holden Station Wagon would make the trip, and worried about the many hazards along the way.

Alan had a week's wages owing, but that would not get them far with fuel and food. Maddie still had little of the money her mother had given her, which she hadn't told Alan about. The men spent several days checking out the car and purchasing emergency spares, including a fan belt, spark plugs and leads, gaskets, a powerful torch, a toolbox, and a jack. Other items included: two five-gallon Jerry cans, one holding fuel and the other for water. Also, a hessian bag filled with water slung on the front bumper allowing it to cool in the breeze. The spare tyre was not the best, but it would get them out of trouble. A cool box filled with emergency food supplies and cans of beer, which the guys agreed were crucial for the trip. Lastly, a ground sheet for the nights when the guys would sleep outside under the stars.

Maddie and Pat said there was no way they would be sleeping outside with all the creepy crawlies and snakes, and would be more than happy to kip in the car with Peter snuggled in his carrycot.

Alan insisted on leaving before sunrise to avoid the peak traffic and to take advantage of the cool morning air. That night, Adrian and Pat slept on the sofa bed.

The following morning, before sunrise, they left Parramatta. After travelling along the Hume Highway for seven hours, they eventually pulled into the small community of East Wangarrata, where they found a rather run-down motel to kip for the night. Maddie went to the office to book a room, while the others drove around the back of the building. They were all aware that if the person on reception saw four of them, they would be asked to pay for two rooms. The girls took the double bed, Alan took the armchair, and Adrian, after finding a blanket and two pillows in the cupboard, dossed down on the floor.

On day two, they bypassed the city of Melbourne, driving over three hundred miles. Eventually, they had to make a pit stop at Ballarat. Then, they made their way to the South Australian border, where they bedded down for the night at the local Youth Hostel.

On day three, they crossed the South Australia-Victorian border and headed to Port Augusta. This was the point at which wheat and wool were loaded onto clipper ships and transported around the world. The Rail industry saved Port Augusta from the worst of the 1930s depression, and when the war came, this industry was crucial to the war effort. Bomber aircraft flew overhead, and air-raid trenches were dug. From 1941, lookouts for Japanese aircraft were posted at the high-water towers.

Over the next two days, they travelled three hundred miles, passing through many small farming areas: Kimba, Kyancutta,

Wudinna, Yaninne, Minja and Poochere. Finally, they arrived at Ceduna – a large fishing village just over 90 miles East of Nundroo at the start of the Nullarbor Plain. The temperature had reached an unbearable 45 degrees. They eventually found a park area where several Aboriginals had sprawled under a giant Gum tree, trying to keep cool. Peter was dehydrated and due for a feed. Everyone was exhausted from the extreme heat. Alan knew they had come too far to turn back.

'C'mon, we'll find out how much to stay the night in the pub. We all need a good night's sleep, and Peter is struggling with the heat. We need to stay here tonight and most of tomorrow and then leave in the cool of the evening.'

Maddie wanted to hit out at Alan and remind him she hadn't wanted to bring their baby on such a risky journey with hardly any money to pay for accommodation and food. She strode off carrying Peter in his carrycot, leaving them all to it and making her way to the nearest pub, hoping they could find her somewhere to cool off and feed her son.

Adrian strode off, swearing under his breath as he went:

'We can't stand here all day sweltering in the sun. I'm off to the pub.'

The publican's wife took pity on Maddie and her wee baby and persuaded her husband to give Adrian some work in the yard. She told him it was time for someone to clean up the junk lying around. Then, she led them inside, telling Pat and Maddie she could use extra help in the kitchen and dining room because they had a birthday celebration that evening. Alan kept everyone amused with his magic and sleight of hand. In return, they were all given a bed for the night. Susan, the publican's wife, gave Alan twenty bob, assuring him how grateful she was for the evening's entertainment – everyone had stayed longer, which meant they had bought more drinks!

The following morning, just as they were getting ready to leave, the cook told them to bring their cool box into the kitchen. They could not believe their eyes when she loaded it with cold drinks, pies, sausage rolls and some tasty leftovers from the party. 'Instructions from the boss,' she said.

They were now ready to embark over the rough terrain and the desolate limestone of the Nullarbor. The next substantial town was Norsman. A trek of over one thousand and two hundred miles and, all being well, three days travelling.

Some of the crevices along the way were up to two feet deep and had filled up with very fine, bull dust, as it was more commonly known. No matter how carefully they drove, many deep potholes were not seen until they hit them. Others who had attempted the journey and had been unlucky enough to hit one had placed a bush or a tree branch over the top. They travelled over low-lying saltbushes and spinifex, managing to manoeuvre their way around as much as possible. Abandoned vehicles appeared at regular intervals along the way. Dumped a short way off the road, they were like grim reminders of the seriousness of any breakdown. Stripped and abandoned, most were riddled with bullet holes.

They had forgotten to top up the fuel cans before leaving Ceduna, so they detoured into a station homestead at Yalata, where thankfully the pastoralist was selling it from fifty-five-gallon metal drums. While Alan was paying for the fuel, Adrian drove the car to where the others were outside an old shack with a rickety sign tacked above the door. 'Joe's Bar.'

Alan and Adrian chuckled as Maddie, who had Peter cradled in her arms, and Pat looked on in amazement at a local straddling the bar. They had never seen such bulging biceps. He was at least six feet tall and weighed 150 pounds, if not more. They watched in bewilderment as he tipped his head back, ensuring he had savoured every drop of beer. It was not until the guy behind the makeshift bar spoke up that they noticed someone else in the room. Until then, they only had eyes for their fellow patron – a huge Boomer - male kangaroo, which, when upright, was almost 6 ft.

'G'day guys, I'm Jack. Everyone's welcome here, even Sheila's. Don't mind Buck. He's famous in these parts. Some who pass through are scared stiff of him, but he wouldn't hurt a fly. G'on, Buck, get outta here! You take up too much room. Besides you've had enuf.'

One gigantic leap, and Buck, the friendly Boomer (a male Kangaroo), was out the door.

'He's an old man now, been 'round here a long time and never fails to come in for a pint. Recon, that's what keeps him going. Ok, guys, what'll be? Pints all round?'

They thanked Jack for his hospitality as they had enjoyed listening to him tell them stories from around the area, but they had stayed long enough. It was time to make up ground before dusk, when they would need to drive even more slowly to avoid hitting wildlife. The kangaroos made the most of the shade provided by the bushes by digging shallow holes beneath them to access the cool earth beneath the surface, while taking advantage of the shade from above and the cooling effects from below.

Along the way, they saw many emus and bustards grazing beside the road. Those which had been ploughed down by speeding interstate trucks lay dead along the roadside. Dingos ran into the bush as soon as they heard the sound of their vehicle, and the car slowed down as a family of emus sauntered across the road. Snakes slithered across the road, and a Bungarrow goanna scurried off out of sight. The cars were few and far between, and they could be easily spotted – way in the distance, one could see the dust flying up. The travellers would stop and chat, updating each other on the conditions ahead and what to expect, other than miles and miles of red dust – sometimes it was so thick they could barely see the road ahead. When the wind blew, it got worse. Everyone and everything in the car, including what was in the boot, was covered in red dust.

Along the way, they came across wrecked vehicles, shattered dreams of those who never made it. Come evening, everyone had to be alert. They constantly shouted, 'Kangaroo to the left!', 'Kangaroo to the right!', or 'Watch out!' – the kangaroos emerged from a low bush and could be in front of the car in a couple of bounds. Maddie was thankful that Alan had insisted on having a kangaroo bar fitted to the front of the car because if they happened to hit one, they would be in big trouble.

The guys took turns driving and sleeping, and Pat and Maddie kept an eye out for wildlife and ensured that Peter was comfortable and calm. Most nights, Adrian and Alan kipped on the ground sheets near the campfire embers that they'd lit earlier to heat Peter's food in the Billy Can – a large empty jam tin with a loop of wire attached for the handle. In another, they heated some baked beans. They threw a bit more wood on the fire when it died down, hoping to keep the creepy crawlies away.

At last, they arrived at the Nullarbor Roadhouse. The station owner, Scobe, as he was affectionately known, informed them that Nullarbor Station spanned over 1.25 million acres, and the homestead was located twelve miles further inland. Scobe served them petrol, which he had pumped from gallon tanks into drums. Then they strolled over to an old stone building where they could buy some drinks. Alan spotted a tyre that would fit their car and asked if they could buy it from him. He refused because, as he explained, it was nearly worn down to the tread; however, he said they could have it if Alan thought it would get them out of trouble.

Just as they left, a rusty old pickup hurtled in, engulfing everyone in red dust. Scobe laughed heartily.

'That's George the Rabbit Trapper, a bonza guy, but one of the craziest trappers around here. C'mon, I'll introduce you.'

He slapped George on the back, sending up clouds of red dust, while Pat was coughing and spluttering.

'G'day, mate. How ya doin'? Come and meet these drongos who've spent days travelling from Sydney and intend reaching Perth all in one piece! I thought you were the crazy one, but not so sure now.'

George shook hands with Alan and Adrian and acknowledged the girls.

'G'day, Cobbers. Nice to meet ya'll. How long ya'round these parts for, cos if ya need some money, you blokes can come trapping with me for a few days. You'll get four shillings a pair and I'm sure Scobe's missus will put the sheilas and youg'un up for two or three nights.'

Alan and Adrian looked at each other and then, noticing the look on Pat and Maddie's faces, they immediately knew they had to decline. As much as the money would help them on their way, they realised it was more important to continue to Perth. So, bidding Scobe and George goodbye, they hit the track, making their way to Madura.

With a population of four, Madura was like many other locations in the Nullarbor, consisting of little more than a makeshift roadhouse. Their accommodation was occupied by two young lads who, having run out of money, had been given a job for a couple of weeks.

After several punctures and minor mechanical problems, they were anxious to reach the end of the Plain. The guys were hanging out for a beer, and they were all in need of a good feed. They were nearly out of cigarettes, and Pat was abusing the guys, as they would not give her one of the last stubs they had. Everyone was irritable, and Peter needed a cool bath and somewhere out of the heat.

They were about half an hour away from Norsman when they got another flat tyre. They packed it solidly with a Spinifex bush, hoping it would bring them to the next stop. Not long after, another tyre went, and with no bushes around, they had to ride on the rim of the wheel to Norsman.

Arriving in the town, as soon as Adrian parked outside a pub, Maddie picked Peter up from his carrycot and cradled him in her arms. She was concerned because there was just one tin of food left, the milk in her breast was drying up, and he was suffering from the heat. She needed to get him into a cool place as quickly as possible.

Tempers were becoming frayed. Alan was angry at Adrian and Pat because they had been spending their money on cigarettes. They knew that Alan still had a little cash, so Pat asked him to buy her some. Alan was furious.

'We need all the money left to pay for fuel and food to keep us going. Tell your missus to back down. I've had enough of her moaning!'

Adrian was also fed up with Pat always thinking about herself.

'Can't you shut up, woman! We're nearly on the bones of our ass, we've hawked our watches and anything else of value. That's it! I don't know about you, but that's all I had of any value, and it was given to me by my uncle Jo!'

Alan readily agreed with Adrian.

'I've already hocked my watch and have nothing else of any worth, if I did, I'd give it up for a good feed or a bed for the night. How about you, Pat? Looks like you've got a couple of really nice rings, eh?'

'No way are you getting those, they were my gran's. I'd give you my wedding ring, but knowing your brother, I doubt it is worth a bean!' She turned and marched off while hurling abuse at them as she went.

The publican took pity on them and bought everyone a round of drinks. His wife, Sally, took Maddie and Peter into the lounge and left them there while she went to the kitchen to prepare some of Peter's milk formula. They all felt a lot better after eating portions of pie and chips. The owner let them all bunk down in the shearer's quarters for the night.

The next morning, just as they were preparing to leave, Sally gave them a hessian bag laden with sandwiches, cold water and two cans of beer for the men. Maddie hugged her, and everyone thanked her for her kindness.

They'd travelled one hundred and forty miles when they ventured through the Yalata Aboriginal reserve, where the Anangu people had settled. Everyone was anxious, as the publican warned them that travellers, especially the white ones, were not welcome. They had just about got to the end of the reserve when they saw several natives, all carrying spears and boomerangs. They were grouped along the roadside. Alan slowed down and told them to remain calm and keep looking ahead. While they were passing, one of the men held his spear up in the air and saluted them on their way. All breathed a sigh of relief.

Diverting away from large potholes and rattling along over areas of corrugation, they eventually arrived at Ivy Tanks, where there was nothing other than two large rainwater tanks. The corrugated iron roofing served as a rainwater catchment system that drained into storage tanks. It was full of bullet holes, but thankfully, there was a small amount of water.

After leaving Ivy Tanks, they crossed the West/South Australian border. Then, proceeding on to Eucla, they came across an abandoned vehicle. The guys took one of the tyres to replace their threadbare one. They were now running on sump oil, as Alan had used one of Pat's stockings to strain the sludge out of the oil.

Having left Eucla, they decided it would be advisable to drive the hundred-odd miles to Madura in the cool of the night. Alan was at the wheel, and Adrian, who was supposed to be watching out for kangaroos, had just nodded off. Peter was fast asleep in his carrycot, which was wedged between Maddie and Pat.

Alan was feeling drowsy and was just about to stop the car when he saw lights blinking in the sky. He started to worry when they loomed closer and closer to the vehicle. His gaze remained fixed on the object while he shouted out to the others to wake up.

'What on earth! Wake up, you lot. Adrian, Adrian for fuck's sake look... the lights.'

By now, they were all awake, and the girls were also becoming alarmed. Then, suddenly, the lights reversed out of sight at an incredible speed and disappeared into the darkness of the night. They all relaxed and started talking amongst themselves, wondering what on earth it had been. The girls were too frightened to say anything until Pat grabbed Maddie by the arm.

'That was scary. We cannot all be delusional! You all saw it, didn't you?'

Maddie, still in shock, nodded in agreement.

'Even so, who would ever believe us?'

Adrian told Alan to stop the car.

'I'll drive now, bro. Sounds like you need a break. Take a nap and you'll take over from me when we leave Madura in the morning.'

When Alan pulled over to the side of the road, he shouted:

'Oh, my God...look! It's back.'

They all watched spellbound—once again, the thing was coming straight at them, but this time, the lights were changing from orange to green as it got closer and closer until it hovered above them. Pat screamed, and Maddie was too frightened to speak. The men, shocked at the sight, remained silent, unsure of what to do. Then, once again, it shot off into the darkness of the night at an incredible speed.

Adrian was the first to speak.

'What the heck was that? I can tell you now that it scared the living daylights out of me. Are you girls okay?'

There were mumbles from the back of the car, and Alan, who had slid down in his seat when he thought the object was going to land on them, said:

'Hey guys... I think we'd better keep this to ourselves. As Maddie said, no one would ever believe us. They'd think we were nutters.'

They all agreed never to tell a soul, knowing they would not be believed. Yet, whatever it was, they knew they had witnessed something extraordinary and frightening.

During their last night on the Nullarbor, they saw many grey kangaroos following the shadows that fell across the nearby mountains and a flock of about twenty wild emus. It was with relief that they all fell into a deep sleep that night.

Making their way to Cocklebiddy, then on to Caiguna and Balladonia, the next stop is Norsman, the first 'real' town for approximately 1600 miles. Dusk would soon be upon them, and with the evening getting cooler, the kangaroos would be emerging in leaps and bounds out of the bushes to find food on the edges of the road. Twenty miles from Norsman, the men became concerned as the engine started overheating. Adrian pulled the car to a stop, got out, and opened the bonnet, allowing it to cool down. Half an hour later, they released the radiator cap to check the water level. It was fine. Then they realised a bigger problem – the head gasket was about to blow. Thankfully, they were able to start the car and slowly limp into Norsman. The following morning, they found a very friendly mechanic who, luckily, had the part they needed.

Once again, they were on their way. Another 452 miles on sealed roads and they would finally be in Perth.

Suburb to Outback

Within the week, Alan had secured a job as a salesman with T&G Mutual Life, despite having no prior experience selling vacuum cleaners door-to-door in Sydney. He knew it would be difficult for the first few weeks, given that the minimal weekly wage was £14.80. He would have to rely on commissions to bolster his earnings. Finding qualified customers was notoriously challenging, and the few leads the company provided were of little help. They explained that the sales entitlements would not be paid until the process was completed and the policies were delivered to the customer.

Peter was four months old when they moved into the fully furnished, neat, weatherboard cottage in Wembley. On the outside, the place appeared to have been newly painted in a soft grey. A small garden on both sides of a slabbed pathway led to the veranda that spread across the front of the house.

Maddie was so happy that they finally had a place of their own. She and Alan made friends with a lovely couple living next door, Molly and Eric, who were in their fifties. Maddie found it comforting to have a friendly face nearby, and Molly was always willing to offer her some advice. She wanted to be a good wife and a mother, and with Molly's help, she was also learning to cook.

After they had moved into the house, Alan had been coming home at a reasonable time, only stopping off for a couple of beers on the way. For the first time, Maddie was starting to feel happy. She loved the evenings at home as a family and how Alan would play on the floor with Peter or help him when he was trying to sit up. He would tell Maddie about his day, and was so proud when he had signed someone up with a sound insurance policy. He cared about his clients and wanted to ensure they got the best policy for their needs.

They still had the clapped-out Holden, which Alan had done much work on upon returning to Perth. Most weekends, they drove to see Daisy and Charles and then to Fremantle harbour to buy fish and chips wrapped in newspaper from the Ciccarello's. Then they would walk back to the foreshore and sit on the grass to eat them while greedy gulls were getting ready to catch any morsel thrown to them.

Maddie should have known that life was too perfect. It wasn't long before Alan returned to his old ways, staying too often in one of the pubs after having a skin full. The later it got, the more anxious she became, watching the clock and listening for the sound of the car in the driveway. Sometimes, he had to meet a customer after work and would phone to say he would be late. When that was the case, she would put his tea in the oven for when he arrived home.

One evening, when he didn't phone, Maddie removed the dried, inedible tea from the oven and threw it in the bin. Then she went to bed, not wanting to be around when he came home. It was easier that way. Sometime later, Maddie was woken from a deep sleep by the sound of the creaking front door. She knew it was Alan and lay very still – she didn't want him to know she was awake. A few minutes later, she heard a crashing noise from the sitting room, followed by Alan's swearing. Getting out of bed and putting on her dressing, Maddie went to the room and found Alan on the floor, on top of the metal smoker stand, where he was futilely trying to pull his trousers off.

Maddie was so angry.

'I've had enough! I cannot take any more, Alan!'

He looked at her through bloodshot, bleary eyes, his lips pursed as he was holding onto one of the armchairs while slowly pulling himself up. Eventually, he managed to sit in the chair, pull his trousers on, and then staggered towards the bathroom.

'Leave me alone! I'm sick of listening to your nagging.'

He stumbled into the bathroom and slammed the door shut. Maddie heard him mumbling to himself, so she decided to make herself a cup of tea, hoping it would help her get some much-needed sleep. Then she changed her mind and returned to the bathroom to see if he was alright or, hopefully, gone to bed. Standing outside the door, she was sure that she could smell gas!

What on earth was he up to?

She pushed open the door and was shocked to see Alan bent over the bath with his head under the old gas heater. Suddenly, she realised that was where the fumes were coming from!

Maddie was in a state of panic; her mind was racing. She had no idea what to do. Then Alan screamed at her. The venom in his voice frightened her even more.

'GET OUT! Leave me alone, you bitch, let me die. GO AWAY!'

Panic-stricken, Maddie grabbed his arm and tried to pull him from under the heater. Seconds later, he stood up and walked out of the bathroom as if nothing had happened. He picked up the car keys that had dropped out of his trouser pocket and made his way out of the front door, slamming it behind him.

It was then that it dawned on Maddie that he had no intention of gassing himself – it was his way of manipulating her.

She went to bed, mentally exhausted.

The next morning, Alan was very quiet and did not mention what had happened the previous night. Maddie was not surprised because, in the mornings after a binge, he seldom spoke of the previous night's events.

Alan arrived home from work early, clasping a bouquet. He put it on the kitchen table, took his wife's hand, and led her to the sitting room.

'Can we talk?' he asked.

Maddie nodded. Alan sat in one of the lounge chairs and, still holding Maddie's hand, pulled her onto his lap.

'I promise I will cut down on my drinking. It will be different from now on. Maybe I'll give it up for good!'

Maddie glanced away, avoiding looking at him. They had gone through this many times before, with Maddie forgiving him, hoping he could change. She loved him… well… most of the time, but wasn't happy. The previous night had shaken her.

Pulling herself up off his knee, Maddie glanced back at her husband.

'Our tea is on the stove, we should eat it before it gets cold.'

Alan kept his word, stopping for a couple of pints and arriving home in time for tea. Occasionally, he had to go out again to visit clients who worked during the day. If he had to see them straight after work and knew he would be late, he'd phone to let Maddie know.

Yet, she wasn't surprised when he gradually returned to his old habits. At least he wasn't out until the early hours of the morning. She often pondered where he went after the pubs closed!

It was a lovely spring morning, and Peter, now nearly six months old, was in the garden with his mother, happily playing in his playpen and enjoying the soft carpet of grass. Maddie was about to peg the last item on the line when she heard the side gate click open. Looking up, Maddie was surprised to see a short, rather dumpy, yet pleasant-looking woman walking toward her. She quickly hung Peter's little vest on the line and, turning to face her, immediately recognised her as Alan's wife. Recalling her manners, she held out her hand to welcome her.

'I'm M-Maddie.'

Elaine returned the handshake, replying.

'Hello…I'm Elaine, Elaine Cox. Is Alan home? I need to speak to him.'

Maddie smiled.

'Unfortunately, Alan is at work, but I can call to check if he's still in the office and let him know you're here.'

Elaine paused for a moment.

'Thank you, that is very kind. Emmm… I can tell by the way you are looking at me that you know I'm Alan's wife?'

'Yes, I do, Elaine,' nodded Maddie. I recognised you from the wedding photos. Come inside, and I'll phone the office and let Alan know you're here. Then I will make a pot of tea.'

Maddie leant over into the playpen as Peter stretched out his arms for his mother to scoop him up. She indicated that Elaine should follow her into the house, and then, after placing her son in the high chair, she offered Elaine a seat and told her to make herself at home while she made the call.

As luck would have it, Alan was in the office.

'I hope she's not come to make trouble,' he said. Maddie told him that she didn't think so and that Elaine seemed very nice. 'Okay, I'll be there as soon as I can. About half an hour or so.' He hesitated for a moment. 'Did she say why she wanted to see me?'

Maddie told her husband that she had no idea what she wanted, but she was sure everything would be fine.

'I'm just going to make us a pot of tea. I'll see you soon.' Maddie hung up before he could respond.

When he arrived, Maddie made a fresh pot and suggested that he and Elaine speak privately in the lounge. They could barely have had time to drink their tea when Elaine poked her head around the kitchen door and bid Maddie goodbye. Maddie was anxious to know what she wanted and why she had left so soon.

Once the front door closed, Alan entered the kitchen, grinning widely.

She wants a divorce and says she will pay for it as she is getting married again. This means that we can get married as soon as it is finalised! Good news, eh!'

Much to their disappointment, their landlord informed them that he had decided to sell, giving them a month to vacate and find another place.

Every day, Alan checked the newspapers for a place to rent—somewhere not too far from town and at a price they could afford. They understood that it would not be an easy task. Then, with only a few days left before they had to vacate, Alan came across an advertisement that he thought looked promising.

'Maddie, come and look at this. It sounds ideal, and we won't have to pay rent!'

Peter was in his highchair and had just finished his breakfast. Maddie wiped the food from around his face and hands. Giving him the spoon to play with, she went to the kitchen table and, standing behind Alan's chair, looked over his shoulder at where he was pointing.

Free accommodation in exchange for caring for an elderly lady. Must be available to move in immediately.

'Emmm...,' she hesitated, 'It's a pretty big responsibility looking after an old lady, and nothing is said about how old she is or how much care she needs. I'm unsure if it's a good idea, but we can always call them. We won't be the only ones attracted by having no rent to pay, but how many would want to look after an old lady in return!'

Maddie called the number and spoke to Mr. Summers, the old lady's son, who informed her that, since there had been no other enquiries yet, they could see him that afternoon after Alan finished work.

Three days later, they packed the car with their belongings and bid farewell to Molly and Eric. Maddie felt sad because Molly had been there when she needed her the most. She promised to return and visit them whenever she could.

The house was well-maintained, featuring spacious rooms and high ceilings. Mrs. Summers was in her eighties, and since becoming ill, she had spent most of her time in her bedroom, occasionally venturing into the lounge in the evenings.

Maddie cared for her, looked after the house, and cooked their meals. Mrs. S was not the easiest person to get along with, and no matter how much Maddie tried to please her, it was never enough. Peter was crawling and getting into everything, while Maddie was running herself ragged as a wife, mother, and caregiver.

Alan's Decree Nisi was granted, and sometime later, the Decree Absolute was granted, too.

Alan and Maddie were married at the Registry Office in Perth a month later. Daisy and Charles were set to be their witnesses, but for some reason, Charles was delayed, so they approached someone on the street.

Daisy pinned a posy of violets onto her daughter's jade-coloured box suit, which Maddie had bought when she returned to England. Alan looked very smart and quite handsome in the light grey suit he had purchased specifically for the occasion. Afterwards, they all went to 'Romano's' – an Italian restaurant in Fremantle, where they made the best chicken and spaghetti.

The following morning, Maddie woke up with a hangover; it was the first time she had drunk alcohol.

Peter, now eleven months old, had a mouthful of teeth and was trying to walk by clutching the seat of a chair, often falling onto his little bottom. Maddie was extremely grateful when her mother bought them a pram, as her son was a solid young lad, and carrying him everywhere made her arms ache. Alan seldom offered to take him, and when he did, he was unsure how to hold him. He only changed his nappy one time, and that was when he was drunk one evening, showing off to some friends.

In the meantime, the Holden had become too expensive as it was always breaking down. Maddie lost count of the times it stalled at traffic lights, needing to be towed or pushed out of the way. There were also the many times they had to push start it—Alan pushing from the rear of the car, rolling it down an incline, and shouting to Maddie to put it into first gear, followed seconds later by him yelling for her to release the clutch slowly. One day, Alan took it to a scrapyard, hoping to get a few pounds, but he was told it was worthless, as most of the parts were unusable.

Then Alan bought an old 1954 Dodge Royal from one of his workmates. He was still with the insurance company, but Maddie knew that he yearned to be back up north on a sheep or cattle station and to have a place of their own, rather than living in someone else's home and taking care of elderly ladies. He was still listed with the Perth Pastoral Agency and hoped something would happen soon.

Maddie had begun to think they would never afford to leave when, one morning, not long after Alan had left for work, she received a phone call from the Pastoral Agency. They told her to inform her husband that they had a position that might interest him. Maddie assured them he would be there first thing the next day.

The next day, Alan strode out of the interview, grinning from ear to ear. He was tempted to stop by the local pub for a few schooners, but he decided against it as there was much to do in a very short time. Besides, he couldn't wait to get home and tell his wife.

'Maddie, Maddie…. where are you? I got the job. Did you hear me? I have a job.'

She called from the bedroom:

'Yes, I heard you. You don't have to shout! That's wonderful news, I'll be there in a moment as I'm putting Peter down for his nap. While you're waiting, can you please put the kettle on?'

While they sat and sipped their tea, Alan explained to Maddie that they would be managing a large sheep station, one hundred and twenty thousand acres, near Meekatharra—a town in the mid-west Murchison region of W.A. He spread out a map to show her exactly where it was, and then produced a folder with details of the property and the work expected of them.

'How soon do we have to leave? How do we get there, or will they arrange transport?'

Alan interrupted her.

'It's okay, sweetheart, you don't have to worry as Sir Ernest Lee-Steere has given us a few days to get ourselves sorted. We will be driving up there, and I assured him we would arrive sometime Sunday evening.'

Maddie panicked.

'We can't possibly leave so soon. There's your job; you have to let them know, and we must tell Mr Summers that we can no longer care for his mother. What is he going to say? Besides, I still have to look after her, pack the clothes, and see Mummy before we leave. I can't just disappear without saying goodbye.'

Alan frowned in frustration.

'You don't have to, Maddie. We'll see everyone tonight, and then tomorrow I'll hand in my notice at the office. If I hadn't agreed to start work by the end of the week, they would have taken on someone else.'

Alan submitted his notice the next day and traded their car for a 1954 Austin A40 Somerset, signing a hire purchase agreement for £180 to cover the changeover cost.

Maddie spring-cleaned the house, packed their clothes and what little else they had acquired in the past few months, and piled everything in the boot and on the back seat. Peter's pram and highchair took up a lot of space. Alan had strapped the folding cot to the roof of the car. They were ready to set off early the next morning. That evening, they bought fish and chips and then spent a couple of hours with Daisy and Charles.

On Sunday morning, they woke up before sunrise, ready to travel the five hundred miles to their destination. The night before, Maddie prepared sandwiches and cake for the trip, along with cold drinks and canned food for Peter. If all went well, they were expected to arrive just after dusk fell.

They stopped briefly at the small farming town of Dalwallinup, bought pies at the roadhouse, and sat on a bench to eat them while Maddie fed Peter, as it was much easier when they were not being bounced around in the car. Moving on, they paused to stretch their legs at Paynes Find—a former gold rush settlement with a population of five hundred that had diminished to around sixty.

It was early evening when they passed through the township of Meekatharra. About three miles out, they saw a battered wooden sign, 'Butta Station,' on the side of the road pointing to a dusty, corrugated road. They drove another thirty-five miles over a wide, ridged dirt road, opening and shutting gates that interrupted mile upon mile of fencing, a few small trees, and scrubland. They saw several kangaroos lying next to the undergrowth in holes they had dug to keep cool. In the distance, a solitary emu stood.

Maddie hugged Peter close to her body, attempting to cushion him from the constant jarring. They'd closed all the windows, hoping to keep the red dust out. The car passed a small, square wooden house with a galvanised iron corrugated roof, and further on, there were two large water tanks. They then drove past several large open-fronted sheds and a stockyard. About six hundred yards further stood a large bungalow made from asbestos with a galvanised roof and a classic bull-nose veranda, surrounded by a small, grassed area with some shrubs and a single tree, sparse of branches and leaves. A rickety fence encircled the house, and a gate, wide open, hung limply on one hinge. At the end of the building, a few feet away, stood a tall windmill, and next to it, towering about fifteen feet high, a metal stand supported a large, rather rusty water tank. As far as the eye could see, there was dust and dry landscape, and the heat caused shimmers on the soil. They had arrived during the dry season.

As the car came to a stop, the dust whipped up by the vehicle settled. Maddie marvelled at the flock of pink-breasted galahs flying overhead and soaring in a glorious cloud above the paddock.

Climbing onto the thick red dust, Maddie stood, taking it all in. She had not expected it to be so desolate and was surprised that no one was there to greet them. Alan had just entered the house when Maddie, holding Peter in her arms, was about to follow him, but was halted in her tracks when she saw a somewhat dishevelled, rotund man coming out of one of the sheds. Although aware that she was being rude, Maddie could not help but stare at this person with such dark skin and a nose so flat and broad. As she watched him saunter towards the house, she presumed he was in his mid-forties, and judging by his thick-set build and protruding stomach, she concluded that they would not get much work out of him. It was then that she realised he was the Aboriginal worker whom Alan had told her about.

Alan didn't seem surprised to see him; striding over, he extended his hand and shook the other man's hand.

'G'day mate. Harold?'

Shaking the man's hand, Maddie marvelled at the Aboriginal's eyes, which looked nearly white against his black skin.

'Yes, Boss? Me Harold. I work for you.' Then he looked at Maddie. 'Jus you, me an de missus.'

Alan turned towards his wife.

'Maddie, Harold is from the Yamatji tribe and will be helping me run this place. As he said, it's just him and us!' Without another word, he patted Harold on the shoulder and motioned for him to follow. 'Okay, mate. Come and help me get this gear into the house. We can talk later.'

After unloading the car, Alan told Harold he wouldn't need him for the rest of the day but warned him he had to be back by 5 a.m. to start work. Maddie watched as Harold wandered over to a long, low building, which Alan told her was the shearing quarters and where Harold kipped down each night.

'Now, c'mon. I don't know about you, but I'm hot, tired, and hungry. Thank goodness you made plenty of sandwiches, and we bought some extra pies. Tomorrow afternoon we will go to Meeka and stock up.' Hesitating for a moment before continuing. 'In the meantime, I'll leave you to get things sorted and unpacked while I survey the land and study the station map – I need to find out where all the paddocks, windmills, and boundaries are.'

Maddie looked around at the bare concrete floor of the kitchen, which was covered in red dust and particles of spinifex bush. It seemed as though it hadn't been lived in for some time, and what made it worse was a window left open, allowing all the dirt in.

Although spacious, it felt outdated and neglected. A large iron stove stood just inside the door, with the flue extending through the ceiling to expel smoke. Sitting on the edge of the furnace were three old flat irons, each weighing about fifteen pounds. A solid pine table occupied the centre of the room, running lengthwise beneath the only window. Perched on a cast-iron stand was an old porcelain double sink with wooden draining boards on either side. A piece of cloth covered the front to conceal the pipes and half-empty bottles. Next to the sink stood a large 1930s kitchenette, and adjacent to that was an old kerosene fridge. Another door led into a larder with ample shelving and a meat safe.

'There doesn't appear to be an oven. How am I to cook our meals?' asked Maddie.

Alan gestured towards an Imperial stove across the room.

'You'll soon get used to it and won't want to use anything else as they are the best you will ever cook on. Now, let's go and have a look at the other rooms.'

He then propelled Maddie toward the sitting room, where she was relieved to see linoleum on the floor. There were two armchairs, a settee, a small cabinet, and an open fireplace. At the other end, a door led into the main bedroom, which connected to a smaller room. Finding linen and blankets in one of the cupboards, Maddie made up their bed while Alan unfolded the cot and placed it in the small room next to theirs.

Peter had not stirred since his last feeding, so his mother carefully lifted him from the carrycot and placed him in his cot, hoping he would sleep through the night. After eating the cold pies and drinking the last bottle of Coke, Maddie and Alan retired for the night.

The following morning, Maddie was awakened early by Peter wanting his nappy changed. Rubbing her eyes to clear the sleep dust away, she noticed that Alan was already up and could hear him moving about in the kitchen.

'Alan, can you see if you can find any tea, please?' she called out. 'Then, as soon as I change Peter, I will make us both a cuppa. Unless you want to do it?'

Alan shouted back, sounding irritated.

I'd already thought of that, but you will have to have it without milk, as we have none. I've stoked the fire so you can heat Peter's bottle, but it will take a while.'

Maddie entered the room.

'Oh,' she paused, 'not to worry. Peter seems quite happy at the moment.'

She lifted the heavy iron kettle from the stove and carried it to the sink. As she turned on the tap, she watched in shock as the water, mixed with green slime, spluttered into the kettle.

'Ugh! Alan, look at this, it's unbelievable! I certainly won't be making any tea with this.' Maddie was dismayed as she watched the water, mixed with green slime, splatter into the sink. 'It's not fit to drink, and how am I going to make Peter's milk formula?"

Going over to the basin, Alan was convinced that his wife was overreacting. 'Yuck! That doesn't look good. I will look at the tank this evening when it's

cooler. For now, you will need to strain and boil it a couple of times to remove any impurities. Meanwhile, continue to strain and boil it. Making his way to the door, Alan called out, 'Looks like I will have to wake Harold. I'm not sure how much use he'll be around the place. Sun will be up soon, so don't worry about breakfast for me.' Giving Maddie a quick kiss on the cheek, he added: 'I see there's an old Ford pickup in one of the sheds. I hope it goes. If not, that will be one of my first jobs. Maybe it will be quicker to saddle up a couple of the horses. Anyway, I'll see you around midday.'

Now, left alone, Maddie had time to assess everything. She could see the water tank and the borehole from the kitchen window. Nearby, there was also a huge drum that collected rainwater. While Peter was sleeping, Maddie decided to take a closer look outside. The electricity was supplied by a generator housed in a shed about 20 yards from the house.

Additionally, there was an antiquated washing machine, a copper tub, a wooden washing board, and a mangle to wring the clothes. Outside the door, a washing line was strung between two posts. It took Maddie a while to absorb it all, but no matter how long it took, she was determined that everything would work out for them.

Over the next few weeks, Alan and Harold drove around the 220,000 acres to inspect the numerous windmills that supplied water for over 8,000 sheep and approximately 1,000 head of cattle. Repairing the turbines often meant climbing down into the well. Once, when Alan was halfway down one of the shafts, he came face to face with a Western Brown – one of Australia's deadliest snakes. It was curled up in one of the crevices. Needless to say, he was out of there before you could say 'Ned Kelly!'

Peter was such a happy baby. When he didn't sleep, he played contentedly with his toys in the playpen. He was now drinking from a cup and could say 'mummy' and 'daddy'. Some evenings, when his father wasn't too tired, he'd crouch on the living room floor with Peter. Alan would roll a tobacco tin on its side to create a circle around Peter and then giggle contagiously as Peter attempted to grab hold of it.

Every morning by 5:30, everyone was up and ready for work. After Maddie cooked them a hearty breakfast, they began their working day. While they worked around the homestead repairing machinery, Maddie rang the bell that hung on one of the veranda posts, calling them in for smoko, a mug of tea and a piece of cake or a biscuit. Then later for their lunch. In the afternoon, when the sun was at its hottest, they took a couple of hours' rest.

It was summer, and the temperatures rose to 40 degrees. Alan found a couple of old camp beds in one of the sheds, so they could sleep outside on the veranda when the nights made it hard to rest. He and Maddie would lie on their backs for hours, gazing at the stars and watching the many satellites scuttle across the black sky.

There had been little to no rain for nearly three years. Spread across the enormous paddocks, several thousand sheep struggled to survive. They dug beneath the dust for burrs from the clover plant, which offered some protein. The drought had reduced their numbers. Carcasses of several sheep lay scattered everywhere. There was nothing they could do but ensure that all the windmills were functioning and providing fresh water for the animals every day. Those who managed to survive huddled beneath any shade they could find, usually near troughs by the water wells. They were malnourished and skeletal.

Aside from their trips to town for supplies, their only contacts were Harold and a Norwegian fencer named Eirik. The latter travelled the countryside erecting and repairing fences that stretched from horizon to horizon, keeping dingoes and foxes at bay.

Erik was a true character, a genuine 'bushie' and a nomad. When he was near Butta station, he would always stop by and spend a few days with them. He and Alan would sit in the cool of the spinifex hut, constructed from spinifex bushes with pipes surrounding the outside and on top to ensure that the water covered the hut, keeping it cool. Most evenings, they would enjoy a large carton of beer. Alan often assisted Erik with the fences, and in return, Erik would help Alan dispose of the animal carcasses near the windmills.

Peter was not handling the heat well, which concerned his parents greatly. During the day, Maddie placed their son in the hut where he played or slept in the playpen. Once a month, they drove into town; while Alan went to Elders farm supplies, Maddie stocked up on provisions such as dried apples, apricots, peas, potato flakes, and large bags of flour and rice as needed. After packing everything into the old Ford Ute, they wandered over to the Royal Mail Hotel to get a cold drink and something to eat before returning home. It was also an opportunity for Alan to spend time with the locals. Maddie usually took Peter into the lounge and chatted with the women.

Due to the drought, the sheep were quite scrawny and not worth the effort of slaughtering and butchering. The goats and kangaroos fared much better on the land.

After hanging the carcass for about a week, he would wait until evening to cut it up. Maddie found many ways to cook whatever Alan managed to provide. Firstly, she roasted it, and then, if there was anything left, it was served cold or fried in batter. She made soup from the bones and any leftovers stored in the cold chest. One day, Alan managed to shoot a very large bustard, a feral turkey, although he knew it was illegal to kill them since they were an endangered species. It lasted a few days and was delicious!

Late one morning, when Alan and Harold were out doing a mill run, Maddie turned on the tap in the kitchen, only to discover that there was no water. Knowing it would be a couple of hours before the guys returned for lunch, she decided to check the windmill at the back of the house. Having just put Peter down for his nap, she was confident he would sleep for quite a while.

She climbed the five metres to the top of the wooden tower. Standing on the platform, she looked down into the tank and found it to be bone dry. Reaching up to the blades, she found that they were jammed. After releasing them, she waited until everything started moving again and then attempted to climb back down, but she couldn't stretch her leg far enough to reach one of the rungs of the tower. Climbing up had been easy, but going down proved to be very difficult. After struggling for quite some time, she realised she had no option but to wait until Alan and Harold returned.

Maddie didn't know how long it would be before Alan came home, and she was worried that Peter would wake up. The sun was beating down on her; she was thirsty and feeling weak. A couple of hours passed before Maddie heard the truck in the distance, and as soon as it pulled into the yard, she started shouting for him. Realising her voice was coming from the back of the house, Alan quickly went there and was shocked to see his wife perched on top of the windmill! Thankfully, Peter was still sleeping soundly.

One time, Alan recorded Harold speaking on a tape recorder and played it back to him, thinking he would be fascinated to hear his voice coming from the machine. How wrong he was! Harold flung his arms into the air, clasped his ears, and turned to run as fast as he could across the paddock, shouting:

'Ungwilla, Ungwilla, Boss, big Boss he Ungwilla'.

This referred to Black Magic Man.

Maddie and Alan didn't think Harold would return. Then, early one morning, he ambled into the kitchen and, without saying a word, sat down at the table to wait for his breakfast. From that day on, he carefully watched the 'boss man', not knowing what the Magic Man would do next.

Another time, Alan instructed Harold to paint the roof of one of the sheds while he went to check out some windmills. Maddie rang the bell, letting Harold know it was time for a mug of tea and a goat sandwich. Time ticked by, and there was no sign of him. Maddie knew that he had been told to paint the shed, so she decided to go and ensure that nothing was amiss. As she approached the building, she looked up at the roof, and there was Harold, lying flat on his back atop the roof, one arm down by his side and holding a paintbrush in the other. He was fast asleep!

'HAROLD!' Maddie shouted. 'I thought you were supposed to be painting the shed.'

As quick as a flash, still lying on his back with his arm stretched out and paintbrush in hand, he frantically pushed the brush back and forth on the roof.

'Miss Gubba, boss woman. I'm painting. Look, Mam, I'm painting!'

Many times, Willie-willies, medium whirlwinds, passed through the property, kicking up dust and bush debris. One time, when Alan and Maddie returned to the homestead after checking a windmill in the next paddock, they found the washing that Maddie had left out to dry scattered all over the ground and covered in red dust. On another day, they forgot to shut the front door before taking a trip into town for supplies, and when they returned, they found twigs, leaves, and red dust scattered throughout the house.

On some days, temperatures soared to 40 °c or higher. The nights barely had time to cool down from the day's heat. They usually slept on the veranda. Lying on their backs, they listened to programmes such as 'Dad & Dave' and the 'Archers' on the old Bakelite radio while watching satellites whizz across the dark sky.

One evening, Maddie was on her way into the house to get a cold drink when she saw a large lizard ambling toward her with its forked tongue flicking nonchalantly in and out. She screamed:

'ALAN! Quick, look!'

Her husband glanced up from the book he was reading, wondering what was causing his wife to make such a fuss. As he did so, the creature, hearing the commotion, flicked its long tail around and retreated. Alan, trying not to laugh, told her:

'Get back here, you idiot! That was a Perentie. It wouldn't hurt you. They're very shy and like to keep to themselves, but you do have to watch out for their long tail. It can be used as a whip. That was a pretty large one, and they are the largest monitor lizards entirely native to Australia and the fourth largest living lizards on earth.'

Maddie watched as the Perentie made its way over to one of the sheds, disappearing around the corner. Once she knew they were not in danger, she thought it was a fantastic creature, with its dark grey body and creamy spots in horizontal rows across its back and down along the larger part of its long tail. She marvelled at its exceptionally long, snake-like neck and powerful limbs, complete with huge, sharp black claws.

Alan burst into laughter.

'The noise you were making was enough to terrify anyone!'

Along with the thousands of sheep scattered across the vast property, there were hundreds of kangaroos, goats, emus, and wild bustards. In a nearby paddock, a mob of brumbies could be seen. Behind some sacks in one of the sheds, they also found a feral cat with two kittens, approximately two months old. Alan didn't stop to consider the consequences when he bent down to pick up one of the babies, but soon he was cursing while desperately trying to pull the hissing critter's teeth off two of his fingers. Meanwhile, the mother cat leapt at him, her claws splayed as she attempted to climb up his trouser leg! The other kittens scurried away.

Much of Alan's working day was spent in the sheep and cattle yards, branding, tagging, and injecting livestock, as well as repairing the fences and windmills damaged by some extremely large willie-willies. Water was pumped from boreholes using the windmills and then transferred directly to either the water troughs or the large manmade dams spread across the vast station land.

Maddie was busy with household chores, cooking three meals a day and occasionally assisting Alan around the homestead. Her days began at five in the morning, and aside from a brief rest, she worked until nine or ten at night, as they seldom ate until the cool of the evening.

She delighted in being a mother and loved watching her son explore his little hands and feet. When he grew tired of that, he'd cling to the bars of the cot or playpen, struggling to pull himself up, his little legs wobbling as he tried to gain his balance.

Maddie, not yet nineteen, had much to learn about life on a north-west sheep station.

When they went into town for their supplies, and before heading home, they would stop by one of the hotels for a cold drink. Maddie would sit on a long bench chatting with the publican's wife. It was a sparse and grim space, and she hated the smell of stale tobacco that wafted from the trough filled with cigarette butts, running along the length of the bar.

One day, Alan occupied his usual spot at the bar, chatting with local graziers. At the same time, Maddie sat by the window, observing and listening to the happenings around her, when a skimpily dressed young woman arrived. She joined the men at the bar, but not for long. After a few minutes, she stood up and walked through a door at the other end of the room. Maddie recognised that it led back to the sleeping quarters. Five minutes later, one of the men at the bar got up and left through the same door.

At the time, Maddie thought nothing of it. About twenty minutes later, the girl returned, once again perched on a stool alongside a rather wealthy-looking grazier. Within minutes, she left the room again, the gentleman not far behind her. This procedure was repeated several times over the next couple of hours. Eventually, curiosity got the better of Maddie. She walked over to the bar, where Alan was in deep conversation with several guys.

'Alan,' she whispered.

Looking at his wife, he realised that they had been there longer than anticipated, so he told her.

'I'll just have another pint and then we can go. Do you want a pie or something to keep you going until we get home?'

'I'm fine, but I do want to leave soon because I need to get Peter home to his bed.' Then she whispered in his ear. 'What I wanted to know is... Can you tell me who that g-girl is?' Madeline tilted her head in the young lady's direction. She sits talking to one of the men for a while, then she goes out that door over there, and he follows. A short time later, she comes back into the bar and chats up another one, who also follows her out of the room!'

Alan threw back his head and laughed heartily. Everyone looked at him, curious about the joke. He then leaned in to whisper to his wife:

'That's the local bike!' Alan put his fingers to his lips. 'Shush. I'll explain when we get home.'

Maddie stared at him questioningly.

'What do you mean? Local bike?'

Placing his finger to his lip, Alan whispered.

'I'll tell you when we get home.'

Occasionally, the guys would go to a back room to play Jackpot Poker. They usually asked Alan to join them. If that happened, they would stay the night in one of the motel rooms. Maddie also enjoyed a game of cards but had never gambled more than a few pence.

One evening, Alan asked the group if his wife could join the game, explaining that she had played before and enjoyed gambling. They reluctantly agreed. The publican's wife, Jenny, found it amusing, so she encouraged Maddie and offered to take care of Peter.

Maddie already knew the three other men sitting at the table. Two were graziers from a local station; the third was unfamiliar to her. She sensed the serious atmosphere, with everyone hoping to win big. Maddie felt quite important being allowed to join the game. They played for about an hour when she was dealt what she thought was a pretty good hand. The stakes were increasing, and it was her turn to declare what she wanted to do! Nudging Alan, she whispered as quietly as she could:

'Is the ten, jack, queen, king, and ace of hearts worth the gamble?'

Within seconds, every hand was thrown into the centre.

The next morning, Alan told Maddie that the other guys had been ready to go all the way and that none of them was dreaming she had a Royal Flush – the highest hand that could not be beaten! Maddie gloated and told Alan that at least she had won £10.

Alan was constantly asking Mr. Spurge to send him a Jackaroo, claiming that even an unskilled young man, who had yet to gain experience, would be more helpful than Harold. Maddie knew her husband was growing increasingly frustrated and wondered how long it would be before he told her it was time to move on!

They had been there for about six months when the manager, Jim, and his wife, Judy, from the neighbouring station, another one of the Lee Steere properties, invited them for Sunday lunch.

Maddie was looking forward to the break, as aside from their occasional visit to Meekathara to buy provisions, they hadn't had a day off since arriving.

They left home with plenty of time to reach their destination, as they had to travel several miles of rough terrain before accessing the bitumen. After that, it would take another half-hour to arrive at the entrance to Bulla station, followed by another twenty miles over corrugations and potholes.

They spent an enjoyable afternoon, and Madeline was happy to see Alan totally relaxed and thankfully not downing his beers too quickly. They had just finished eating when they heard the familiar sound of Sir Ernest's private plane circling the property and eventually landing some distance from the homestead. Jim excused himself and, jumping into an old Ute, sped off to collect him.

On their return, Alan waited for his boss to alight from the vehicle and then made his way over to greet him. As he approached, Sir Ernest waved him to one side, saying that he wanted to have a word.

A few minutes later, Alan stomped back to the group, his face contorted with anger. Maddie knew the look well and realised that everything was not okay. Shaking hands with their hosts and thanking them for the invitation, he then turned towards his wife, instructing her to gather their things and get into the car. Embarrassed and unsure of what was happening, Maddie thanked Jim and Judy for their hospitality, and then, clutching Peter to her body, she hurried over to join Alan in the truck. The engine was already running, his foot poised on the accelerator, and as soon as Maddie shut the door, he shoved the gear into place and sped off, sending clouds of dust into the air.

Maddie sat silently, waiting for Alan to explain what had made him so angry. She observed him gripping the steering wheel tightly, the muscles in his lower arms tensing as his biceps bulged. Aware that she anticipated an explanation. Then, gritting his teeth.

'The BASTARD!' Alan was enraged.

'He said we had no right to be away from the property, that we were employed to work on the station, not to be off socialising. I told him that the only time we left the damn place was to stock up on provisions at Elders store. I wanted to punch him in the face and told him we were sick of slaving on his property for fifteen hours a day, seven days a week for a measly pittance!'

Maddie bit her lower lip while trying to think of what to say to calm him down, but she decided it was best to keep quiet – she knew as sure as eggs were eggs that they would soon, once again, be moving on.

Three days later, with the car crammed to the rooftop, they headed south towards the coastal town of Geraldton—about 400 miles south of Meekathara. Maddie sat hunched against the window, chewing her fingernails and trying hard not to cry. At nineteen years old, with a young baby to care for and no idea where they would sleep that night, she wondered what lay ahead for them. She had been quite happy living on the Station. Even though it was not always easy, she enjoyed the experience and loved the vastness of the countryside.

A storm was brewing; the orange sky darkened with thunderous clouds clustering in the howling wind as it swept across the lowlands. Spinifex rolled across the road and plains, while the dust rose like a great screen, blocking everything behind it. As the wind began to subside, an eerie stillness enveloped the area.

They had driven for several hours when they pulled into the small township of Mount Magnet. With a population of around 500, it was the longest-surviving gold mining settlement in Western Australia and still had three hotels. Evidence of Mount Magnet's gold-rush heyday was visible in its wide main street, which had been constructed to accommodate a camel train turning unhindered. A traveller once asked: 'What's here at Mt Magnet?' and the reply was: 'Five gins and a dingo.'

They were thirsty and hungry, and Peter needed to be fed, so Alan pulled up outside the Commercial Hotel. Upon entering, they made their way to the bar, where the publican was chatting with a customer. He greeted them warmly, and after pouring Alan a cold beer from the keg beneath the bar and a shandy for Maddie, they ordered two Mrs. Mac's pies and went and sat at one of the tables. Maddie put Peter's little shoes on, and they watched as he began to totter around the room, happy to have some freedom after being in the car for several hours. Occasionally, he fell back onto his little bottom and giggled as he scrambled to his feet.

They travelled on for another four hours, eventually arriving in the town of Geraldton – a major west-coast seaport and home to the Yamatji and Wajarri aboriginals. As it was too late to continue to Perth, they checked into a hotel for the night. Maddie settled her son on the large bed in their room and packed pillows around him to prevent him from falling off the edge. She then joined her husband in the lounge. After enjoying a substantial meal, Maddie went back to their room, leaving her husband to join the men in the saloon bar.

The next day, they drove the 260 miles to Perth, where they checked into a large caravan park in Como, on the city fringe. They managed to hire one of the larger caravans with an annexe attached, which enabled them to store most of their belongings inside.

Alan was taking on a few odd jobs here and there, but nothing permanent, so he had no choice but to register for the dole until something more permanent turned up. The owners of the park, Duncan and Mary, asked Maddie if she would be interested in earning a few bob cleaning the two large ablution blocks. At five-thirty each morning, Maddie headed off to work, leaving her husband to listen out for Peter in case he woke before she returned. In the afternoons, she helped out at the small onsite shop, and while her son gurgled away happily in his pram, she attended to the customers. Mary very generously gave Maddie a discount on all her purchases.

They had been at the park for nearly two months when Alan spotted an advertisement in the *'To Let'* section of the local paper, headlined *'Rent free!'*

Maddie's first thought was: '*Not again.*' Alan interrupted her thoughts.

'Honey, it's always worth asking, and surely, we'd be far better off being in a house rather than cramped in a caravan. It can't do any harm to ring and find out. Do you have any coins for the phone box? I'll need several in case I run out halfway through the conversation.'

Alan took the ten- and twenty-pence pieces that Maddie handed him, and grabbing his coat, went out of the van and made his way to the other side of the park, where the public phone box was. He was back within minutes.

'Mr Toms or Tims, I can't remember what his name was, but that doesn't matter. He said to call and see him after lunch today.'

Maddie wanted to know more.

'Does it say why it is rent-free? Surely, for the time being, we'd be better off staying where we are, as it is close to town and easier for you to find work.'

She had just finished feeding Peter his breakfast and was wiping all the bits of egg off his face and hands. It was one of the few mornings when he had not tipped the plate upside down onto the tray. She gently lifted him out of his highchair and added:

'I can't go then. I'm working in the shop until 1 o'clock. Can't you phone and say we will be there around 2:30? If not, you will have to go without me.'

Alan frowned.

'You need to come with me. Go and tell them you can't do it today. I'm sure they'll understand. We can't hang around, and he said he has another couple coming to see him in the afternoon.'

Maddie apologised to Mary for not being able to work that afternoon.

They drove along Albany Highway until they arrived in the area of Cannington, where they kept a lookout for the address they'd been given. As they drove past a neat 1950s triple-fronted brick veneer house, Alan knew at once from the description he had been given – this was the one. Turning the car around, he drove back and pulled to the curb outside the building.

As they made their way up the pathway to the front door, Alan was about to knock when the door swung open, revealing a man in his forties who smiled broadly. He was smartly dressed in jeans paired with a dark blue t-shirt and extended his hand to Alan.

'G'day, er, Mr. Cox?'

'Sure am, Mr...' Alan hesitated, not remembering the man's name. 'Yep, I'm Alan. Mr Cox was my father!' Then nodding towards Maddie, he added, 'This is my wife, Maddie.'

'Ha, ha. Yes, quite so. Please, call me David.'

They followed David into a long, narrow hallway that led to a spacious kitchen.

'Sit y'rself down while I put the kettle on. In the meantime, I can tell you what the setup is.' He hesitated a moment and finally asked: 'Would you prefer a beer, Alan, and are you happy with a cup of tea, Maddie?'

Alan gratefully accepted the offer of a beer, while Maddie opted for tea.

David told them that he was a widower with two young boys, Alexander, who was fourteen, and Robert, who was sixteen. He needed someone to take care of the house and his boys while he was prospecting up north. They chatted for a while, and then David, leaning back in his chair and delving into his trouser pocket, produced a tobacco pouch and started to roll a cigarette. He then glanced at Maddie:

'Do you mind?' She shook her head. Then, sucking on his cigarette, he blew the smoke away from the table. I return home every month or so for a few days, then I head back into the bush again. It's a good life, but hard yakka. I couldn't earn anything like it in the city.'

Alan nodded, as he understood exactly what he meant. David looked at them questioningly.

'So, what do you think, are you willing to take it on? If you are, you'd have to come as soon as possible, as I leave in five days.'

Alan looked at Maddie.

'Sounds fine to me, how about you, luv?' he asked.

The thought of living in someone else's house again was daunting. Still, Maddie knew they needed to find somewhere soon because there was little room in the caravan for Peter to play, and she wouldn't let him outside on his own with all the cars coming in and out of the park, many of which took little notice of the speed limit. Maddie nodded.

'I'm sure we can manage, but before we leave, could you please show us around the house?'

'Of course, my dear. I don't suppose Saturday would be too soon, would it? That would leave you a couple of days to sort yourselves and familiarise yourselves with the place before I leave? If so, come over early in the morning, and I'll introduce you to the boys before they go off to school. Monday, I'll be up with the birds and off like a dirty shirt!'

It didn't take long to pack their belongings into the car once again, a chore that Maddie was becoming quite skilled at! They had met Adrian and Robert, David's two boys, the day before. Adrian, the younger one, was a bookworm, and when he wasn't at school, he spent a lot of his time either in his room or out with friends. Robert kept to himself most of the time, only showing his face at mealtimes.

David, true to his word, departed early on Monday before everyone was awake.

***

Eventually, Alan took a part-time job with a large building company. Although this position was not ideal, it was sufficient to keep their heads above water, especially since they had no rent to pay. After work, he joined the other workers at the local pub for a few rounds, often staggering in around midnight.

One morning, Maddie woke up to find the pillow next to hers untouched. She leaned over to glance at the little bedside clock on the table and was surprised to see it was nearing six o'clock. Peter was awake and happily babbling to himself in his cot in the corner of their bedroom.

She wanted to curl up and go back to sleep, but couldn't. She needed to see Peter. Maddie shut her eyes, hoping the nausea she'd experienced for the past few days would subside. Then, dragging herself out of bed, she made her way to the window, and, drawing back the curtains, watched the early morning commuters heading to work along the busy highway.

She turned toward her son, who was starting to get restless.

'Good morning, little fellow. And how are you today? Ready for your bath?'

Reaching upwards with his arms outstretched, Peter stood on his toes, grasping the top of the cot railing and waiting for his mother to scoop him up. He was nearly fourteen months old, walking well and getting into a lot of mischief. He tugged at his mother's hair as she lifted him into her arms and carried him into the bathroom. She placed him on the rubber mat in the bath and tested the water as it filled the tub. Maddie splashed water on his belly while she pushed his little yellow rubber ducks up and down the tub. Peter laughed with his infectious giggle as he tried to catch them.

After drying and dressing him, she put Peter back in his cot and went into the kitchen to scramble some eggs for his breakfast. Then, she prepared the boys' breakfast and ensured they had everything they needed for school, including packed lunches. Not long after they left the house, Maddie thought she heard the front door opening, followed by a quiet click as it shut.

Alan was home. Yet another one of his nights out with his drinking mates and goodness knows what else! The meal she had cooked for him last night was now in the bin. She didn't move from her position at the sink, furiously drying the breakfast dishes and refusing to turn and look at him.

Maddie felt his arms encircling her waist and nearly gagged from the stench of stale beer and whiskey. She pushed him away, stepped to one side, and ran to the bathroom to throw up!

Alan behaved as if staying out all night was acceptable.

'Hi Hun. Is there a cup of tea in the pot, and can you rustle up some bacon and eggs as I'm starv'n? He pulled the kitchen chair out from the table and plonked himself down. I'm taking the day off to look for a full-time job. They are putting off some of the part-timers at work, and I know it will be last in – first to go.'

Maddie barely acknowledged him, knowing that anything she said would spark an argument. He would use that as an excuse to storm out of the house again and accuse her of pushing him to drink. She remained silent.

Alan ate his breakfast in silence, occasionally glancing at the paper he had brought home. Now and then, he circled one of the ads in the situation's vacant columns. After finishing his meal, he took a final gulp of his tea, got up from the table, and went to the bathroom.

'Thanks, luv. I'll have a shit, a quick shower an' shave, and then I'm going to the job centre to see what's on the board, although I'm not holding my breath as I'm certainly not taking any old job!'

Sometime later, he emerged from the bedroom, grabbed his keys off the kitchen table, and, giving Maddie a quick peck on the cheek, walked towards the front door.

'Seeya tonight, luv. I won't be late.'

He arrived home just as Maddie was preparing for bed. He walked into the bedroom, clutching a bunch of flowers. Without looking at him or acknowledging him in any way, Maddie continued to undress.

'It won't happen again. I'm cutting down on drinking, and I'll only go to the pub on Fridays and maybe play a game of darts with the boys on Saturdays.'

Maddie had heard it all before. She knew he truly meant it, and at that moment, she felt sorry for him—she desperately wanted to believe that this time things really would change. He shoved a small, gift-wrapped package into her hand.

'I do love you.'

Maddie opened the box, and inside, she found a diamante bracelet. She kissed him on the cheek.

'Thank you. It's lovely.'

She wanted to say: *'I don't want it. Return it and get your money back!'* He was buying her forgiveness, but she didn't want or need that. How could she throw it back at him to hurt him the way he was hurting her?

Just as Alan was losing hope of finding full-time work, one of his mates called to inform him that the foreman at Hanson's Building Supplies had just quit. Alan wasted no time getting to the yard, where he sought out the boss, who, after verifying his credentials, hired him on the spot. As he walked out of the yard, he let out a sigh of relief – it was the first time in quite a long while that he had felt so optimistic about the future. They were living rent-free with very few bills to pay, and now, at last, he was back in full-time employment.

As promised, Alan had reduced his drinking, stopping for a quick pint before heading home.

Maddie, although still feeling out of sorts, kept putting off seeing the doctor, as she was certain it was nothing to worry about. Then, one morning, while walking down to the local shops with Peter fast asleep in his pushchair, she started to feel nauseous, but after stopping for a few minutes, she continued on her way. She was waiting to be served in the local butcher's shop when she thought she was going to faint. Luckily, an elderly lady who was standing next to her noticed that she had gone very pale and called for someone to bring her a chair and a glass of water. They asked if there was anyone they could call to come and fetch her, but Maddie, refusing politely, said that she was feeling much better. After buying some stewing steak for their tea that night and thanking everyone, she made her way home.

The following day, shortly after Alan left for work, Maddie spent the morning vomiting in the toilet. She called the doctor's office and was given an appointment for that afternoon.

Dr. Warner knew Alan and Maddie well; ever since they had moved to the area, he had been their family doctor and was fully aware of the issues within Maddie's marriage. He checked her blood pressure and heart rate, confirming that all was well. As she got up to leave, he stopped her.

'Sit down, my dear. We are not finished yet. I think it would be advisable to take a blood and urine test, as you appear to be anaemic. I'll send it off today, and I'll give you a ring as soon as I receive the results.'

Maddie left the surgery feeling much better after speaking with him. David Warner watched her as she walked out of his consulting room, aware that he would be giving her news she might not want to hear.

The following afternoon, Maddie received a call from the surgery's receptionist, who informed her that Dr. Warner wanted to see her. Maddie left Peter with her next-door neighbour, Eunice, who had two young children of her own and also loved Peter. They helped one another out whenever needed.

Upon arriving at the surgery, Maddie was pleased to find only one other person in the waiting room. It wasn't long before her thoughts were interrupted.

'Dr. Warner will see you now, Mrs. Cox.'

As she walked through the open door, the doctor gestured toward the chair.

'Come and sit down, my dear.' Then, leaning forward in his chair with his hands clasped together under his chin, he began: 'Maddie, it is as I expected. You are nearly three months pregnant.'

At first, Maddie couldn't grasp what he had told her.

'No, I can't be. I'm on the pill!' But as soon as the words came out of her mouth, she knew there had been a couple of times she had forgotten to take it and hadn't given it another thought, believing she would be very unlucky to conceive during those instances.

His face showed concern for his patient; he worried about how she would cope with taking care of two young children and a husband who prioritised drinking over his family.

'My dear girl, I'm afraid that no birth control method is one hundred per cent reliable. I'm going to prescribe for you, as your anaemia is due to you being low on iron. I want to see you again in four weeks, unless, of course, you have any problems before that.'

Maddie cooked Alan's favourite meal of liver, onions, and bacon, which thankfully the boys enjoyed too. After they had all eaten, Alan returned to reading the paper while the two lads helped her wash and dry the dishes. They stayed in the kitchen to do their homework, while Maddie joined Alan in the sitting room.

'Alan, I went to see Doctor Warner a couple of days ago,' she said, hesitantly waiting for him to respond.

'What did he say? Is everything okay, hon?'

'When I saw him the other day, he took some blood and urine samples because, as he explained, I appeared anaemic.' Alan continued reading the paper, so Maddie carried on, hoping to get his full attention. 'I went back today for the results.'

Alan looked up from the paper.

'Are they okay? There's nothing wrong with you, is there?'

Maddie blurted it out:

'I'm pregnant!'

'Wow! That is a surprise. When is it due?'

'Dr. Barton said that he thought I was about twelve weeks, so in another six months.'

He extended his arms towards her.

'Don't worry, I'm sure everything will be okay. Have you told your mother yet?' Maddie just shrugged her shoulders.

It was three months until their unborn child was due to be born when David phoned to say he was driving down from Karratha and would be with them in a day or two. Before hanging up, he told Alan he had quit his job. There was something in the tone of his voice that made Alan think, and he felt sure that he was coming back for good. Alan was on edge the entire weekend but thought it best not to mention his fears to Maddie.

On Sunday evening, David phoned from the railway station to tell Alan that his car had broken down and asked if he would mind giving him a lift home. Thankfully, Maddie had made a large lamb casserole, so she dished up an extra plate, and she put it in the oven to keep warm for when they returned. She realised that David would be hungry and in need of a cold beer.

After they had finished eating, Maddie cleared the table and washed the dishes while the guys took their beers into the sitting room. Neither spoke as David placed his tobacco pouch on the little coffee table. He took out a packet of Rizla papers and offered it to Alan. They continued to sit in silence as they evenly spread some of the weed along the middle of the thin paper. Then, they lightly licked the edge and rolled them into shape. Maddie had joined them and watched as they puffed away on the rollies.

Before Alan had a chance to say anything, David spoke, and just as Alan had feared, he told them he was home to stay since the boys were at an age where they needed their father. He explained that their mother had up and left them three years ago, leaving him to raise his sons. Realising it was short notice, he didn't hesitate to assure them they were welcome to stay until they found somewhere else.

Alan scoured the papers every evening when he came home from work, but was unable to take time off to help Maddie find somewhere. She looked through the windows of the local estate agents, hoping to find a property available in the area that was close to where Alan worked. Several days later, Maddie came across a promising advert displayed in the newsagents. She went inside and asked the man behind the counter if he could kindly write the phone number for her.

Driving along Railway Parade, Maddie noticed that most of the houses were either weatherboard or asbestos, while some of the more modern ones were brick-clad. Further up the road, Alan pointed out several very old places that, as he said, were built post-war by the State Housing Commission, when there was a severe housing shortage throughout Australia. Then, in 1945, soldiers were returning from service, and a couple of years later, they were needed for refugees and British migrants.

They turned onto Redcliffe Street and were halfway down the road when Alan pulled up to the curb. Maddie looked at her husband.

'Are you certain this is the place? Look at its state! Surely this is not the one we've come to see!'

While they debated whether this was indeed the right house, a vehicle pulled in behind them, the front door opened, and a young man emerged.

'Mr and Mrs. Cox?'

Alan gave a nod. 'Ur, yes. Yes, we are.'

'G'day. I'm Doug.' The men shook hands and the agent, smiling at Maddie, remarked: 'I've not been here before, so I don't know what sort of a state it's in. C'mon, let's take a look.'

They followed him up the pathway, which was flanked by weeds and a couple of woody Geranium bushes outside the front door, adding a splash of colour to the shabby exterior. Before unlocking the door, the agent turned towards them:

'Looks like it could do with a bit of work.' I believe that it has not been lived in for quite some time. If you would rather, I can show you something else,' he hesitated a bit and went on. 'It will be much more expensive, but a whole lot better for you and your family.'

Alan frowned.

'Yes, and we'd have to pay a bond and two weeks in advance, whereas you said the owners are waiving the bond to this place. I can certainly see why! But as we are not in a position to afford anything else, can you please show us inside? Surely it can't be that bad?'

As Doug pushed the door open, Maddie gasped!

'Oh my God, this is awful!'

Then, as they made their way through to the other rooms, they saw that they were just as bad, if not worse, than the previous one. There was one bedroom, a small sleepout, and a kitchen where the stove was covered in fat and heaving with dead cockroaches. It made Maddie feel ill just looking at it. Then, stealing a look around the bathroom door, she quickly slammed it shut—she'd seen enough! Throughout the house, the floors were covered with faded, cracked linoleum. As for being advertised as fully furnished, that was a joke, as most of it needed to be taken to the dump.

Maddie made her way to the front door with the intention of returning to the car. Alan called after her.

'Maddie, wait, wait a moment.' He turned to the agent. 'You said if we clean it up and paint the inside, the owner is prepared to forego the first two months' rent. Does that still stand?' Then he turned to his wife. 'At least that would give us a bit of time to save for a bond on a decent place. What do you think?'

Maddie stood, biting her lip—something she had been doing lately when feeling anxious—now thinking of her grandfather, knowing he would be devastated if he learned anything about the life they were leading. Close to tears, she turned to look at her husband, and knowing they had no other choice but to take it, she said:

'We don't have any other option, do we? You'll have to ask David if we can stay on for a few more days. We can't possibly move in until I've scrubbed every room. The kitchen will take a day on its own! I'll have to ask Eunice if she can take care of Peter because there's no way I would bring him here until it is reasonably habitable.

Alan shook Doug's hand.

'Okay, we'll take it.' Then he turned to Maddie again. 'I'd ask for a couple of days off work, but we can't afford to have any of my wages docked. They go through gallons of paint, so maybe I can get a couple of large tins on tick, and then, at the weekend, I can tackle some of the rooms to freshen them up.' Then he put his hands around her. 'Things can only get better, and they will. I know they will.'

David told them he was happy for them to stay a little longer, mentioning that he was looking forward to some home cooking after working in the mines.

Alan wanted Maddie to ask her mother to lend them some money for essential household items. She told him that he would have to ask her himself since she was too embarrassed; they hadn't been able to repay what they borrowed over a year ago. That evening, Alan called in to see Daisy and Charles.

Maddie spent over a week working her way through the house, spending hours on her hands and knees scrubbing the floors, scraping fat off the stove, and cleaning the inside of the few cupboards in the kitchen. They took a trip to Gregson's Auctioneers in Perth and managed to place successful bids on two old but comfortable armchairs, a kitchen table and two chairs, a three-quarter-size bed, and some old scatter rugs for the floor. They still had the box of cutlery and a small amount of crockery that Maddie's mother had given them when they returned from Sydney.

The first time it rained, the ceiling in their bedroom began leaking. Neither of them could use the bathroom, and the water heater was also out of order. They discovered an old tin bath buried under piles of rubbish in the back garden and cleaned it up. By filling a metal bucket with water and heating it on the gas stove, they managed to take a bath. At least the old Colda Electric fridge was functioning.

Maddie found some curtains in one of the charity shops and cut them down to fit the bedroom window. The place was still a dump and very basic, but at least it was clean. They were living off the 'smell of an oily rag!' Thankfully, Maddie's mother was too busy working to have time to visit them, as she would have been upset and angry to see how they were living.

Now in her fourth month of pregnancy, she looked forward to having a baby brother or sister for Peter; however, she worried about the future. They lived hand to mouth and never stayed anywhere long enough to call a place 'home'.

Alan had started drinking heavily again, and Maddie, although depressed about the way they were living, would not allow herself to wallow in self-pity. She remembered once hearing a quote by Nietzsche: *'What doesn't kill you makes you stronger.'* He said it was because it's only the strong who survive, and that makes them stronger. She didn't realise it at the time, but she was strong, and that would be her salvation in the years to come.

One morning, while preparing breakfast for her husband, Maddie could hardly drag herself around the kitchen. She felt weak and had a severe headache, which was unusual for her. She was relieved when Alan left for work, as she didn't want to concern him, believing it would probably disappear before he returned home.

After bathing and feeding her son, she placed him in his cot, hoping he would sleep for a couple of hours. Then, pouring herself a glass of water, she dragged herself back to bed, yearning for a few minutes of sleep, but her mouth and neck began to throb. The pain worsened, making it difficult for her to open her mouth to drink from the glass. She knew she could not remain in bed all day—there was her son to care for and household tasks to attend to. She edged to the side of the bed and, pushing herself up and placing her feet on the floor, realised she didn't have the energy to stand. She dragged herself back into bed and slept fitfully on and off until she acknowledged it was time for Peter's next feed. She felt mortified, as it had been several hours since she had put him in his cot. Although her jaw and neck still ached, she managed to pull herself out of bed and get dressed.

When Alan came home, he immediately sensed that his wife was unwell – she appeared pale and was not her usual self.

'Maddie, what's wrong? You don't look well at all.'

With a forced smile on her face, she managed to answer:

'I'm fine, don't worry. I have a headache, and my throat is a bit sore, but that's all.'

Alan replied, concerned.

'You don't look fine to me. The surgery doesn't shut until late, so don't you think it would be a good idea to see the doc?'

Maddie wouldn't hear of it and promised Alan that she would go in the morning if she
had not improved.

The following day, Maddie's condition worsened. Alan called the surgery to ask if Dr. Warner could come to the house, as his wife was too ill to leave her bed. He arrived within the hour and, after examining Maddie, told them she had a severe case of tonsillitis. He advised Alan to take a couple of days off work to care for her and their son.

Since the two months were up, they were now paying a weekly rent of 5/6p. Alan had been promoted to head foreman, resulting in a slight wage increase. The house, though still old and shabby, was clean. They hoped the day would come soon when they could afford to move into a decent place, somewhere not riddled with cockroaches and where they could take a proper bath.

As Maddie walked home one afternoon after taking Peter to the clinic for his latest check-up and vaccinations, she was lost in thought, wondering what to cook for tea. Making her way along Railway Parade, she heard a car pull up beside her. It was Alan. He asked her to put the stroller in the boot, but she declined, telling him she'd see him at home.

'Ok, honey, see you in a bit. I've got some good news.' He could see she was about to question him, so he held up his hand, saying: 'It'll wait 'til you get home.'

Walking through the door ten minutes later, the first thing Maddie did was put the kettle on. Then, sitting at the table, they waited in silence for the tea to brew and for Maddie to pour it. After taking a sip from his cup, Alan eventually spoke.

I had a call at work today from the Pastoral Employment Agency. They asked if I was interested in a position that had just come up, as manager of a farm north of Perth. I think they said Reagan's Ford. Anyway, it's about an hour away from Gin Gin.'

Maddie, although happy that they would finally move out of the hovel they were living in, asked.

'Are you going to take it? Did you ask about the accommodation and when they want us to start work?' Maddie barely paused for breath!

Picking up a biscuit and dunking it in his tea, he watched as half broke off and sank to the bottom of the cup. 'They have arranged an interview with the owner in two days.'

Maddie silently prayed for life to improve, knowing it could not get much worse!

Kybie – Regan's Ford

Leaving Perth and driving inland for about half an hour, they passed through the town of Bullsbrook and the RAAF military base at Pearce. Continuing for another thirty-two miles, they arrived at the settlement of Gingin, where Maddie pointed out a small supermarket and asked Alan if he would like an ice cream and a cold drink, to which he replied affirmatively. While Maddie was in the shop, Alan ensured that Peter, who was strapped in the canvas seat they had managed to hook over the rear bench, was okay. He was a very calm child, and at just over a year old, he was walking, albeit unsteadily, and was becoming increasingly curious and mischievous. He was uttering quite a few words. Apart from 'mamma' and 'dadda', he was attempting to say other things that his parents did not quite understand!

Alan would have liked to spend a bit longer knowing that this would be their closest town for stocking up on provisions and non-essentials for the farm. Before leaving Perth, he had made a point of reading up on the area which had a population of around four hundred and was claimed to be one ot the oldest rural towns in Western Australia. Initially, it was given the aboriginal name JinJin, meaning either 'footprint' or 'place of many streams.'

Within a few minutes, Maddie ventured out of the shop clutching two cans of lemonade, one ice-cream in a cone and a small tub for Peter. Leaning into the car, she handed Alan the two cones and, after having put the other purchases on the seat, she went back into the shop for the packets of potato crisps she had been unable to carry. Then she opened the rear door of the car, released the straps which were holding Peter, lifted him out and took him into the front seat so she could feed him. After Maddie had finished cleaning up the melted cream off his face and hands, she strapped him back into the car seat.

Driving back onto the highway, they continued their journey. Maddie tore open one of the packets of crisps and, taking out a small blue sachet, she sprinkled the contents onto the crispy slices of potato before handing the packet to Alan. She preferred hers without salt.

Five minutes later, they turned off the highway and headed towards Regans Ford, with a further forty kilometres to reach their destination. They were now in the Wheatbelt country. Most of the road was sealed until about halfway, when they encountered corrugation. Maddie asked Alan to stop the car so that she could cradle their son to protect him from being jostled about.

As they drove along, admiring the countryside, Alan pointed out areas of land that had been divided into plots, most of which lay barren and unproductive. He told Maddie that after World War II, many soldiers were given a block of land and had the opportunity to start a farming life. The allotments brought triumph for some and despair for others.

Finally reaching a crossroad, they felt relieved to see a rickety wooden sign indicating that Mogumber was to the right and Kybie Farmstead to the left. They turned left. After a short drive alongside a paddock of white gum trees, they arrived at the entrance of the farm. As they proceeded up the long, treeless driveway, they were surprised to hear the drone of a helicopter overhead. Reaching the end of the drive, they caught sight of an asbestos fibro bungalow nestled among some eucalyptus trees. Approaching the house, they startled a large flock of pink and grey galahs that had been perching in the trees. The sound of their collective squawking as they flew was deafening.

Alighting from the car, they were surprised to see the helicopter hovering over the paddock adjacent to the house and watched it land vertically on the ground. The blades were still whirring when a man jumped down from the cockpit. Within moments, he was striding towards them. After exchanging greetings, Alan was the first to speak.

'Roy, I'd say that's arriving in style. It's a beauty!'

'It sure is, mate. I've only recently obtained my licence. It's the first time I've flown outside the city area.'

Alan and Ray made their way towards the house, with Maddie a short distance behind, clinging to her son's hand as he was still unsteady on his chubby legs; yet it was clear that he wanted to walk. While they looked through the house, Roy told them that they were the first to live in it since the old homestead, built some fifty years earlier, had been demolished. Maddie couldn't stop smiling and could hardly wait to settle in. After living in other people's houses, taking care of teenage boys and an elderly, cantankerous lady, and then living in a hovel for the past few months, this felt like a palace!

There were two moderately sized bedrooms, a lounge, and a large, well-equipped kitchen with an Aga. Proudly pointing to the numerous electrical items, such as a large food mixer, a milkshake maker, an electric knife, and, of course, a toaster and an electric jug, Roy told Maddie that he owned an electrical company in Perth. She was in her element.

Opening the bag that he had placed on the kitchen table when they first entered the house, Roy produced milk, tea, sugar, and various other items, telling them that it should last them for the next couple of days until they went to Gingin. While the men were talking, Maddie busied herself with making a pot of tea and, after leaving it to steep for a few minutes, she opened a packet of ginger biscuits, hoping Alan wouldn't dunk them in his tea in front of Roy.

'C'mon, lad, we'll take a drive around the property, and I'll show you the boundaries and the work that needs doing. At around 8,000 acres, Kybie isn't that large, but there's plenty to take care of. There are 1,250 sheep and a hundred head of cattle at the last count. I'm interviewing a young lad in Perth next week as you'll need an offsider, as some of the fences need repairing and there are holding yards to be built.'

Just as they were getting ready to leave, Roy asked. 'Can you ride Maddie?'

'Yes, my grandfather taught me at a very young age. I love to ride.'

'Great, come with me. I have a surprise for you. Oops, I nearly forgot; there are also eleven horses, three cattle dogs, some chooks, and a rooster.' Maddie was about to ask who had been taking care of them when Roy continued. 'A friend from one of the neighbouring farms has been coming over for the past couple of weeks to ensure they have food and water and to check that they are okay.'

As they walked around the back of the building, the first thing she spotted was the most beautiful Palomino stallion, standing at sixteen hands high, with a yellowish-golden coat shining brightly in the afternoon sun. She was speechless! As soon as he saw her making her way over to the corral, he came ambling towards the fence and sniffed gently at her hand as she reached out to stroke his silky black nose. Leaning forward, she blew softly into his nostrils to let him know she was a friend.

A few days after returning to Perth, Roy rang to let Alan know that he had just interviewed Joe, a seventeen-year-old Dutch lad. He mentioned that Joe seemed nice enough but didn't have much going on upstairs; however, he was confident that Alan would soon knock him into shape. Maddie went over to the shearers' quarters to check that one of the rooms had clean bedding, and Joe would be taking his meals with them in the house.

Alan's first task was to install a new generating plant as the old one had packed up, and then to build a hot water system, which he accomplished by connecting the Donkey, - 44-gallon drum – to the water tank raised above the ground so that a fire could be lit beneath it, thus heating the water for the bathroom and kitchen, which would eventually be extended to the laundry.

Every morning, it was Joe's job to load the cylinder with firewood and set it alight, providing them with plenty of hot water for the day. As much of the wood was green, the only way to ignite it was by drenching it with kerosene, which Joe obtained from a large drum in one of the barns. One such morning, Maddie noticed that he had left the partially filled jar on the ground next to the heater. Picking it up, she placed it on top of the kitchen window ledge and then went to find Joe, telling him that it needed to be kept out of Peter's reach at all times.

One morning, Maddie was hanging out the washing on the line while Peter sat on the ground beside her, playing with some clothes pegs. When his mother asked, he reached up and pressed one into her hand, thinking that it was a great game.

'Peter, pass me a peg?' Then, realising that he had gone very quiet and was not responding to her request, she glanced down to find that he had wandered off. Although she was not too concerned, as the gate into the yard was closed, so he couldn't have gone far. It was then that she spotted him sitting on the ground near the heater. He had the glass jar in his hand, the one with the kerosene, and was holding it up to his lips.

'Oh NO!' Sprinting over to her son and fearing the worst, she quickly scooped him up in her arms and, putting her nose to his mouth to smell his breath, screamed out to Alan, knowing he was working around the yard somewhere and would surely hear her. Within seconds, he rounded the corner, and running over, Maddie showed him the empty jar; without asking, he knew what had happened. Running to the barn to get the car, they drove the twenty-minute journey to the hospital while Maddie clutched her son, soothing him and praying they would arrive in time.

Upon arriving at the hospital, Peter was rushed into the theatre. After having his stomach pumped, the staff assured Alan and Maddie that, although their son was going to be alright, they wanted to keep him in overnight. Returning to the farm, Alan sought out Joe and, after giving him his marching orders, informed him that he would be driving him back to Perth in the morning. He then contacted Roy to let him know that he needed another offsider as soon as possible.

A week later, Jack arrived. He was a quiet, personable man in his mid-forties, and to Alan's relief, he had ample experience from having previously worked on a farm. Jack's wife remained in Perth due to a lack of accommodation for married couples. One day, while Jack was checking on the windmills, he stumbled upon an abandoned building in one of the paddocks a mile away. That evening, he mentioned it to Alan, asking if it would be possible for his wife to join him if he could make it habitable in his own time. Alan was intrigued by the idea, noting that it had been deserted for many years and that a considerable amount of work would be required, but he agreed to go there with Jack on Sunday.

The land surrounding the building was barren. Aside from a half-dead tree leaning drunkenly against the front entrance and a few low-lying bushes and vines that had crept up and over the rotting verandah, there was nothing. Constructed from timber and iron, it appeared sound enough from the outside, apart from the doors and windows that had rotted away, leaving a gaping hole in the iron roof. A few feet away, a rusty corrugated water tank stood on a stand, and next to it was a small lean-to with an old wood burner in the corner.

The interior required a complete renovation to make it habitable. The front entrance led into a small hallway with a door to the right that opened into the kitchen. There was an old

Coolgardie safe, a simple cupboard made of wired mesh and pressed metal, with a wet hessian bag hanging over the side, which would have kept the food at a cooler temperature. The old Metters wood stove would shine like new with a bit of spit and polish. Opposite the kitchen was another small room, and at the end of the short hallway were two small rooms, along with another that had been a bathroom. It would be a huge task to undertake, but Alan felt confident that Roy would grant his permission and hopefully provide much of what was needed to make the place liveable.

Roy raised no objection and was happy for Alan to obtain whatever they needed for the repairs; however, he insisted that the work be done in their own time.

Jack toiled mosts nights until dark, undertaking repairs on the roof and creating new windows and a door to keep any critters out. Alan assisted whenever he could. Occasionally, taking Peter with her, Maddie helped by sweeping the floor and removing rat droppings. Alan suggested that they take an old blanket and the playpen so that Peter would be safe while the work was ongoing. Eventually, after many hours of toil, Jack felt that, although there was still much more to be done to the place, the time was right for Daphne to join him and add her touches to make it feel like home. Jack drove to Perth in the old Bedford truck to collect his wife and the few bits of furniture they possessed.

Occasionally, Maddie would visit, bringing food and offering to help spruce up the place. She couldn't help but notice that Daphne seldom smiled, appearing sad and withdrawn, but did not like to pry.

Although Jack was proving to be an asset on the farm, he was becoming increasingly unreliable. Some days, he arrived late, and on other occasions, he did not come to work until the following day, always with a seemingly valid excuse. Then the day came when Alan was erecting one of the fences and hit his thumb. He'd had enough, and throwing the hammer onto the ground, he marched into the house, grabbed the keys for the truck, and, storming out, yelled to Maddie that he was going to see what the issue was. She didn't blame him for being so angry, as it had gone beyond a joke, as when Jack did eventually turn up, he always had an excuse. Daphne was unwell. He hadn't slept, or the old truck wouldn't start. The excuses were wearing them down. Alan realised that, like himself, Jack enjoyed a drink, but there were times he knew he'd had too much, and it was affecting his work.

It wasn't long before Maddie heard the Ute roaring up the driveway, followed by Jack trailing behind in the truck. After parking near one of the sheds, the two men alighted and continued with their work.

They worked hard constructing fences and erecting a corral for Ferdinand the bull, as well as planting over one hundred olive trees along the avenue leading up to the homestead. Then, once a month, they drove to the sheep and cattle sales in Mogumber, a half-hour drive east of Regans Ford. It was a modest settlement boasting an old stone post office/store and a small tavern. A short distance away was the Aboriginal community. In 1951, the government handed control of the settlement to the Mogumber Methodist Mission, renaming it Mogumber Native Mission.

Gertrude, the Holstein cow, supplied them with rich, creamy milk, which Maddie left to set, giving the cream time to rise to the top. When skimmed off, it provided them with fresh clotted cream to spread on their bread and jam. When there was a surplus, she made butter by whipping the cream, watching as it transformed into soft creamy peaks, and eventually, the pieces would start clinging to the beater and separating into butterfat. It was then washed, drained, and formed into butter pats—a lengthy and slow process, but worth the effort.

One day, Mr Spurge phoned Alan to let him know that there was a cattle sale at Mogumber and wanted him to attend, as he needed to find out what prices they were fetching. Alan left early that morning, and after the sale finished, he stayed in the pub until late. The following morning, Maddie was awoken by Peter's crying, as he wanted his nappy changed. She was sitting in the kitchen, feeding her son, when she suddenly realised that Betsy would be waiting to be milked; otherwise, her udders would become swollen, sore, and fit to bursting.

As soon as she finished feeding Peter, she settled him back in the cot, knowing that he would soon be fast asleep. Then, she went into the bedroom she shared with her husband.

'Alan, Alan, wake up! You need to milk Betsy.' Alan rolled over, moaning and turning his back on her. 'Leave me be, it's early. Go back to sleep.' Maddie shook him.

B-but... Alan, suffering from the night before, was not in the mood. 'BUGGER OFF!' It's about time you learnt to milk the bloody animal.'

Once Peter had drifted off to sleep, Madie made her way to the stockyard. As she approached, she spotted a dingo bitch lying with her muzzle resting on her paws, ears pricked, and her yellow eyes watchful. As Madie suspected, Betsy's udder was bulging with milk. She sighed—it was not going to be an easy task to get her from the yard into the shed for milking. Picking up the lasso that hung on the gate, she held it behind her back and slowly walked towards Betsy, expecting her to dart away. Therefore, she was surprised when she allowed Madie to slide the rope over her head and then ambled behind as she led her to the lean-to. After pushing her head into the bail, Madie quickly clamped it shut. Then, seizing the rope that Alan had slung over a pillar, she struggled to tie Betsy's back leg to the post, which proved extremely difficult as the irate cow kept lashing out with her leg. Feeling exhausted, she retrieved the old packing box she had seen Alan sitting on, and finding the steel bucket, she placed it beneath Betsy's udder. Perched on the crate, she stared down at the teats, trying to visualise the squeezing action Alan had used to produce the milk. Leaning over with her head against Betsy's belly, she pulled gently on the teats and, to her amazement, produced a few dribbles of milk, and then, persevering, she was soon squirting the white liquid into the bucket. Everything was going well until the cow lifted her tail and dumped a steaming pile of muck onto the ground! Despite the smell emanating from the foul mess, Maddie continued to squeeze the teats, although she was aware that Betsy was becoming restless, as evidenced by her stamping her feet and attempting to pull her head out of the bail. Then suddenly, *wham!* She kicked free of the rope and, thrusting backwards with both legs, struck Maddie on the shin, sending her off the box and landing flat on her back in the middle of the cow pat: a bruised shin, a deflated ego, bucket emptying as the milk soaked into the ground. Struggling to get up, she saw Alan striding across the yard.

'What on earth are you doing, woman? Why didn't you wake me?' Then, reaching down, he hooked his hands under her arms and, lifting her, was careful not to get the dung all over himself.

'Can you get back to the house without my help?' He asked. Too upset and feeling sorry for herself, Maddie chose not to reply and slowly and painfully hobbled back to the house, leaving Alan to finish off.

After taking Jack to task and telling him that his job was on the line, Alan was relieved that he was arriving on time most mornings, although he was not working at full capacity.

Every so often on a Saturday evening, Maddie and Alan, taking little Peter with them, drove the eighteen miles along the gravel road to the pub in Mogumber. Although the settlement had few houses, the pub was always busy. The owners, Ma and Pa Trip, made everyone feel very welcome. Ma spent most of the evening tickling the ivories, with everyone singing along to songs by famous artists such as Peggy Lee and Dinah Shore. Ma's favourite was 'The Biggest Aspidistras in the World', best known as Gracie Fields' song from the film 'Keep Smiling' in 1938. When Pa decided it was time to head off to bed, he would entrust one of the patrons to manage the bar, and just before closing time, when the local policeman walked in, the door was locked and the curtains drawn as they continued well into the night. Alan and his family had usually left by that time.

One such evening, arriving home, Alan went into the lounge to pour himself a nightcap before making his way to bed. Picking up the whisky bottle, he noticed that it was empty. He shouted out to Maddie, who was in the kitchen getting herself a hot drink.

'Maddie, what's happened to the whisky?' She entered the room holding her cup, a frown on her face. 'There's no need to shout!' Alan, ignoring the remark, pointed to the bottle and spoke.

'Have you suddenly taken a liking to whisky? Because, as you can see, the bottle is empty, and the last time I looked, it was half full.'

Maddie laughed. 'You are joking. You know perfectly well that I hate the stuff. The smell is enough to put me off.'

Then, pausing for a moment, she pointed to the top of the television where there were several miniature bottles of alcohol. 'I suggest that if you are that desperate, you open one of those!' Alan walked across the room and picked up a small bottle of brandy. As he started to unscrew the top, he realised that the seal had been broken. After removing the cap, he sniffed at the contents and, taking a sip, exclaimed, 'What the fuck is this? It's not brandy.' He then handed it to his wife. 'Taste it.'

As Maddie disliked any spirits, she took a sip gingerly. 'Tastes like cold tea to me.' They then opened another bottle and another, and then, realising they had all been emptied and refilled with tea, they looked at one another, both thinking the same. There was only one other person who had access to the house.

Alan rose earlier than usual the following morning and, after dressing, made his way to the cottage. Daphne, already dressed and preparing breakfast, was surprised to see Jack's boss on the doorstep. Inviting him into the kitchen, she swiftly scooped up some items from the table and put them in a drawer.

John, wasting no time, spoke. 'Daphne, I need to speak with Jack.' 'Bu...Bu.... he's...," she stammered. Interrupting her, Alan laid his hand on her arm. I'm genuinely sorry, but there is something important I need to ask him.

Daphne ran from the room, and upon entering their bedroom, Alan could hear her desperately trying to awaken her husband from a drunken stupor. When she returned to the room, her entire body was shaking, and tears were pouring down her ragged face. Then sobbing uncontrollably,

'I k-knew that this w-would happen one day. He's had s-so many jobs, but they n-never last, and we move on and f-find another. I thought that it would be different h-here, knowing t-that he couldn't go to the pub every day, or b-buy....b-but, oh God! What am I to do, Alan? He's now making his own!'

Alan retorted. 'Making his own what?'

Daphine indicated the drawer where she had shoved the item from the table. Walking over and pulling it open, Alan immediately understood what she had been trying to convey, as there were several tins of boot polish and bottles of methylated spirits inside. Jack had become so desperate, sinking into alcoholism, that this was what he had resorted to—lethal doses to satisfy his thirst, anything to make him see the world differently. Stroking his chin thoughtfully as he took in the situation, Alan was attempting to figure out the kindest way to tell Jack's wife he could no longer employ her husband.

'I'm so very sorry, Daphne; I truly am, but it's not working out. I cannot justify keeping Jack on. I wish there were another option, but unfortunately, there isn't. I assure you, though, that you have time to sort things out, and Maddie and I will do all we can to help.

Daphne nodded as she had known that would be the outcome once they found out. 'Thank you, thank you so much. I am so very grateful.

Roy did not send anyone to replace Jack, informing Alan that it would be simpler to employ casual labour from the Mogumber Mission as required.

Maddie was expecting their second child in about six months, but that had not stopped her from slowing down to help Alan around the homestead. It had been raining heavily for a couple of days, and many roads were submerged under water. However, Alan was hopeful that the road to Mogumber would be safe to travel, as they looked forward to joining the crowd at the pub on Saturday evening, where voices were raised as they sang along with Ma, while she pounded away on the old piano.

It was just after six when they set off, with Maddie seated in the front beside Alan and Peter secured in his seat at the back. They were about five miles from their destination when they encountered a stretch of water that covered the road. Maddie was concerned, stating.

'I think we should turn back as that looks quite deep to me.'
Alan, unconcerned, said. 'If I take it slow, we should be okay.'
Maddie chose to remain silent, as her husband was usually correct in such situations. They were nearly halfway across when the water began to seep into the car. It quickly rose to the tops of their seats and up to the car's bonnet. Then the engine stalled. Unable to push the doors open, Alan wound down his window and managed to squeeze himself out. Making his way around to the other side, he signalled for Maddie to lower her window and do the same. This was nearly impossible due to her bulging

stomach. However, she eventually emerged unscathed. Then, reaching inside, Alan lowered the back window and, unbuckling his son from the car seat, gently pulled him out of the car.

'Now what, Alan? We are in the middle of nowhere, not a building in sight. We can't stand here all night. So, what do you suggest we do?'

'We have no choice but to walk, and hope that someone comes along. If not, we will have to keep walking until we eventually arrive at Mogumber.'

As they trudged through the water, Alan carried Peter, with Maddie following behind. As always, seeing the humorous side of their dilemma, she started to giggle, which annoyed her husband. They hadn't gone far when Alan handed their son to Maddie, stating he was becoming too heavy. So, she had no choice but to perch Peter on her hip, away from her stomach. They had walked for what Maddie thought seemed like many miles when Alan turned and shouted to her.

'Look, look ahead, there's a farmhouse in the distance.'

Maddie was too exhausted to reply, and her back ached. They had just reached the entrance to the property when the farmer's wife spotted them and came running towards them. Taking Peter from his mother's aching arms, as she ushered them into the house, she called out. 'Karl, come quickly, we have visitors.'

As soon as Karl saw the bedraggled pair, he knew what had happened, as many times before, travellers had attempted to navigate what they believed was a small pool of water after a heavy downpour. His wife, Laura, instructed Maddie to take off her shoes and dry them by the fire, while Karl asked Alan to follow him out to the shed. Shortly after, Maddie watched from the window as they made their way off the property, with Alan standing on the back of the tractor, a tow rope slung over his shoulder. Much later, they returned with Karl towing the car and Alan sitting inside, navigating it. Extending their gratitude to the lovely couple, Alan insisted that they would be okay to travel on to their destination. Arriving at the pub, they spent the rest of the evening enjoying the company, and when everyone was leaving, Ma insisted that they bunk up in one of the guest rooms. Travelling home the following morning, they were relieved to see that the water had subsided enough for them to continue on their way safely.

Maddie, now eight months on, found life much happier since coming to the farm, as Alan was no longer drinking as much and seemed content with a few beers or the occasional glass of whisky. This did not mean that he never got drunk; it was just that it happened less frequently. Having nowhere to go, he was not staying out all night, doing goodness knows what!
In the evenings, Maddie would sit darning the holes in Alan's socks or carefully unpicking the frayed collars of his shirts, turning them over and restitching them in the hope of making them last another season. At other times, they would sit for hours playing rummy and poker.
When it was time to scatter the lupins in one of the paddocks, Maddie and Peter sat on the wagon while Alan drove the tractor, and she scattered them along the furrows. She continued to ride the beautiful stallion, despite Alan's objections.
Not long after Jack's departure, Alan's brother Adrian arrived at their doorstep with his wife Pat and their one-year-old daughter, seeking work and expecting to stay at the homestead with them. It had been over a year since they had last seen them, when they were staying with their sister Rhona in Sydney. Alan looked quizzingly at his brother.
How did you know where to find us?' Adrian shrugged his shoulders. 'That was easy, as I knew where your mother lived, Maddie, and she told me you were on a farm near Regan's Ford. Upon arriving in Gingin, being such a small place, I knew that if I asked around, someone would know you.'
Realising that he could scarcely turn his brother away, especially since they had a young child with them, Alan reluctantly agreed. 'Okay, you can stay in the old building up the road and I will phone my boss and see if I can offer you work; to be honest, I need all the help I can get since the last bloke left.'
The brothers worked well together, and on occasion, they would spend an evening together, each eager to discover where their paths had taken them since they last met.
Adrian entertained them with tales of his many escapades, reminding them of the time in 1966 when he and two mates,

armed and masked, robbed one of the major banks in Adelaide. Neither Alan nor Maddie had heard the whole story before, so they were intrigued to know the entire story. Always eager to proudly share his finest moments, Adreian was happy to oblige.

'Well. After I managed to slip through the net and flee with my share of the loot, I sprinted as fast as I could to where we'd left the car with the keys inside for a quick exit. I drove like a maniac until I found an abandoned plot of land. After dumping the car, I zigzagged to the laneway at the back of the house. The bloody gate to the yard was padlocked on the inside, so I had to throw the bag, filled with thousands of pounds, over the picket fence. Then, with great difficulty, I scrambled over, grabbed the bag, kicked open the door, and shouted out to Pat.

Pat interrupted. 'I knew something was wrong as he was sweating like a pig and pacing the room like a caged animal. It was then that he showed me the sack of money, pulling out bundles of notes and shoving them at me, telling me to go to the butchers and buy some chickens! He wouldn't give me time to ask questions, just told me to drive there as fast as I could.'

Getting his two pennies' worth in, Adrian said. 'Yes, you stupid bitch, you wasted valuable time.' Pat began to protest, but he interrupted her. 'As soon as Pat left the house, I threw everything that was in the freezer into an old bin outside the back door, and when she returned, we stuffed the chickens with most of the notes and packed them into cold storage. Then, grabbing some clothes, I crammed them into a holdall, shoved a handful of notes into my pocket, and gave the rest to Pat. I had no time for anything else, so I scarpered back out the way I came in.'

'You know the rest, serving time in Pentridge, and you two coming to see me. What you don't know is that I was released after five years for what they said was impeccable behaviour. Funny, eh, me on good behaviour!'

Alan and Maddie had listened in amazement as James recounted his adventure, if you could call it that! Adrian was curious.

'Adrian, a few years have passed since then. What have you been up to? Have you had a decent job for once?' Jimmie smirked. 'Well, mmm, that's another story!'

Patting his brother on the back, Alan commented, 'We're all ears, so you may as well tell us, as by the sounds of it, there is much more to tell. Am I correct?'

Adrian, as always in his element when boasting about his past, continued. 'One time after having a skinful in the local pub, I went to get into my car when a couple of coppers drew up alongside me. The cocky one asked me to produce my driver's licence, while the other officer took out the breathalyser. However, just as I was about to take the test, the officer who had taken my licence stepped over and took the other copper aside, showing him the document, and they started whispering. I heard them say that my name was familiar to them and that they needed to check on me. So I shouted out, telling them not to bother as I had robbed a bank.'

Maddie gasped. 'What happened next?'

'It was hilarious as after locking my car, they escorted me to the police station, where it was confirmed that I had indeed robbed a bank but had served my sentence and was free to go. However, the best was yet to come. They forgot to test me for drink driving!'

'There's more if you're interested?' Maddie was the first to comment. 'There's more? I would have thought you would have behaved yourself after being released?'

Adrian grinned. 'Well, what you don't know is that, when I got out of prison and returned home, I found that Pat had raided the freezer and spent most of the money that had been stuffed in the chickens!' Once again, Pat interrupted. 'Well, what did you expect? You were away all that time, and I needed to live. 'Well, not that well! I served my time only to be released and left with nothing. That's a joke!'

Have you ever used a gun for any purpose other than robbing a bank? 'Well, now that you ask, there were a couple more escapades. But, in my defence, I have turned over a new leaf since then, as Pat will confirm. Right, Pat?' Nodding her head. 'Yeah, he's different now.'

'Anyway, there was one other time. It was when I was out of town. Remember, this was a few years ago. I needed a quiet drink at a local pub, but when I walked in, it was packed with locals. I was about to leave, but I changed my mind, went to the boot of my car, and took out a rifle that I had kept there, just in case I ever needed it. I then re-entered the pub, calling out, "Where is the bastard? If I find you, you're dead meat!" Believe it or not, the bar emptied in a flash, and the publican, mouth agape and scared out of his wits, didn't know what to do. So, I put the rifle down on the bar, asked him to pour me a scotch, and sat there enjoying the peace. That was until a carload of coppers arrived!'

Rising from her chair, Maddie asked if anyone would like a hot drink before going to bed. 'How about one for the road, eh, Alan?' 'Okay mate.' Alan replied.

Whilst Maddie and Pat were in the kitchen, Alan poured his brother a neat whisky. Adrian, eager to share one more incident with his brother before the evening drew to a close, continued the conversation.

'You will laugh at this one, brother of mine. A couple of mates and I devised a plan to steal some expensive fur coats from one of the large department stores. After observing the movements in the shop and determining how to remove them safely, we developed a strategy.

Adrian looked at his brother, shaking his head in bewilderment as he waited with bated breath to hear about his next adventure.

'Anyway. We stole a van and parked it outside the store's entrance, leaving the driver in the cabin. The other bloke and I, dressed in white dust coats, entered the building, wheeling a clothes rail covered in white sheeting. We then went over to where the coats were, positioned our rail next to the one with the furs, and covered the coats with our sheeting. After that, we casually wheeled the expensive furs out to the van, pushed the rail up the ramp, and, jumping into the cabin, drove off.

'Okay mate. I reckon that's enough for one night. Time for bed.'

Autumn was nearly over, and with only a couple of weeks until Maddie was due to give birth to their second child, she remained determined to help around the farm and ride the magnificent stallion that Mr Spurge had gifted her. The white Gum paddock was full of mushrooms, so when time permitted, they foraged under the trees, where large clusters could be found. They watched Peter tottering around on his little legs, eager to assist, as he grabbed with his tiny hands, plucking them from the stems and crushing them in his eagerness to help.

The Moor River flowed through the property at the back of the Kybie, and on the other side was a larger farm. The only contact Alan had with them occurred one late afternoon when a young man came roaring around in his 4x4 to inform them that their bull had swum across the river and was attempting to mount one of their cows!

Later, when discussing this with Maddie, he suggested that they should visit their neighbours. Maddie was pleased with the idea and suggested.

'Let's take the basket of mushrooms we gathered this morning, as there are far too many for us.' Alan nodded and added. 'Okay, that's a good idea, but save enough for us to have on toast for breakfast tomorrow.'

Maddie, her enlarged belly resting against the side of the playpen where Peter was happily playing with his building blocks, leant over to lift him out. Pushing his mother away.

'No, no, go 'way, go 'way!' He then continued to play with the blocks, stacking them one on top of the other until, in frustration, he swept them down in a heap. 'Come on, Peter, they might have a friend for you to play with. Please be good for mummy.'

After kicking his legs in a minor tantrum while fighting to get his way, he calmed down, allowing his mother to wash and dress him in clean clothes. After putting a couple of nappies and a bottle of juice into a bag, they were ready to go.

They drove to the end of the drive, passing all the olive saplings that Aland and Adrian had planted. Then they turned left, making their way down to the main road. After turning left again, they drove a short distance until they reached a small bridge that crossed over a ford. Two hundred yards further on, they came across the sign for *Coolonga Farm*. Following a short drive up an avenue of white eucalyptus trees, they were startled to see a large, old homestead. The corrugated iron fascia seemed to have withstood the years well, but the asbestos roof was in dire need of repair. There was a small area of lush green grass where they had planted some rose bushes.

As Alan alighted from the car, the young man appeared around the corner of a large open shed, filled with antiquated machinery. He was then taken aback when the man scurried off in the direction of the house and, after reaching the front door, ran inside, slamming it shut behind him. Alan, looking at Maddie in bewilderment, asked.

'What do you think we should do? It doesn't look like we are going to be welcomed here. Maybe we should leave.'

Maddie shrugged her shoulders, not knowing what to think or say. Remained silent, Alan was the first to speak.

'This is silly. We can't just stand here and wait to see if he comes out of the house.' 'Ok,' retorted Maddie. 'You go and knock on the door, and I'll wait here with Peter. If no one comes out, we'll go home.' Not receiving a response, Alan was about to return to the car when the door opened, revealing a man who appeared to be in his mid-thirties.

'G'day.' Then, pointing towards the trees lining the river, 'We're your neighbours, over the other side. One of your men came yesterday to tell us about our bull, so we thought it was about time to come and introduce ourselves.' After a few seconds of surveying Alan, he appeared to relax, and, approaching the stranger standing on his doorstep, extended his hand.

'G'day mate. Sorry, but we ain't had a visitor here for donkey's years. Ma and Pa never put foot out of the place, leaving me t' see t' things. Anyhow, I'm Jed, Jed Darche.'

Maddie, having walked over, was standing next to Alan, with Peter in her arms. She smiled at Jed, marvelling at his thick, black crop of hair, finding him quite handsome in a rugged sort of way. There was hardly an ounce of fat on him, reminding her of a lean greyhound. 'Hi, I'm Maddie.' Jed acknowledged her with a nod of his head and then beckoned for them to follow him into the house, saying.

'C'mon in, but mind you, don't pay too much attention to the folks, as they are wary of everyone. We haven't done much work on the place in a long time, but it's clean and tidy.

Although they seemed shy, Alan and Maddie quickly warmed to Jed's parents. It was evident that Jed inherited his good looks from his mother and his hair and swarthy complexion from his father, although time had not been kind to him. His back was hunched, and his hands were gnarled and rough, indicating how hard he had worked for much of his life. Ma had scurried off to the kitchen, returning with a pot of tea and cake. Meanwhile Jed produced cold beers for the men. Sitting on the floor, Peter played happily with his father's tobacco tin. Maddie observed Ma Darche watching him with a hint of sadness on her face. It wasn't long before the elderly couple were chatting easily with them, sharing stories of their time on the farm and explaining how they acquired the property many years ago, shortly after they married during the Second World War. Jed cast a wistful glance at his parents and continued to explain to his visitors that they had little contact with the outside world, apart from his trips to the cattle sales in Mogumber. When the old Bakelite radio broke down, his Pa refused to replace it. Not wanting to overstay their welcome, Alan and Maddie thanked them for their hospitality and made their way out to the car, about to drive off when Ma Darche appeared at the door, waving her hand and asking them to come again.

After their initial visit, they returned many times. Maddie loved to sit with Ma over a cuppa while Alan, Pa, and Jed compared notes on farming, discussing the welfare of their sheep—how many had been born or, as sheep often do, died.

Then, one Sunday, having driven over to see the family, Jed was in the courtyard with a sheep that had injured itself while attempting to jump a barbed-wire fence. Meanwhile, Alan and Maddie were seated in the kitchen with Pa, while Peter curled up on the sofa. Ma, who had just made the obligatory pot of tea and some fresh scones, entered the room carrying a tray laden with the teapot and cups. Maddie rose from her chair to assist when suddenly Pa flung himself out of his chair and lunged at Ma, grabbing hold of her dress and dragging her beneath the table. Meanwhile, Ma screamed, and the tray and its contents went crashing to the floor! Alan, witnessing the commotion, jumped to his feet, stunned by what was unfolding before his very eyes! Getting down on her hands and knees, Maddie peered beneath the table to see the couple clinging to one another, looking petrified! Then Pa, wrapping his arms around his wife, whispered.

'It's okay, Doris, it's safe. They've gone.' As Alan helped the couple out from under the table, he was baffled by what had just occurred, so he asked. 'Whose gone?
'THOSE BASTARDS.....The bloody JAPS!
'The Japs?' Alan, shaking his head, looked at Maddie, even more bewildered. Then, he hit the palm of his hand against his forehead. 'Oh my God! You really do not know that the war was over many years ago?' Meanwhile, Jed, hearing the commotion, immediately rushed into the house to help calm his parent. Maddie slipped into the kitchen to prepare a fresh pot of tea. Jed, feeling embarrassed, apologised.

'They will have heard your boss's helicopter circling the house, preparing to land on the paddock. And having never left the farm, they have no idea what goes on in the world. I've tried telling them, but they refuse to believe me.'

Peter was eighteen months old when the time came for the arrival of a baby brother or sister. He enjoyed playing in the small, fenced area outside the front door, as it was the only patch of grass surrounding the house. Although he was an inquisitive little lad and had never tried to wander off, they kept the gate locked.

One afternoon, Maddie was at the kitchen sink preparing vegetables for their tea while keeping an eye on her son from the window as he played with a couple of toy trucks. After filling a pot with water for the potatoes, she took it over to the stove on the other side of the room. When she returned to the sink, she looked out of the window to ensure that Peter was still playing happily. However, there was no sign of him! 'You little bugger, where have you disappeared to now?' Not overly worried, she made her way around to the rear of the house, expecting to find him there. Instead, she saw that somehow, he had managed to unlatch the gate.

'Oh, no!' Maddie was now worried as there were all sorts of mischief he could get into around the property. Running out of the gate and rounding the corner towards the small field next to the corral, she saw Peter, laughing in glee, making his way towards Ferdinand the bull. Somehow, he had managed to crawl under the electric wire fence without getting zapped. Maddie stood frozen in fear, not wanting to frighten either her son or the generally ferocious bull, which stood firm, gazing directly at Peter. As he toddled closer to the massive creature, Maddie realised she had to act quickly, so she manoeuvred herself, hardly daring to breathe, under the fence without getting electrocuted. For a moment or two, she remained still, just watching. Then, slowly rising, she edged her way towards her son and, holding out her hand, quietly spoke to him.

'Peter, come to Mummy.' He stopped and turned to look at her just as Ferdinand was beginning to look agitated. Maddie became frightened, hoping that he wouldn't charge towards her son. Then, pointing at Ferdinand, Peter said, 'Mama, Mama. I want to play with big Boo.' Moving closer, she was able to reach out and take his hand, then gather him into her arms, being careful not to make a sudden move. She made her way to the electric fence. Then, she carefully pushed him underneath, telling him not to move until she joined him. Peter made it known that he was unhappy because he had not been allowed to play with Boo.

Not long after that incident, Alan went into Ferdinand's coral to top up the hay rack. Unfortunately for Alan Boo, as they were now calling him, was not in the best of moods. After finishing loading the hay, Alan was about to leave the corral when the very angry bull started snorting loudly, and before Alan could retreat, it came stampeding towards him. Then, lowering his head, he shoved Alan against the fence. Quickly regaining his footing, Alan managed to get to the gate before the bull made another attempt at him. The next day, although stiff and sore, he was, thankfully, uninjured.

With only ten days until her baby was due, Alan drove Maddie to her mother's, taking Peter along. He returned to the farm the following afternoon. Maddie kept herself busy around the small flat, and on the day before she was due to give birth, she walked nearly three miles to visit her friend Molly, taking Peter in the pushchair. When she arrived, she was exhausted. Fortunately, Molly and her husband were at home. After enjoying their company and having some time to rest, Maddie's relief was evident as they insisted on driving her home.

In the early hours of the morning, the nagging pains Maddie had that day grew stronger and more frequent. She waited a while to ensure it was not a false alarm, but as they came closer together, she decided to wake her mother. Daisy awakened Charles, informing him that they were off to the hospital and to keep an eye on Peter. Then, not bothering to remove her curlers from beneath the hairnet, she threw a dressing gown over her nightie and was ready to go. Maddie was waiting by the front door with a small case.

As they made their way through the streets of Subiaco, Daisy had no idea where the hospital was, especially since everything looked so different in the dark. She began to panic, as it felt as though they were driving in circles, going up one road and down another, only to end up back where they started. Eventually, they encountered an early morning road sweeper and, pulling over, asked for directions. Eventually reaching their destination, Maddy exited the car and waddled up the hospital's steps. A duty nurse located a wheelchair, and after taking her details, swiftly took her to one of the wards.

Daisy phoned Alan the following morning to inform him that his wife was in labour and would update him when she had more news. He had anticipated the call and arranged for a local lad to oversee the farm until his return. After finishing the morning chores, he packed an overnight bag and, making his way south, stopped off at Bullsbrook, an hour down the track, for a quick pint. An hour later, he was still propping up the bar as he chatted with some of the locals. Before leaving, he rang the hospital to ask how his wife was doing and whether she'd had the baby yet. He was taken aback when she informed him that his wife had given birth to twins!

'TWINS! It can't be. Surely we would have known before now that she was carrying two babies?' Putting the phone back on the hook, he returned to the bar, letting everyone know that his wife had given birth to twins. As they congratulated him, shaking his hand and slapping him on the back, John called out to the barmaid.

'Hey, luv, drinks all round. I've just learned that my missus has given birth to twins. Having stayed longer and drinking more than he had intended, it was now time to continue his journey to

Perth. But having had a skinful, he asked if anyone was going that way and could give him a lift. Charlie, who bred pits on his property on the far side of the aerodrome, offered to take him.

'Yep, I'll take you.'

'Great, thanks, Charlie. A quick pint and we can be off.'

'Okay mate, no problem. Give me a shout when you're ready.'

After a couple of rounds, Alan phoned the hospital once again to inquire about his wife's condition and to ask if they could inform her that he was on his way. The nurse responded.

'Are you Jack or Alan Cox?' Puzzled as to why he was asked. 'Alan Cox, I've just had twins.'

'Definitely Alan, not Jack?'

'Of course, don't you think I know my own name? Is there a problem, nurse?'

'Mmm…I'm sorry, Mr Cox, but I think there has been a misunderstanding. Your wife is still in labour.' Alan could hardly take it in; first, he was informed he was the father of two babies, and now this nurse was telling him his wife had not yet given birth!

'What the fuck are you talking about! I phoned earlier and was told that my wife had given birth to twins. How could you have made such a mistake?' He slammed down the phone, dreading the prospect of telling everyone and knowing he would look like a complete fool. So, choosing to remain silent, he approached Charlie, who was still perched on a stool at the bar. Realising that Charlie was not in a fit state to drive, he made his way to his car, turned on the ignition, and headed towards the city.

Meanwhile, Maddie was nursing their newborn son, James Alan. At just over seven pounds, he weighed significantly less than his big brother, and whereas Peter had blonde, curly hair, James had dark, straight hair. Whatever life threw at her, it did not matter, as she would always have her two beautiful sons.

Alan drove back to the farm, telling Maddie he would return in a week to collect her and the two boys.

A week later, he was making his way back to Perth, once again stopping at the Bullsbrook pub for a quick pint. He was preparing to move on when Charlie staggered over to him.

'Hey, mate, if you want t' get t' see your wife before the bairn is born, we'd better make a move!' Alan chuckled to himself, remembering what someone had told him.

"You'd never know that Charlie was drunk until the day he's sober!" He had fond memories of the old man, who was one of the town's characters.

Charlie and his wife, Mary, lived in a dilapidated tin shack with shattered windows that swung on their hinges, rusted walls, a sagging ceiling, and shabby linoleum that barely covered the floors. But it was their home. They had a cow named Betsy, and if, after a night of drinking, Charlie didn't get down to the paddock in time to milk her, she would amble over and stick her head through one of the windows or push the door open to make her way into the kitchen. Then, with the mightiest bellow, she would let them know she was there. Being drunk for most of the time, they were used to this, and ambling downstairs, Charlie would pull an old fruit box and metal bucket out from under the table and proceed to milk her in the kitchen.

Alan and Maddie got on well with the 'odd' couple and visited them whenever they passed by. Although their home was somewhat dilapidated, with chooks and ducks wandering around the kitchen or perched on the table, and occasionally one of the pigs would join the clan, it was always clean.

Charley was a wonderful character, loved by everyone. He worked as a janitor at the airbase, but he was also one of the finest pig breeders in the state. Frequently, his pigs would escape and be seen wandering about the town, causing havoc, before making their way home across the airstrip. The time everyone still talked about was when the local baker came barging into the pub screaming obscenities at Charlie. 'Get you fat ass off that stool and see what your fuckin' pigs have done to my store. Without saying a word, Charlie got off the stool and, followed by all the other patrons, joined the irate baker as they made their way to the shop. Everyone gasped when they saw one of Charlie's sows and ten white piglets foraging through torn flour bags. By then, everyone was howling with laughter, except for Charlie and the baker. Charlie, who was not in the least perturbed, looked at the baker with an amused expression and then nodded towards the pigs. Saying

'They can't be MY pigs, as mine are pink... These are white! Then, chortling, knowing very well that everyone knew they were his.

'But whoever they belong to, I'm sure if you can catch 'em you can keep them!' By this time, the sow and her piglets had wandered out of the bakery and were trotting up the street. Meanwhile, Charlie, still laughing, jumped into his old Austin Ute and, rattling an old kerosene tin, made his way home across the airfield, with the sow and her piglets following behind.

Peter adored his little brother, often gazing into James's pram, playing with the chubby little fingers and stroking his hair. James was just a few months old when one afternoon, while hanging the washing on the line, Maddie heard the familiar hum of Mr Spurge's helicopter approaching the farm. He usually landed in the paddock across the road from the homestead. She was certain that Alan was not expecting him, so she assumed he had come to see what progress her husband had made around the property. Maddie was confident that Alan would have heard the roar of the rotor blades, as he was nearby in one of the barns working on the generator, which always gave him grief.

Maddie made her way back to the house, knowing Roy would be hanging out for a cup of tea. Alan entered the kitchen and scrubbed his hands to remove the oil and grease. Said. 'I'd better get down the paddock pronto as he won't want to be walking in this heat.'

Roy Spurge had not come for a social visit; he was there to inform them that his son Mark would be taking over the management of the farm. He assured them that he had been very pleased with all they had accomplished during their time there but was also delighted that his son, who had previously shown no interest in the farm, now wished to take it over.

'I'm not kicking you off. You must take your time in finding somewhere to live and, hopefully, securing a new position very soon. That said, I know that Mark would like to move up here in the next month or two.'

'Th...thank...' Maddie got no further as Alan, his temper rising, shot back. 'We'll be out of here by the end of the week.

I'll find somewhere for us to live and don't you worry, I'll soon have another.'

Maddie was too upset to speak, astonished by Alan's rudeness to the man who had always been so gracious to them and appreciated that he would want his son to follow in his footsteps. Once more, they would be homeless. The only difference this time was that they had two small children. Her mind wandered back to her own childhood, when her mother moved from job to job, house to house, never having a home of their own until arriving in Australia.

Roy made his way back to the helicopter, with Alan not offering to drive him. Instead, he stomped out of the house, slammed the door behind him, and shouted. 'Well, that's that, isn't it!'

Maddie felt sad at the thought of leaving the place she had come to love, which she had thought would be her forever home for some time to come.

1963

One month until Christmas, Alan and Maddie were working on a small farm in the hills near Serpentine, thirty-four miles south-southeast of Perth. With a population of about 400, it was a relatively small settlement. They lived in a two-bedroom asbestos dwelling that the owner, Mr. Carter, had transported to the property.

The flooring throughout was typical linoleum. There were no curtains, but that was not a necessity since they were too far from the road to be seen. Although there was very little furniture, it was sufficient. There wasn't a wash house, and the Maytag wringer washing machine sat outside the back door, covered in dust and dirt. As there was no hot water, Alan's first job was to build an outside boiler, similar to the one in Kybie.

The farm was little more than a smallholding, meaning that Alan's role would be to maintain the house and the surrounding property.

A mile up the road, a petrol station and a convenience store were run by a lovely lady named Mary. She always treated Maddie kindly and extended her credit until they received their first pay packet. Alan's first wage should have been transferred into their account a couple of weeks ago, but every time he checked with the bank, it had not been deposited. He phoned Mr. Carter, only to be told it had probably been held up in the Christmas rush.

Alan often spent beyond their means, meaning they lived hand to mouth for much of the time.

Maddie visited the bank manager to request a small overdraft. Although reluctant, he must have taken pity on the young mother with two small children and arranged for a small overdraft to tide them over.

Eventually, Alan was paid, but the ensuing months continued as before. What could they do? They needed work and a place to live. Alan put their name down with the State Housing Commission, hoping they would qualify for a state house. He told Maddie they would stand a better chance of being moved to the top of the list if they relocated the family to a caravan park.

When Alan informed his boss that they were leaving, he was pleased to know that Mr Carter had been happy with the work he had done in a relatively short time, and said he was sorry to see them go. He then paid monies owed and sorted out their account at the service station.

They settled at a caravan park in Como, and Alan found a job with a local building company. Shortly after moving to the park, a telegram arrived from State Housing, informing them that they had been allocated a house in the new suburb of Cloverdale and advising them to contact the agency immediately if they still required it. The SHC provided homes at a very reasonable rental rate. If residents continued living in the same house and decided they wanted to buy it, the rent paid during those years would be deducted from the purchase price.

Since leaving Gingin, Maddie had not felt as excited about a house. It was a brand-new brick veneer home on a large corner block. Many were still empty, ready to welcome families to the estate. Those who had already moved in were mainly young couples with children. The little furniture they had was stored in Charles' garage, but it was sufficient until they could afford to buy more. Maddie hoped that it would be their forever home.

Their next-door neighbours, Terry and Rae McAndrew, were the first to welcome them to their new home. They had three children: Richard, Laura, and Simone.

Alan had to give up his job at the builders because it was too far to travel each day. He registered for unemployment, and within days, he began working with a removal company. Then, not long after that, Charles's mother, Mia, asked if they would be interested in running a delicatessen for her. She told them she had closed it down some time ago but was considering reopening it. Apart from selling the usual items, she wanted to offer takeaway foods such as burgers and hot chickens. As Alan was working, most of the management of the place would fall to Maddie, but Alan believed she would be more than capable of handling it. This opportunity would provide a boost to their income. Maddie said she would try it to see if she could juggle her time between the shop and caring for their children.

At twenty months, Peter was getting into mischief, but James, only three months old, required less attention as he slept most of the time. Inside the shop, a couple of steps led down to a small flat where crates of cool drinks were stored. It was ideal for the children, as she could lay them down for their naps and be sure they would be safe.

Maddie shut the shop door around midday for half an hour and went down the stairs to the flat to get herself and Peter something to eat and take care of Jammie.

Life was hectic, with the shop opening every morning at 9 a.m. and not shutting until around 5:30 p.m.

Alan helped whenever he could, especially on weekends, lifting heavy crates of cool drinks and handling other necessary tasks. Occasionally, when Charles stopped by, he and Alan would head to the pub, and that would be the last time Maddie would see Alan until later that night. Sometimes, Maddie prepared their meals in the shop, bringing them home to heat up for their tea.

Caught up in her life, Maddie barely noticed when she started losing weight, which worsened as Alan reverted to his old habits—drinking and returning home late.

She had only been at the shop a few months when Mia came in to see her and told her that she didn't need her anymore, having decided to run it herself with the help of a young girl who would assist her. Maddie then knew that Mia had used her to build a clientele, which she had accomplished relatively quickly. She was not sorry to leave as Mia kept putting off paying her, saying that she was family and families helped one another.

Alan, still eager to start a business, contacted his elder brother Stephen, who had recently established a septic cleaning business. Stephen was happy for Alan to enter the same field, mainly because they would be operating in different areas. He offered to sell his brother one of his older trucks at a reasonable price since he was buying a new one. He mentioned that Alan would need to outfit it because he was removing all the equipment for the new lorry. Alan jumped at the opportunity.

Once the lorry was ready, Maddie advertised the business in the local phone directory and shops. They then asked Terry, who had recently been made redundant, if he would like to come and work for Alan. He said he was not so sure about working in a job where they sucked out everyone's shit! But in the end, he agreed to give it a go as he needed the work.

They were going well, and finally, the bank account moved from red to black. Needing more furniture, they took a trip to Gregson's Auctioneers in Perth. They were fortunate that day, as few people were bidding, allowing them to purchase some decent items very cheaply. They already owned a television that they had acquired through hire purchase.

They met up with Daisy and Charles quite regularly, usually on the weekends, going on picnics, and occasionally they'd hire a babysitter for the night so they could join them at the Fremantle Club. Maddie still didn't drink alcohol, preferring to sip juices. She loved to dance and would have stayed on the floor all night dancing to the five-piece band. Alan wasn't a dancer, so he seldom took her onto the floor, but she was never short of a partner. Anyone who asked her to dance would always turn to Alan for his permission. He never minded since he didn't enjoy dancing. Additionally, it gave him more time to drink. However, if anyone returned a second time to ask his wife to dance, he let them know that he was not happy.

Alan was still doing the occasional magic shows. Maddie always assisted him, handing him the props, catching the doves as they flew around the room, putting her head or hand into a chopper, and occasionally being locked in a large trunk with chains and a padlock. A large piece of cloth was held up to hide the trunk, and within a couple of minutes, Maddie had to make a quick exit. They had been asked to perform a show for the local Cub Scouts' group as part of their end-of-year presentation evening. Alan had had quite a few beers before going on and was feeling quite full of himself as he started the evening with a one-liner, he thought was rather funny:

'Good evening, everyone. My name is Mr. Magic. I might not pull a rabbit out of a hat for you, but I sure can pull a hair out of my ass!'

Most adults were horrified that he had said that in front of the children, but the boys found it hilarious. Maddie didn't know where to put herself—she was so embarrassed!

Once, Alan was asked to perform at a show on a Saturday at the Esplanade Hotel in Fremantle. As Daisy and Charles headed to the club that night, he suggested Maddie join them, stating he would come along after finishing the performance. He left home before Maddie, smartly dressed in black trousers and a tailcoat, which he always wore when entertaining adults. He told her he would put his top hat on when arriving at the club.

At the club, Daisy, Charles, and Maddie sat with all the usual friends at a long table. Maddie's back was to the glass door entrance of the ballroom, and she was chatting away with everyone when one of their group said, in a low voice,

'Oh dear, it looks like Alan has arrived!'

Maddie and Daisy swivelled around in their chairs to see why everyone looked so uneasy. Maddie cringed when she saw Alan, his battered top hat clutched in his hand, weaving drunkenly between the tables as he made his way over. Without his jacket, his tailcoat was covered in dust, and his shirt was torn, hanging out of his trousers; he looked as though he had been in a fight. Daisy was horrified, and Maddie wished she could crawl under the table. He plopped down next to Charles, saying nothing. He didn't seem capable of holding a conversation.

The room, which had gone silent, was starting to return to normal, and their friends tried to forget he was there. About ten minutes later, he told Maddie it was time to go home. Charles said he would drive them, but Alan insisted on getting a taxi. She knew now was not the right time to argue with her husband, as she was sure he would get nasty, given his mood.

When they returned home, Alan staggered to the bedroom and collapsed onto the bed. Within seconds, he was out cold.

'Thank God for that,' Maddie thought.

The next morning, since it was Sunday, Alan slept in. Maddie remained mortified at the thought that he dared to show up at the club in such a drunken and dishevelled condition. She had never felt so embarrassed. Later that morning, when he finally emerged from the bedroom, he told Maddie what had happened at the hotel, mentioning that there had been a guy drinking at the bar for most of the evening who had called him a 'poofter.' Pursing his lips, he told her he wouldn't take that from anyone and that he had marched up to the bar, grabbed the guy by his shirt collar, and told him to come outside. Saying, " I'll show you who the poofter is! " After giving the guy a good hiding, he went inside and downed a few more schooners.

The sewerage business was flourishing. Terry had overcome his apprehension about sucking up shit for a living! There was never a dull moment, often having their wives in fits of laughter as they shared anecdotes from the day.

One antidote occurred on a public holiday when they received a call from a gentleman asking them to come and empty their tank, as it was either full or blocked. Alan told him he would call back when he found out if his offsider was available. He went next door and asked Terry if he was willing to help, reminding him that he would be on double time. Alan reconnected with the client and informed him of the price and that payment would be required upon completion.

Arriving at the house and assessing the location of the manhole for the tank, Alan drove slowly and backed down the rather steep driveway leading to the garage. The family sat on the balcony with friends, laughing together, drinking wine, and enjoying the day off work. No one offered the workers a drink!

When they had finished their job and the hose and equipment were rehung back on the truck, Alan made his way up the steps to the balcony.

'It's all clear now, shouldn't give you any more problems. It was pretty full, and there was a blockage. That's why it took a bit longer.' Alan passed the invoice to one of the occupants. 'I'd prefer cash, being a holiday, but a cheque will suffice.'

The guy to whom Alan had handed the invoice said:

'No worries, mate. I'll send you a cheque next week.'

Alan, not one to be easily dismissed, especially since he had not shown the decency to offer a word of thanks, came straight back at him.

'Sorry mate, but you knew what the terms were. It's a bank holiday, and you're bloody lucky that we came out. I'm not going till I get the cheque, and if you don't pay up now, there'll be a tank load of shit down your driveway!'

Smirking, the bloke evidently thought that Alan was scaremongering.

'I said I'll get it to you next week. Is that a problem?'

Without another word, Alan ran down the steps, jumped into the truck, and drove it to the top of the driveway. Then, turning on the vacuum pump, he got out of the cab and went to the rear of the truck, standing poised to open the valve at the bottom of the tank, allowing the sewage to flow back out of the tank and down the driveway.

'Cheque or shit, please yourself!'

Within seconds, the guy pulled out his wallet and handed over a wad of cash. Alan and Terry laughed all the way home.

Another incident they used to tell was when they were called out to the house of an elderly lady. She had a little Australian Silky Terrier that kept biting at their ankles and barking. They had removed the manhole cover and saw it was chock-a-block, full to the top. The dog continued to snap and bark at them. The woman was in the house and either didn't see or hear what her precious dog was doing, or was ignoring it. As her pet got closer, the tank opened and Alan gave it a nudge, sending it to flounder on top of the waste matter! They quickly fished it out and watched as it tore up the garden and dashed straight through the house's back door. When confronted by the mutt's owner, they said her dog had got too close and fallen in. Not guilty!

Then there was a time when the husband of the house stood and watched as they pumped out his tank. They were rodding it in an attempt to clear a blockage, and when they showed the fellow the handful of condoms that had caused the obstruction, he turned a deadly shade of white and charged off to the house. Seconds later, an ungodly row erupted. The husband was shouting:

'Well, who the bloody hell do they belong to? They sure aren't mine!'

One Sunday, after having lunch with Daisy and Charles and staying until late, as Alan pulled into the driveway, Maddie said she thought she heard a baby crying. At first, they believed it was coming from their neighbours across the road, but as they got out of the car, they realised it was coming from inside their house!

Quickly unlocking the front door, Alan discovered the sound was coming from the boys' bedroom.

'Bloody hell! Maddie! In here!'

Maddie couldn't believe her eyes! A baby, no more than a couple of months old, was lying in a urine-drenched bassinette, his little face purple from crying! A bottle, half full of stale, congealed milk, lay by his side.

Lifting him out, she clasped him to her breast, hoping to control his sobbing. She then asked Alan to go and see if the neighbours had seen or spoken to anyone who may have noticed something.

Slowly, his crying gave way to gasping sobs. Maddie gave him a quick bath and dressed him in some of James' baby clothes. Hunting around in the cupboards, she found a tin of Ideal milk, mixed it with warm water, and poured it into the now clean bottle. Although very hungry, he was so exhausted that he could hardly drink.

Alan returned a few minutes later and said those he had asked had not seen anything unusual. They decided against phoning the police, hoping that someone would come and collect him. Although Maddie was not hopeful, she agreed that another few hours wouldn't make much difference. They would contact the authorities if no one came to claim him by morning.

While they were still trying to puzzle out who could have left such a young baby with them, a knock on the door interrupted them. Alan sprang to his feet, hoping it was someone with information, but he was astounded to see his young sister standing there.

'Sarah! What are you doing here? How did you find out where we live?' Then it suddenly dawned on him. 'It's you, baby. It is, isn't it?'

Without waiting to be invited, Sarah entered the house.

"That's no way to greet your favourite sister. Aren't you pleased to see me?'

Overhearing the brief conversation, Maddie realised that it was Alan's youngest sister, whom she had never met.

Alan could not contain his fury and burst out in anger.

'There's no need to tell me, Sarah! I know that's your baby. It's just the sort of thing you'd do.' Then, shaking his sister by the shoulders, he went on. 'Why, why on earth did you leave it here? Are you crazy? What if we had been away for a few days? What would have happened to your child then? How on earth did you get in?'

Sarah stared at the floor, not wanting to make eye contact with either of them, especially her brother.

I squeezed through the bathroom window and then unlocked the back door. I knew you'd be home – I spoke to one of your neighbours and she told me you'd gone to your mother-in-law for lunch.' She raised her eyes, looking straight at Maddie. 'My brother, Adrian, told me you were nice and a good mother. I had nowhere else to go?'

'You still haven't told us why you left him here,' replied Maddie. 'Did you intend to leave him and never come back? Or has your conscience got the better of you?'

Sarah shrugged her shoulders.

'I left him with milk, and he was warm... I don't know what all the fuss is about.' Maddie was losing patience with her.

'The fuss, as you call it, is that you are his mother! You cannot just abandon your child like this. If you really cannot cope, there are people and organisations out there that will help you. What on earth possessed you to do such a thing? Does your child have a name?'

Once again, Sarah shrugged her shoulders and blurted out.

I'm almost nineteen, and we already have two little boys. Neither of us wanted this one.'

Sarah stayed the night, leaving early the next morning before anyone was awake, taking her son with her. They never did learn his name.

Although concerned for Sarah and her baby, they knew there was little they could do to help.

That evening, when the children were tucked up in bed, Maddie told Alan she wanted to know more about his sister. She realised it must have been extremely hard for all of them when both their parents died, especially Sarah, who was the youngest. Putting his paper aside, Alan nodded in agreement, admitting that it had not been easy for them.

Sarah was eleven when our mother passed away. They sent her to live with one of the aunts. Agnus and her husband Bill were strict but very kind. Sarah has always been headstrong and determined to get her way, always rebelling. At thirteen, she ran away and didn't return home for about a week. Aunt Agnes asked if I would take her to live with me and Elaine.'

Alan paused, lighting another cigarette and taking a swig from the can of beer. 'She didn't get on with Elaine and wouldn't adhere to any of the house rules, staying out most nights and not telling us where she was going or where she'd been. The final straw came when she stole my cheque book and, forging my signature, cashed it in.' Taking another swig from the can, Alan continued. 'I needed to go north where I could earn more money, but that meant Sarah would have to be left with Elaine, who made it very clear that would not happen! None of the relatives were prepared to take Sarah, so the only option was to put her into the Home of the Good Shepherd.'

Maddie looked at him with a questioning expression. 'What is that place?'

Leaning back in the chair, Alan took a couple of puffs from his cigarette, which had burned down to a stub.

'It's an institute for wayward children. There was nothing else I could do, Maddie. She wasn't there for long. Aunty Maureen took her back to live with them. Then, when she turned fifteen, Sarah started dating Dan. The last I heard was that she was pregnant, and she and Dan had driven to South Australia and married in a registry office.'

Maddie didn't know what to say, as despite everything, she did feel sorry for his sister.

Maddie had a contraceptive diaphragm fitted. Life was too complicated; she was always on the move, and with Alan's drinking, she constantly worried about the future. A future she was not prepared to bring more children into.

Life went on, and the bills continued to pile up. Nothing changed. Alan was drinking as much as ever. Where had he been? Who had he been with? She knew he'd had several fleeting dalliances, but never brought the subject up, knowing he would deny it. So far, he had never hit her, yet she always felt as though she had received a good hiding.

Maddie knew there were times she should have kept her mouth shut instead of venting her anger. But she needed to let him know that it was affecting their marriage and how unhappy she was. She knew she had to keep believing he would reduce his drinking. The diamante necklace, the bracelet, and the other presents. They were conditional gifts – he thought she would be happy that he was home and that he had promised to change. She didn't want to accept them. She always hoped he meant to drink less and return to the family like most other husbands. But that never happened. He would last three or four days, maybe a week, before reverting to his old ways.

Trying hard not to cry, Maddie blinked away the tears as she listened to Dr. Warner confirm that she was pregnant. She almost voiced her thoughts aloud. '*How could that be! James wasn't two yet!*'

Leaning back in his chair, Dr. Warner gave Maddie a few moments to compose herself. Then, he told her that she appeared to be exceptionally fertile and that, as he had mentioned on a previous occasion, no contraceptive offered one hundred per cent protection. The doctor advised Maddie to tell her husband that, in the future, he should use a condom. Maddie had never heard of a condom, and when Dr. Warner explained what it was and how it worked, she knew it would be a waste of time. Covering her mouth to prevent bursting into a fit of giggles, she imagined Alan in his drunken state fumbling around, trying to put a piece of rubber on his willie!

No, the perfect solution would be separate beds. That would suit her fine! However, that would never happen. Despite her doubts, she decided to ask Alan if he would use one. Although she anticipated his reply, she had to laugh when he retorted vehemently:

'No way! It'd be like taking a shower while wearing a raincoat!'

It was a very sad time for Maddie when her mother told her that Jimmie, her beloved grandfather, had died at the age of 71. Maddie cried inconsolably. She had just lost her mentor. Jimmie had instilled in her all that was good; he had given her the strength to overcome all adversity as she navigated the twists and turns of her life. The sense of profound loss and the memories of being enveloped in his loving arms would never diminish.

Alan was happy to let Maddie take over the finances to ensure all bills were paid on time, and when there was a problem, she was the one who went to see the bank manager. Maddie paid all the invoices by cheque to maintain a record of incoming and outgoing transactions, doing her utmost to avoid being overdrawn. However, as Alan insisted on having a chequebook as well, it became an impossible task because Maddie was unable to reconcile the books until he handed it over. She would then discover that they were overdrawn because Alan had been writing cheques without considering their financial state. At that point, it was time for Maddie to see the bank manager.

The business had been ticking along, but the debts were piling up, and the overdraft was at its limit. In the end, Alan sold to a rival company, leaving enough from the sale and the 'goodwill' to pay what they owed. Alan then went back to selling insurance.

Maddie was due to give birth any day. Not sure of her due date, she ensured that everything was ready for their baby's arrival and her trip to the hospital. As with her other two pregnancies, she was on her knees scrubbing floors, gardening, and going for long walks. Then, one afternoon, she had just come home after taking the children to a nearby park when she felt a spasm. She wasn't concerned, as the contractions were not strong and still far apart. Later that afternoon, they became more frequent and intense. Maddie knew it was time, so she stopped what she was doing and went into the bedroom to retrieve the case, placing it near the front door. She then phoned Alan and had just finished explaining that he needed to come home and take her to the hospital when there was a knock on the door. Alan told her not to put the phone down.

'I'll hang on, you get the door and get rid of whoever it is.'

Maddie walked across the room and opened the door to find two men dressed in overalls.

'Mrs. Cox?'

Maddie regarded them with a puzzled expression.

'Yes. Can I help you?'

As one of the men pushed past her into the sitting room, Maddie questioned him.

'Excuse me, but what do you think you are doing barging your way in here? Please leave!'

Looking at Maddie sympathetically, he handed her a piece of paper.

'I'm sorry, mam, but I'm afraid we're here to repossess the television, as you are way behind with the payments.'

Maddie couldn't understand. Alan had told her he had sorted it out the week before.

'My husband paid it last week. We don't owe you anything! Then she remembered that Alan was waiting at the end of the phone. 'One moment, please. I will speak to my husband.'

As she reached for the handset, one of the men remarked:

'Ok, Miss, but that won't make any difference as we have our orders.'

Maddie was dismayed; it was clear that her husband had not paid the television rental.

'Alan, th-there are t-t-two men here; they say you hav....'

Alan interrupted her:

'I know. I heard what was said. Put him on the phone, and don't worry, I'll sort it out.'

Passing the handpiece over, she observed his face as he listened to Alan's words. Seconds later, he turned to her with the phone still in his hand.

'Your husband would like to speak with you.'

Then, passing over the receiver to Maddie, he joined his mate at the door, and, without another word, they made a hasty retreat!

'Maddie! Are you ok?'

She picked up the handset, remaining silent as Alan waited for his wife to respond.

'Yes, I'm fine, but why did you tell me you had paid the bills when you evidently hadn't? And what did you say to the guy that made him leave so quickly? He even forgot to take the television!'

Alan erupted in laughter.

I told him that your waters had broken, and you were about to give birth. I mentioned that if they stayed much longer, they would be the ones who would take you to the hospital.

Although she was annoyed with Alan, she couldn't help but smile to herself.

'Well, if you don't hurry, I WILL be giving birth at home!'

Alan arrived home half an hour later. After dropping the boys off next door, they headed to the hospital. When they arrived, Maddie was taken to one of the wards, and it was not until late that evening that she was transferred to a trolley and brought down to the delivery room, where the walls were lined with cubicles, each with a curtain and a high bed. They set Maddie onto one of the beds and then left her alone. Now and then, a nurse would look in and perform an internal examination to check on her progress. Soon, Maddie felt the urge to bear down and knew it was time.

Everything was going well until one of the nurses attempted to place an oxygen mask over Maddie's nose and mouth. Maddie panicked and began fighting to remove it. There was urgency in the nurse's voice as she struggled to reposition it.

'Please, Maddie. Maddie, leave it on... She's slipping away! We're losing her!' Their voices were getting fainter... *'Maddie, can you hear me? Maddie! Maddie!'*

She floated above, able to see herself lying on the bed and hear what they were saying, but unable to respond. Then everything returned to normal and calm, and Maddie cried tears of joy as one of the nurses placed the little bundle in her arms.

'Maddie, you have a beautiful little girl.'

Maddie had already told Alan that if it were a girl, she would like her to be called Kimberley, or Kim for short. Their baby was swaddled in a blanket, keeping her warm and secure as she suckled hungrily at her mother's breast. Maddie marvelled at her daughter's pink, scrunched-up face, tiny hands, and feet.

When she finished feeding her daughter, the doctor and one of the nurses entered the ward. He told her she was a lucky lady because the mask she had refused was intended to provide her with oxygen. Maddie wanted to share her experience of the vision she had of herself floating over her own body. She knew that in those few moments, she had left her physical form.

Before moving on, the nurse sat on the edge of Maddie's bed and carefully unwrapped the blanket. She told Maddie that while her baby was positioned in the foetal position, her left arm and leg had bent backwards, so they had carefully placed them both into the correct position by tucking her leg into the nappy and her arm into the sleeve hole of her singlet. She assured Maddie that there was a very good chance that, by doing this, both limbs would realign. By the time Maddie was released from the hospital, Kim's leg and arm had healed.

Maddie made an appointment to see Dr. Warner, requesting the implantation of the coil into her womb. There would be no more babies.

Alan belonged to a darts club, seldom missing a meeting. One time, Alan was unable to attend because their car was in the garage for repairs. He stayed at home with his wife, and they watched television. It was after ten when Maddie, feeling tired, told Alan she was going to bed. A knock came at the front door as she was leaving the room. Alan and Maddie looked at each other, wondering who on earth it could be at such a late hour.

Opening the door, Alan was surprised to see that it was Mervyn, who lived with his wife and two children two doors down. Alan always thought he was strange, but why would he call on them so late in the evening? Aware that the man was agitated, Alan spoke first.

'Hi, is everything okay? Is there something you need?'

Mervyn's eyes were nearly popping out of his head, and his mouth had dropped open. He didn't reply. Instead, he quickly thrust a large bone into Alan's hand.

'I've b-b-bought a b-bone for your dog.'

Then, without waiting for a reply, he backed away from the door, turned quickly, and fled out of the courtyard and back home. Alan, in a state of bewilderment, slowly turned to look at his wife while still holding the bone.

'What was that all about? We haven't got a dog!' Then, after mulling it over for a few minutes, he added: 'Ha, ha, I know what he was up to!'

Maddie lifted her eyebrows.

'And what, may I ask, is that?'

Alan's arms were crossed, and his mouth set into a firm line.
'He knows that I am out every Wednesday, and with the car not being here, he assumed that was where I was!'
Maddie chuckled.
'Well, as you know, he's not known in the district as 'Merv the Perv' for nothing!'

Alan was an excellent salesman and was recently awarded salesman of the month. Having been with the company for a while, he received his first commission from completed sales. Financially, things were looking a bit brighter. Bills were being paid on time, and hire purchase payments on the car and television were up to date.

Peter and James loved having a little sister and always vied for her attention. Peter was the quieter and more serious of the two. James was boisterous and full of mischief. Kim was already crawling everywhere.

Maddie enjoyed caring for the house and gradually became a skilled cook. She was learning to sew, making clothes for all the children and fleecy sheets and pillowcases for the children's beds. Aside from saving money, she took pride in her accomplishments in such a short time. She bought many children's clothes from charity shops, most of which had hardly been worn. Knowing he would disapprove of their children wearing second-hand clothes, she didn't inform Alan.

Occasionally, Alan performed magic shows at local primary schools or children's birthday parties. One day, he took Maddie to see his friend Jacko, an amazing ventriloquist. He could throw his voice as if it were coming from the other side of the room. He was utterly obsessed with his puppets, caring for them as if they were his children. Maddie found this rather strange.

One Saturday, Alan arrived home with a large box of puppets, telling Maddie that Jacko didn't want them. After negotiations, he had managed to buy them for a song! Maddie could hardly believe her eyes when he produced five hand puppets one by one, all made of *papier-mâché*: Punch, Judy, the Baby, Percy the Policeman, and the Crocodile. Then he went out to the car again and returned with a wooden theatre, decorated with stars and bright red curtains hanging on both sides of the stage. Alan already had plans to incorporate the Punch and Judy show into his magic, telling Maddie that he would be the voice of Punch, the Policeman, and the Crocodile, while she could be Judy and the Baby. He had it all planned.

Since acquiring Punch and Judy, their first performance was at an orphanage. It took place in one of the local parks among the trees. Alan wore the baggy clown outfit that Maddie had made, as he wanted to inject a bit of humour into the act. The children and staff had a fantastic time playing games and enjoying a picnic lunch. Alan performed his magic show, and Maddie's help followed it with a slapstick act featuring Punch, his wife Judy, and his friends. As everyone was packing up to leave, Alan decided to swing from the branch of one of the trees. He grabbed hold of the lowest branch, and while pulling himself up, a loud crack was heard! The next moment, he was lying flat on his back on the ground. Everyone found it hilarious, and the children wanted him to do it again!

When the Royal Show came to Perth every year, Alan worked in George Stewart's Boxing Troupe in the Side-Show alley. Banners with pictures of the many troopers were displayed, and on either side of the stage, a drummer beat away, calling everyone to come and watch the fight. George stood on the stage, spruiking through a large horn and promoting the show, encouraging the crowds to gather.

'C'mon, just one likely fella. The money's not bad if you manage to go the distance.'

Aboriginal men and youths could gain respect by boxing and earn some money. Many young men and Aboriginal youths joined the boxing troupes purely for the excitement and, of course, the money to be earned from a successful fight. Boxers in some troupes slept under blankets on the sawdust of the tent floor, while others snoozed in fitted-out vans. George could also be seen driving around in his big Cadillac, tooting the horn and calling out for boxers to join up and travel with the show.

George grew up in tough times. As a kid with undiagnosed dyslexia in a Christian Brothers School, he suffered constant ridicule as a result, and so George ended up letting his fists do the talking. He was a talented boxer who fought in the ring and with bare knuckles in the street for a stake. He was barely out of his teens when he was already working as a security guard and a standover for card games in the various gold diggings around the bush. He ended up drifting down to the waterfront, where he worked on merchant ships around Australia. His capacities as a fighter were recognised and put to use, mainly protecting union leaders from attacks by the police and rivals. Back in WA, George operated a successful marine salvage operation. He started with a tent and an old bus, and then ran the George Stewart boxing troupe, which toured the country towns and featured some of Western Australia's most renowned Noongar fighters from the southern and Wheat Belt areas.

George Stewart was one of the toughest men around. Years later, he wrote the story of his life, 'The Leveller.' Alan and Maddie became friendly with George and his wife. They told anyone who asked that they had never witnessed his violent side.

Within the troupe, Alan often worked as the geeman—mixing with the crowd outside and heckling the fighters on stage. It was a way to draw the crowd inside. He was paid five pounds a day and a pound for each fight he participated in. Alan and the other troupe members would get a good workout without injuring one another. Their opponents would throw left hooks that were caught on the glove, yet they would still fall to the mat. At other times, a volunteer fighter from the crowd would truly make them earn their pay. If they were fighting one of the local lads, they had to be cautious of one of his friends or his girlfriend tackling them with her handbag, especially if they were giving him a bit of a thrashing. They were all actors playing a part.

The show also attracted several young Aboriginal boys who looked rough, mean, and 'ready to rumble,' But, more importantly, they were seeking respect, equality, and a bit of money to put in their pockets.

Peter was four when Maddie took him to the Royal Show, leaving James and Kim next door with Rae. Alan told her to bring him to Side Show Alley, saying he thought he was old enough to watch a wrestling match. A group of blokes had gathered inside the tent. Several were taking off their caps and rolling up their sleeves, ready to fight the champion, who was bare-chested, showing off his muscles. It gave aspiring boxers, particularly those from disadvantaged backgrounds, a chance to hone their skills in front of intimate yet boisterous crowds, earn some pocket money, and have the opportunity to become the hometown hero.

Alan was standing near the back of the tent when George invited a member of the crowd to get into the ring and test his strength against one of his greatest wrestlers. Before anyone else could take up the challenge, Alan was pushing his way through the spectators, elbowing his way towards the ring.

'I'll take him on. Looks like a pushover to me!'

George beckoned for Alan to enter the ring and then, so that the crowd could hear, he explained the Queensberry rules, which, of course, Alan already knew as he'd wrestled Stan many times before. They knew the score and were always told beforehand who would win the match.

Alan nodded at his opponent and then, without further ado, the fight began. Seizing the big guy by the neck, he rammed his head into the tent pole, punched him in the face, and they rolled around on the ground, tying each other up in knots! They never did hit the pole, and the punches didn't connect. Then Stan had Alan in a hard hold, and thrusting his head into the tent pole and then picked him up and dropped him heavily on the floor.

Peter pulled his hand free of his mother's and before anyone could stop him, he had run into the ring and in no time, he was already kicking at the nasty man's leg, yelling at him to let go of his daddy. The crowd roared with laughter.

Never again did Maddie take Peter to watch his daddy wrestling.

Another time, the troupe's strong man, Big Bob, came striding out into the ring, prancing about, flexing his muscles, and holding a solid tin plate against his stomach. George asked someone from the crowd to come up and hit the plate with a sledgehammer, as Bob was provoking the audience.

'Come on, try your punch! It's good for the indigestion!'

Once again, George shouted out to everyone.

'Come on up, there must be someone in the crowd who can fell Big Bob?'

Two or three hands went up, all eager to have a go at 'felling' Big Bob. One of the hands belonged to Maddie's husband! George pointed at Alan and said:

'C'mon, big guy, step up here. Show us what you can do.'

Everyone was clapping while Alan was striding into the ring. Of course, no one knew he was part of the act. As Alan picked up the sledgehammer, Bob flexed his muscles and, clenching the plate with both hands, pulled it flat against his stomach. Alan swung the hammer with all his force, aiming for the centre of the plate. Unfortunately, he struck the side of the plate and hit Bob's hand! None of the crowd realised what had happened as Bob hardly flinched, but Alan knew he was in big trouble – Bob would be out to get him as soon as they left the ring. He was outraged!

'I'll get that guy and ram his head so hard into the pole, he won't know what hit him!'

Everyone thought that was part of the act, but Alan knew better! Bob had so many fights over the years and so many repeated blows to the head that he was becoming punch drunk. Alan was worried that he would recollect who it was who'd hit him. So, after collecting the nine pounds owing to him for the day, he went to find Maddie and told her it was time they went home.

The times when Alan had gone easy on the drinking, he and Maddie had many good times together. They worked alongside each other companionably. In many ways, it was a good partnership. Those were the times when Maddie loved him.

It was the mood swings and the excessive drinking that killed anything she felt for him. Then there were the heated arguments.

That was when Maddie realised that although she loved and cared about him, she was not in love with him. He had caused her too much hurt.

One afternoon, after putting the children down for their nap, Maddie was down on her hands and knees washing and polishing the kitchen floor when she heard the front door open and shut. Then Alan poked his head around the kitchen door.

'Any chance of a cuppa, love?'

Maddie filled the jug with water and, setting it to boil, looked over at her husband, who was leaning against the sink and looking pleased with himself.

'How'd you like to do a bit of travelling, go off somewhere before Peter has to go to school?'

Maddie hoped he was not serious. Surely, he was joking. They had moved too many times, and she loved living where they were. They had made some very nice friends and had a lovely home. The monthly rental payments were coming off the purchase price of the house. She had hoped that one day they would own it.

'Why would you want to go off travelling when for the past few years all we have done is move from place to place, never spending more than a few months anywhere, and sometimes we stayed only for a few weeks? You surely cannot be serious?'

'I want to go back over East,' he said. 'There are more jobs, and I have heard the wages are higher. I don't want to live here for the rest of my life.'

Maddie was so upset; she could hardly get her words out.

'B-but I don't want to leave here. This is the nicest place we've ever lived. It's our home, and we have three young children! I don't want to drag them from place to place like gypsies!'

'Maddie, oh come on, Maddie. This could be our last chance. Anyway...' Alan hesitated, looking very sheepish... 'I've chucked in my job!'

Maddie was flabbergasted.

'W-what do you mean? S-surely you haven't q-quit your job. W-why? You were doing so well, and we have a lovely home now and good friends.' Maddie felt as though her whole world had turned upside down. She could see that he had made up his mind and, as always, had no alternative but to go along with his plan.

Putting his arm around Maddie and pulling her towards him, he said:

'It will be okay, I promise you. This is our last chance, and once on the road, you'll enjoy the adventures.'

They sat and talked for over an hour, with Alan sharing his plans with his wife and trying to convince her that it was a chance to see more of Australia before the children started school. He said that he'd seen an excellent second-hand Bond wood caravan.

The next day, Alan took her to see it. Maddie agreed that it was indeed in good condition. There was a small sink, a gas burner, cupboards, and a fold-down table that transformed into a small double bed. Additionally, there were two single beds at the other end. Although there was an annexe running the length of the van, it was far too small to accommodate all five of them.

They sold their furniture and took some boxes of personal items to Maddie's mother to store in her garage. Although still very unsure, Maddie knew she had to make the best of it, and in doing so, she got caught up in Alan's enthusiasm as he did his best to assure her that everything would be okay.

Early 1965

Alan fitted a tow hitch and a solid bar on the front of the car to protect them from collisions with kangaroos on their journey across the Nullarbor. The caravan, at just under fourteen feet in length, provided just enough room for the five of them. On both sides of the van, there were two double beds. Peter and James would sleep in the top two, and Kim in one of the bottom ones.

The cupboards were small, but adequate, and there was some storage space under the bench seats.

Maddie stocked up on tinned food, packets of food, and other essentials they would need for their journey. They stowed the annexe under one of the single beds and the clothes in the wardrobe and drawers, both of which were very small. Everything else went into the boot of the car, along with a large container of water and two jerry cans of fuel.

Maddie had difficulty saying goodbye to their good friends, Terry and Rae, and promised to write very soon to let them know they had arrived safely, wherever they ended up.

The first night, they pulled into a caravan park in the town of Kalgoorlie, 370 miles northeast of Perth. It was one of Australia's most famous towns due to the gold rush around 1889. During that time, almost a hundred hotels and eight breweries had been established – a complete contrast to the lonely tents and huts that had previously scattered the area. The region, once populated by barren bushes and hopping kangaroos, was now bustling with human activity. Alan pointed out the notorious red-light area where about twenty prostitutes worked at any given time. It became famous for its corrugated iron 'starting stalls.'

The following morning, they travelled over 100 miles to Norsman, setting up camp for a few days to give the children a break from the long hours in the car. They spent their time meeting up with fellow travellers in the park, swapping stories while everyone shared their food as they cooked sausages and burgers on the communal barbecue.

After travelling for several days and nights, they arrived on the outskirts of Adelaide, where they camped overnight in a layby. Two more days of travel took them to Melbourne, and then they embarked on the last leg of their journey: crossing into New

South Wales and making their way to the township of Campbelltown.

Alan signed up for the dole, but before receiving his first disbursement, he was called for an interview with a large packaging company. He commenced work the next day.

One morning, when Alan was feeling rather amorous and the little caravan was doing a little 'rock and roll!' there was a loud knock on the door, followed by a bright and breezy voice, '*Milko.*'

Quick as a flash, Alan retorted.

'Two pints please!'

Later that morning, after Alan had left for work, the milkman returned. With a twinkle in his eye and a knowing grin, he handed Maddie the bill for a week's delivery of milk.

'Sorry, love, I didn't like to disturb you earlier!'

Alan was quite content working for the packaging company, so when they asked if he would be willing to move to their other establishment up in Newcastle, he jumped at the chance. His boss arranged for Alan and Maddie to stay at the Stockton caravan park, which he explained was a five-minute ride on the passenger and vehicular ferry that would take them from Newcastle to the peninsula.

Stockton was an old-fashioned seaside town featuring a blend of 19th-century cottages and a beach that stretched for twenty miles along the coast.

They had barely moved there when the doctor confirmed what Maddie already knew: she was pregnant again! Alan wasn't at all concerned when she told him, but Maddie cried. Kim was barely three months old, and by the time this bairn was born, she would have four children, none of whom would have started school.

Before leaving Perth, Maddie's doctor had told her to remove the coil for a while and go back on the pill. But therein lies the tale... Maddie lost the pills while travelling over the Nullarbor. She searched high and low, telling herself they had to be somewhere! It was impossible to lose them in such a small space! She told Alan that it would not be wise to do anything until they reached civilisation so that she could buy some, but it was like talking to a brick wall! Returning from the pub, her protests were ignored!

Alan seemed to enjoy his work and had begun making friends. He spent most Saturdays in the pub with drinking buddies, rarely returning home until the bell for last orders rang. His wages were paid into the bank every fortnight. Until then, they often lived hand to mouth. Nonetheless, Alan rarely missed a Saturday night out with the crowd, always taking his turn to buy a round of drinks for everyone.

One Saturday, with only ten shillings jingling in his pocket, Alan told Maddie that he wouldn't see his mates because he was going to the betting shop. Someone had given him a tip on a rank outsider at 50/1, and he planned to invest all of it.

Maddie had just finished giving the children their lunch and wiping their faces and hands when Alan flung open the caravan door, grinning from ear to ear! Then, plonking himself down at the table, he pulled a wad of money out of his pocket and, with a flourish, threw it onto the table. 'Looks like we'll eat well tonight, eh!'

One evening, a horrific incident occurred at the park. A couple in their mid-thirties, whom Maddie had spoken to a few times, were having a heated argument. As the shouting and screaming grew louder, the residents began to emerge from their vans, curious to know what was happening. Then, to everyone's horror, the man flung open the van door and started dragging the hysterical woman across the grass, yelling obscenities! Many stood back, too frightened to intervene, and by the time Alan and a few burly blokes reached the couple, the brute had viciously punched her in the head. Together, they managed to pull the brute away and held onto him until the police arrived. The woman was unconscious and in terrible condition, as he must have given her a severe beating before dragging her out for all to see!

They had been there for six months when, once again, Alan wanted to move on. Two weeks later, after submitting his notice at work, they were already travelling south. After a couple of overnight stopovers, they pulled into the Werribee Caravan Park – a small community located twenty miles from Melbourne.

Alan never shirked work, and although he had registered for the dole a couple of times, he always found a job before any payments were made to him. Even though he didn't have a trade, he acquired several testimonials over the years. Still, he disliked taking orders and became argumentative and unresponsive when he believed he could do a far better job. He wanted to be the boss of his own company.

It wasn't long before Alan was hired as a supervisor in the Department of Works, overseeing road maintenance. He then decided that the old Holden was not good for his image. He took out a hire purchase loan, trading it in for a sleek second-hand Mark 7 Jaguar.

On the morning of 14 February 1966, Australia's shops, banks, and ticket offices opened their doors to usher in the age of decimal currency. Curious citizens formed long queues to exchange their pounds and pennies for brand-new dollars and cents. Maddie wondered if she would ever be able to manage the exchange, as it seemed so complicated!

As the park laundry didn't have a washing machine, Maddie had to do everything by hand. She would rest her large pregnant belly on the edge of the concrete laundry tub to lean over into the sink. The sheets and towels were the most challenging, as washing and rinsing them until all the soap had disappeared was a tedious task. Then, winding each item around one of the taps, crossing the ends over one another and squeezing out as much water as possible, she struggled to hang the still-dripping clothes on the line, which was strung between two poles. Her hands were sore from scrubbing, rubbing, and wringing.

It had been over eight months since they left Perth and made their way to the East Coast of Australia. At the age of twenty-two, Maddie was about to give birth to their fourth child. She always ensured that everything was clean, that there was food in the cupboards, and that all the laundry was washed and ironed. Eunice, who had two young children, befriended Maddie when they arrived at the park and later told her friend that she would look after the children while Maddie was in the hospital and Alan was at work.

One day, after arriving home from a barbecue lunch with friends, Maddie began to experience mild contractions. She didn't inform her husband, knowing it would be some time before she needed to go to the hospital. The sun had just set, and the evening warmth enveloped them in stillness, so they took the children for a short walk before putting them to bed. Despite feeling extremely uncomfortable, Maddie's contractions were still infrequent, allowing her to get a good night's sleep.

The next morning, Maddie sat the boys down for breakfast when, in the middle of feeding Kim, she inhaled sharply as a searing pain shot through her body. Inhaling deeply and then slowly exhaling, she eventually felt the pain subside. Shortly after, there was another pain, and then another. They were now coming every four to five minutes and lasting what seemed like an eternity!

After waking Alan, she went back to feeding Kim and encouraged her boys to finish their breakfast. Then, having dressed the children, she took them over to her friend Eunice, who lived on the other side of the park.

Ten hours later, Maddie nursed her little boy, watching as he suckled at her breast. Holding his tiny hand in hers, she marvelled at how perfect all her children were. She knew then that, although it was not going to be easy, everything would be alright. She had been blessed with four healthy children, and she had more than enough love to give to each of them.

While Maddie was in the hospital, Eunice took care of the children until Alan came home from work. They were always bathed and dressed in clean clothes, ready for Alan to take them to the pub for their tea. He took the day off work when Maddie was due to come home the following day, so he needed to get everything clean and tidy for her return. Although he had seldom cooked a meal, except for barbecues or eggs on toast, he decided that it could not be hard to throw some meat and vegetables into a pot and cook a stew! That evening, after he had dished it up to the boys, he was feeding Kim when he noticed Peter and James pushing their food around the plate with their forks.

'Come on, boys, eat up.' Then, putting another spoonful into his daughter's mouth, he urged them again. 'Look, your sister loves it.'

Peter looked up at his dad and, screwing up his face, retorted: 'Dad. She ain't said nothing yet!'

The next morning, Kim had diarrhoea. Thankfully, by the time Alan collected his wife from the hospital, everything was back to normal. When Eunice recounted the incident to Maddie, they both ended up in stitches, as evidently, every time Kim dirtied her nappy, Alan bathed her!

Alan returned to work, and Maddie had settled into a routine with her four young children, but it was not easy living in such a small caravan. Peter, who would soon be five, and James, three and a half, had several playmates at the park and spent a lot of time on the swings and kicking a ball around. The mothers kept an eye out for each other's nippers.

Each morning before heading to work, Alan collected the morning paper because he liked to read it while having his breakfast. Then, one morning as he turned to the next page, he looked in shock.

Adrian John Mathews has been extradited from Darwin. Reading on, he was alarmed to see the words *'Armed robbery'*!

Maddie was at the kitchen sink washing up the breakfast dishes when she heard her husband.

'By God. I don't believe it!' Maddie replied, only half interested. 'What don't you believe?'

'Come and take a look for yourself! Do you remember the other day we were wondering where Adrian and his dippy wife were?' Maddie nodded. 'Well, listen to this. My brother has made the headlines!'

As Maddie sat down next to her husband and looked in amazement at the headline, Alan proceeded to read.

Adrian John Mathews, who has been on the run since being involved in an armed robbery, has been extradited from Darwin. He and two other men robbed a city bank in Melbourne. They were all armed and disguised. Two were captured shortly after, but Mathews managed to escape. One of the bank staff had noticed a very distinctive tattoo of a lady on the calf of Matthew's leg. It was that which helped with the capture when an off-duty policeman in Darwin was having a drink in a local pub and at once recognised the tattoo and made the arrest.'

Maddie was astounded. She had quite liked Adrian and found it hard to believe that he had committed such a crime. Alan continued.

'There's more. It states that he has been sent to HM Prison Pentridge for seven years! That is here in Victoria. It's a top security prison. I wonder what happened to all the money and if his accomplices were caught!'

Alan worried about his brother's ability to cope with being locked up among some of Melbourne's most hardened and violent convicts. After voicing his concerns, it was decided that they should pay him a visit.

From the outside, the jail was imposing. Upon entering through the two massive steel doors, they found themselves in a large courtyard. They were taken to the main building, where they were signed in and searched. The cigarettes and toiletries they had brought with them were thoroughly checked to ensure nothing untoward was inside. They were then taken along a corridor leading to a large, bleak room, where several cubicles lined one side of the wall, and officers were strategically placed throughout the area, keeping a close eye on the inmates and their visitors.

Scanning the cubicles, Alan was the first to spot his brother at the far end, sitting behind a glass partition. Adrian wondered who his visitor was, as, other than his wife, who seldom visited, no one would know he was there.

After getting over the initial shock of seeing his brother and sister-in-law, Adrian's cheeky face lit up with a broad grin as he asked how they had found out where his new abode was! He said he'd been given the opportunity to obtain some academic qualifications, specifically in reading and writing, which he was rubbish at! He was working in the woodworking workshop and making a very special table inlaid with a draught board. Hoping to get out early for good behaviour, he was keeping his nose clean and managing to ward off any unwanted attention by delivering threats of what would happen to them when they had all served their stretch! They'd barely had time to talk before the time was up.

Alan promised they would return soon.

The couple, who had managed the park for the past four years, decided it was time to move on. The owners approached Alan and asked if he and Maddie would be interested in taking it over. Although they were tempted, they declined to do so. As the position didn't come with a house, they would have to continue living in the caravan, which, with four young children, would not be possible.

Having been away for nearly a year, Maddie was ready to go home to Perth. Since giving birth to Joseph, she had thought about it constantly. It was time to settle down, to live in a house, and for her mother, Daisy, to get to know her grandchildren. She wanted to write to her best friend, Kay, to explain why, over five years ago, she had left in such a hurry without saying goodbye. Too ashamed to let the family know that she was having a baby! Writing it all down would have been easier, but she needed to see her dear friend and apologise for any hurt she had caused.

Joseph was two months old when Maddie received a telegram from England informing her that the money bequeathed by her grandfather had been released. Maddie had not expected to be left anything, assuming it would go to her mother, Daisy. Two days later, she received a letter from her mother confirming that they had each been bequeathed over £8,000.

Maddie couldn't wait to share the news with Alan, so she called his boss to find out which site he was at. Within minutes, she was bundling the children into the car and heading to the site, where she found her husband astride a bulldozer, clearing bushland.

When she told him about the money, it took a few moments for it to register. But when it did, Alan reached for his coat and lunchbox and jumped off the dozer.

'That's just the break we needed. We can leave. Go back to W.A. C'mon, what are we waiting for? Let's go!'

Maddie wondered what on earth he was doing.

'You can't walk off the job and leave the dozer here! We are not leaving immediately. You have to hand in your notice, and we need to make plans!' Maddie could not believe that he would walk away and leave the vehicle in the middle of the bush.

'No! They can come and collect it. I'm getting the hell out of here! I hated the job anyway. I'll phone as soon as we get back and tell them I'm quitting. Quitting as of today!'

None of the children had been christened, so Maddie said she would not leave until they were. Eunice and another couple from the park attended the hectic but memorable day. The children had all behaved incredibly well. Maddie was so proud.

A week later, Alan walked off the post, and they were on their way home to Perth. Before leaving Melbourne, they arranged to visit friends at the Air Force Base at Point Cook. Merle had lived near them in Cloverdale, and Maddie looked after her two young boys while she and her new husband went to Bali on a belated honeymoon. Additionally, Merle's brother had worked part-time with Alan on the sanitary truck.

Upon arrival, they were able to park in the driveway since it was just long enough to accommodate both the car and the caravan. After spending a couple of hours catching up on events from the past year, it was time to continue on their journey. While Maddie was rounding up the children, Alan said he'd reverse out of the driveway, ready to leave.

When he started the car, he was just about to reverse when he heard a loud 'clunk' coming from the front of the vehicle. Leaving the engine running, he got out to inspect the problem. He lay down on the ground and, looking underneath, found the issue: a broken axle.

They were going nowhere!

Barry, Merle's husband, called all the local garages to check if they could get a new one. As soon as he informed them it was a Mark 7 Jaguar, they said it would have to be ordered and could take up to three weeks to arrive. Thankfully, their hosts were more than happy to let them stay until the part arrived. Much to everyone's relief, the part came eight days later. Two more days passed, and they were on their way.

Making their way back to Western Australia over the same track they had travelled twelve months ago, they were approaching the Eula Pass when they heard a loud thud. Alan glanced up at the rearview mirror to check if the caravan looked okay.

'Oh shit! The van has come adrift!' Quickly pulling over, they climbed out and walked to the back of the car, where they discovered that the tow hitch had separated from the caravan and was resting on the tow bar, thankfully undamaged. They could hardly believe how lucky they were; had they started the climb, the caravan would have rolled back down the hill and been smashed to smithereens.

Alan started inspecting the tow hitch on the back of the car.

'I don't believe it.... the bastards, they only spot welded. Not a single bolt! How the hell did they think that would hold?'

Alan remembered passing an abandoned car about half a mile back. Taking some tools with him, he drove off to find the wreckage and returned with two tyres complete with rims. Together, they managed to prop the tow bar up onto wheels. In another couple of hours, dusk would settle in, and Alan needed to be on his way.

'I'll go back to Madura – it's more likely to find someone who can weld it back on and secure it with bolts! It'll take at least a day to get there and another to return, and that's without any problems arising. I hate leaving you here on your own with the kids, but there is no other option.'

Many tales have been written over the years about people disappearing while travelling across the Nullarbor. Cars running out of fuel or breaking down, along with their occupants abandoning them, most hoping to reach safety but often found much later, having perished in the arid desert. Their skeletal bodies were seldom discovered in such a vast, barren wilderness.

After feeding the children, Maddie allowed Peter and James to play outside for a while, assuring them that if they strayed too far from the caravan, they would be in big trouble! Later, when they were all safely tucked into their beds, she sat at the table with the Tilly lamp casting a warm glow as she updated her diary.

Sometime later, Maddie heard the sound of a vehicle approaching. Pulling back one of the curtains, she peered through the window. She could see nothing except for red dust rising in the distance. She listened to the drone of the vehicle as it grew louder, and then everything went quiet... That was until she heard a door slam and then… voices. Pulling the curtain back a fraction, she peered outside. Parked alongside the caravan was a Volkswagen Combi bus.

Maddie swiftly closed the drape, feeling a tightness in her chest; her heart was beating so fast that it scared her. She barely had time to think when someone knocked on the door. She froze! Alan had told her to keep the door locked. What was she supposed to do? The person knocked again. It was a man's voice!

'Hello. Maddie! Are you alright?' Then, pausing for a moment, he waited for her to respond. 'Maddie, there's no need for you to worry. We came across your husband travelling in the direction of Madura, and when we stopped to speak with him, he told us what had happened. We promised that we would stop and check that you and the children were okay.'

Warily unlocking the door, she was relieved to see a middle-aged couple staring back at her. Letting out a sigh of relief, Maddie pushed the door wide open and stepped outside. She didn't want the children to be disturbed. Declining Maddie's offer of food and drink, they told her they had travelled a long way that day and were ready to hit the sack.

When Maddie awoke the following morning, they were gone. Each time she saw red dust billowing in the distance, she hoped it would be Alan. There had been a motorbike towing a mini trailer, an old Chevy car, and an eight-wheeler interstate truck. There was no sign of her husband until the evening of the second day.

1966

Australia changed to decimal currency in the year 2000. The conversion from pounds and pence to decimal currency was met with great excitement. A complete change was needed to avoid confusion. Educational information was sent to individuals, banks, and businesses on how to cope with and use the new currency, ensuring a smooth launch of the new coins and notes. It took several months before shops ceased showing prices in dollars, pounds, shillings, and pence.

Alan was now selling vacuum cleaners door-to-door. His salary was poor, but he received dividends for each machine he sold. He had a knack for sales, but he disliked knocking on doors and cajoling the woman of the house into buying something they didn't need or want. Unfortunately, his sweet-talking didn't yield many sales. Maddie was not surprised when Alan told her he was thinking of quitting.

Maddie knew her husband was in a foul mood when he entered the caravan that night.

'Not a good day?' she asked.

'You could say that!' he replied. Then, reaching into the fridge, he took out a beer, flipped off the top of the bottle, and sat at the table.

'Today I had three doors slammed in my face! I'm not sure which is worse – that or getting my foot in the door, going through my sales pitch, giving a demonstration, and then being told they had recently bought a new Hoover! In another house, I spent ages going through my spiel and showing the woman how efficient the machine was. I was quite confident that I would secure the sale. That was until she told me she was the cleaning lady and suggested that return another day! By which time I had vacuumed the entire carpet!'

Alan sold three of the most expensive models the following week, and his boss awarded him a bonus. Maddie always knew that her husband had the gift of the gab and got along well with most people. He was trusted and well-liked. However, she was aware of the darker side of her husband.

She was concerned that if they were not careful, the inheritance left to her by her grandfather would dwindle. Alan had mentioned buying a new car! She felt more secure having money in the bank and not needing to count every penny before spending it or worrying if Alan's wage would last until the following week. Maddie suggested to Alan that they buy a place of their own rather than look for somewhere to rent. He thought it was a good idea, so they started driving around the areas, looking at all the 'for sale' signs.

Agents had shown them a few places, but nothing had caught their interest. Alan was focused on buying an old house cheaply and renovating it. Maddie was unconvinced, but as usual, she went along with him. She wanted to stick to her budget and didn't want to spend all her inheritance on a house. After several weeks of searching, they received a call from one of the agents, informing them that a property had just come on the market and could be precisely what they were looking for – an old asbestos house that required significant work and included a quarter-acre plot adjacent to it. They arranged to meet him at the house later that day.

Arriving a few minutes early, they could look around the area and the exterior of the dwelling. Sitting on stilts and featuring a wide veranda, Alan immediately saw the potential. He told Maddie they could enclose a section of the veranda to create more rooms. When the agent arrived, he guided them up the rickety wooden steps. Entering through the front door, they found themselves in a tiny lounge. There were two doors: one leading into a small kitchen and the other to the main bedroom. Another bedroom connected to the substantial kitchen. In the bathroom, as they called it, there was a tin tub, an old gas heater, and a semi-attached sink! Alan, noticing the expression on Maddie's face, immediately knew she was not impressed.

'I know exactly what you are thinking. Our priority will be a bath, and we can handle the rest as we go along. Just think of the potential this place has.'

Maddie understood that what he said made sense, but...

I agree with what you say, but where will we all sleep? There are six of us and only two bedrooms!

The big question was how much the owners were asking for it. The agent said they were asking for 6,000 dollars but would probably accept less, as he was anxious to get rid of it. Alan negotiated him down to $5,500 but needed time to work this out since they were still converting the exchange rate from British pounds to Australian dollars. After conferring with Maddie and being not one to procrastinate, Alan extended his hand, shaking on the deal.

'Yes, we'll take it.' By the end of the month, all documents had been signed and the deeds handed over.

With the help of friends, they began renovating. The back veranda was enclosed, creating a spacious kitchen and dining room that stretched the length of the building. The verandas on both sides of the house were also enclosed, allowing for three additional bedrooms and what Alan called a 'party room.' They discarded the old cooker but retained the large butler's sink. Finally, after replacing all the floor coverings, they decided enough had been done to enable them to move in. It was liveable. However, before they could move in, they needed furniture. They had sold everything when they left Perth to travel to Sydney.

They bought most of it at the auctions—a comfortable three-piece lounge suite, a large pine table with six chairs, and enough beds. Aside from the furnishings, Maddie wanted everything else to be new and was thrilled at the prospect of shopping for it, so she was pleased when her mother asked to accompany her.

The bathroom remained the same, with everyone bathing in the large tin bathtub. Alan, having put on a significant amount of weight over the last few years, found it a real struggle to get into the tub. He was not a pretty sight, his legs hanging over the end and arms draping on either side. Thankfully, it wasn't long before it was replaced by a porcelain bath. A friend plumbed it in for them, and to Maddie's joy, they had taps! No more carting water from the kitchen.

She laboured for Alan, standing on ladders and tables, balancing asbestos sheets and holding them up to the ceiling while he secured them. She carried long lengths of timber and mixed cement. Alan didn't like painting or wallpapering, so they usually argued when he tried to help. Much to his relief, Maddie didn't mind; she said she was happier doing it alone. She worked late, often past midnight, as it was easier when everyone had gone to bed.

The garden? No, they didn't have a garden; they had a builder's yard! Alan was always going to the tip and bringing back old iron beds and anything he thought would come in handy, telling her, 'It will be useful one day, you wait and see.'

He was often right, as the pieces of junk he brought home were frequently used to mend or create something. Maddie always picked up lengths of wood with nails and sharp metal fragments because she worried the children would step on them.

One morning, Maddie was carrying a laundry basket out to the clothesline when she stepped on a piece of wood with a large rusty nail protruding. She was wearing rubber thongs on her feet, but that did not prevent the nail from piercing through the sole and deep into the side of her heel. Struggling to pull it out, Maddie felt faint. Then, closing her eyes and giving it a quick yank, she removed it and hobbled inside. After washing her foot, she disinfected it with Dettol; then, drying it off, she applied an antibiotic cream.

When Alan arrived home from work, he insisted that she get a tetanus injection. After examining the foot, the doctor informed Maddie that, since the nail had penetrated so deeply, it had pierced a nerve. Over the next few weeks, Maddie walked on the side of her foot because it was too painful to put pressure on her heel accidentally.

One day, when Daisy was visiting, she noticed that Maddie's leg had a distinct curve. She realised this was due to walking on the outside edge of her heel for such a long time. Alan took Maddie to the doctor, who sent her to the hospital. She walked out on crutches, her leg plastered right up to the knee!

Joseph was barely six months old and still dependent on being carried around. Maddie learned to cope quite well, but it was very tiring. Alan did what he could, and Peter, now five, felt very important as he helped his mummy. The plaster had to remain for six weeks.

She still had two weeks before it was removed, and Maddie was complaining because the cast was rubbing against her leg and causing a lot of discomfort. She asked Alan if he would remove it.

'I can't do that. They said six weeks! It's not ready to be taken off yet.' He was firm in insisting that she had to wait.

'I don't care! I can no longer stand it. It's driving me crazy! You can do it with the bolt cutters, you know you could if you wanted to. Please!'

Shaking his head, Alan reluctantly agreed.

'Don't blame me if you get into trouble with the doctor. It's not easy to get the cutters between your leg and the plaster, but if you insist, I will have a go after tea when the children are in bed.'

Once the children were asleep, Alan retrieved the bolt cutters from the shed. The space between the plaster and her leg was not wide enough.

'I'll see if I can find something else, and if not, you will have to wait until you go to the hospital.'

A few minutes later, he returned, wielding a hacksaw!

Maddie regretted asking Alan to cut it off as she envisioned the saw cutting through the plaster and slicing into her leg. If only she had been patient and endured it for a few more days. *NO!* I don't want it off that badly. Forget it. I'll do as you say, and I will wait!'

'You wanted it off, so I'll take it off. Don't worry, it'll be ok, but you must sit perfectly still and trust me.'

It seemed to take ages, but eventually, he could peel all the cast off. Maddie's leg had straightened, but it had wasted away, and the released smell was disgusting!

They were not pleased when, one weekend, his sister Sarah, Dan, and their three young boys, Tommy, Billy, and Jamie, arrived on the doorstep. The last time they'd seen Sarah was when she had abandoned her baby in their house. Maddie noticed Sarah did most of the talking while Dan looked on like a wet rag! She told her brother that she and Dan were married and they wanted to return after spending some time away. Dan hadn't yet registered for the dole. They were broke! Alan and Maddie knew they could not turn them away.

While Maddie organised everyone's sleeping arrangements, Alan went to the shop to stock up on food. The children, all around the same age, were getting along well, even though her sister-in-law's boys were rougher.

After everyone had been fed, Maddie sent the children to play in Peter's bedroom while she, Alan, Dan, and Sarah relaxed in the sitting room. They listened to Sarah relate where they had been since Maddie and Alan had last seen them. While Alan went to work, Darren and Sarah visited the dole office, leaving Maddie to care for all the children. Peter was now attending Naval Base School, where a single teacher taught a single classroom to a handful of students.

Much to Maddie's relief, Sarah and her tribe moved out in two weeks.

Life continued much the same. Peter, now six and a half, and James, nearing four, had made friends with two boys who lived around the corner. They could cut through the wasteland, meaning they didn't need to go on the road. Luke and Jack's mother didn't like her boys getting dirty. By the end of the day, Peter and James always ended up grubby, but nothing a good dip in the bath couldn't rectify! They rarely visited the doctors unless they had injured themselves, like that time when Joseph jumped off a stack of bricks and landed on a dog's bone, driving the sharp end into his foot. Or when Peter had his appendix removed.

Once again, Maddie began losing weight. Initially, she wasn't too concerned, as renovating the house and caring for four children kept her busy from morning until late at night.

And then, there was Alan! Come six o'clock, Maddie's stomach would start churning. She knew that if Alan hadn't come home by around seven, he would not be home until late or early morning. She would listen for the sound of their car pulling up in the driveway, and if she had already gone to bed when he eventually arrived home, she'd lie entirely still, hoping he would assume she was asleep. Then she would listen to him stumbling around the bedroom, trying to undress himself without waking her up. Maddie would stay awake for ages, sobbing into her pillow. Many times, she begged him to get help, but he always said he didn't have a drinking problem.

'I'm not a drunk. I can stop whenever I want. But I don't want to!'

She'd ask him how he would feel if it were her staying out until all hours and coming home drunk. He would never reply!

His mood swings were unpredictable, leaving Maddie unsure of what to expect. One minute, he would be happy, charming, and considerate; the next, it felt like waiting for a ticking time bomb.

Maddie's biggest regret was that he seldom cuddled the boys and always insisted they shake hands with him when they went to bed. They had to grow up to be men, not sissies, he'd say. Yet, he never once kicked a football or played a game with them. It was different with Kim – he would always kiss her before going to her bed.

It was still dark when, one morning, Maddie woke to hear the front door creak open and close a few moments later. Alan had gone to a Buff meeting that night and hadn't returned by the time she went to bed just after midnight. Glancing at the clock on the bedside table, she saw it was just after five. Maddie rolled over, facing away from the bedroom door, not wanting her husband to know she was awake. She heard him come into the bedroom, and seconds later, he was feeling his way toward the bed and sitting on the edge to take off his shoes and socks. Then she felt the mattress shift as he stood up again. She couldn't stand it any longer. She'd had enough of his lies and did not know where he had been or who he was with. And *why?*

She slowly sat up and turned to face him. He looked ridiculous standing there with his trousers down around his ankles. As soon as he realised Maddie was awake, he hoisted them up to his waist, then, bending over, picked his shoes off the floor. As he walked towards the door, he said.

'Hi, Hun, go back to sleep. I'm going to work early today. I have quite a lot to do. I tried not to wake you.'

Then, without waiting for a reply, he retreated from the bedroom. A few seconds later, she heard the front door slam. The sound of the car engine started up, and then he was gone! Alan was home early that night, and nothing was mentioned about his early morning start.

Another time, when he had stayed out until all hours, he realised he had left his door keys at home. So, finding that the sash window to the sitting room hadn't been latched, he very quietly pushed it up and partially heaved himself onto the sill. Then, putting one leg through the open window, he tried to find something to take his weight, eventually resting on the edge of a small table. This enabled him to swing the other leg over the sill and into the room. However, in doing so, the table toppled over. Alan lost his balance and landed with an almighty crash on the floor!

Maddie woke with a start, unsure whether she had been dreaming or if the noise had come from inside the house! Quickly getting out of bed, she took her dressing gown off the hook behind the bedroom door, nearly tripping over the hem of her nightgown. As Maddie made her way to the sitting room, her first thought was that someone had broken in. She wondered if she should call the police instead of trying to confront the intruder herself! In the end, she decided to peek around the door cautiously.

'ALAN!' She could not believe her eyes –her husband, with his trousers down to his knees, was sitting atop the metal cigarette stand, which had buckled beneath his weight. Alan stared at her, his bloodshot eyes half-closed and a grin on his face.

'Hi! I'm home!' Maddie turned and walked out of the room. She heard her husband's unsteady steps as he entered their bedroom sometime later. A few seconds later, she thought she heard water flowing. Maddie reached for the bedside lamp, and after switching it on, she saw Alan standing with his back to her, peeing inside the wardrobe.

Later that year, they secured a contract with the Cogburn Council to produce over 2,000 copies of the local newspaper. Maddie collected the editorial from the council, took it home, and assembled the layout before passing it to the printer. Once the printing was complete, they collected the finished editions and took them home again to collate. They were then rolled up, secured with elastic bands, and ready for delivery. Peter and James wanted to help, so they put the bands on. Once everything was done, they used one of the council's flat-top trucks to deliver them far and wide around the district of Cogburn.

They were well compensated for their work, but Alan remained unhappy.

'We can produce the paper ourselves. All we need is a printing machine and someone to run it for us!'

Maddie had some money left from her inheritance, allowing them to buy the printer while still leaving enough to get the business up and running. Alan visited various estate agents to see if they could find an affordable building to rent. He became disillusioned, stating that anything he was shown was either unsuitable or the rent was too high.

Then, one of the agents called to inform them about an old building in Fremantle and asked if they would like to see it. He assured them that they would hold it until Alan finished work. Fortunately, he arrived home earlier than usual, eager to learn more.

'Where are the car keys, Maddie? I'll get the motor running while you gather the children. Don't worry about changing them; they are alright as they are. Come on, hurry up! We don't want to miss out!'

The agent had opened the shop and was waiting inside for them. It was one of several buildings nestled between a dry cleaner and an electrical appliance shop. The first room overlooked the main road and was relatively small, but a larger room was located at the back. The previous occupants had left a lot of junk, filth and neglect. The rental the owner was asking for was reasonable.

Alan was enthusiastic and could see the potential. He mentioned there was enough room in the back for the machines and that they could use the front room as an office. Maddie knew he was eager to start his own business, so she tried to understand his reasoning. She worried that taking on something they knew very little about was a considerable risk, but she also had a lot of faith in him. He was very astute when it came to making things happen.

Alan installed shelves while Maddie cleaned and painted the two rooms. As soon as they looked presentable, they went to the auctions and purchased a couple of desks, more shelving, and, most importantly, an old but reliable Mercedes Letter Press.

The next step was to find a printer operator, a salesman, and an office girl. Then, all being well, they would soon be up and running.

Terry Hanley came to work with them. He was one of the best printers in the area. He then introduced them to Mick, who was an excellent compositor. The compositor gathered type, sorted by letter, size, and kind, from a compartmented box. He set each letter on an iron rule, called a 'composing stick,' to form words and lines. The type had to be set 'backwards' as printing reversed the images. When several lines were done, the compositor set them in wooden cases called galleys. Sometimes, woodcuts were added to illustrate notices and advertisements. The galleys were tied with string, gathered, and locked in a page-size iron frame, or 'chase,' and secured to the stone bed of the press. A carriage carried the chase back and forth beneath a pressure plate or platen.

While Peter and James were at school, Maddie Kim and Joseph went to the factory, allowing her to help collate the magazines and newspapers. The children were well-behaved, happily playing with their Lego blocks, their brother's tin soldiers, and Dinkie cars.

Knowing they could not afford a loan, Alan decided to bring a partner into the business, preferably one who would be a passive investor. He thought of Bill, a guy he had met in the pub some time ago. Bill often called to talk with Alan and watch the editorial pages being printed. Alan had come to know him quite well and knew he was very well-off. He was the local rag-and-bone man and could be seen driving his two-ton truck around the streets, collecting unwanted household items that he later sold to merchants. Bill was married to Jennifer, who was significantly younger, and they had three young children. Alan arranged for himself and Maddie to visit him at his home.

Bill answered the door in a tank top and shorts. Maddie's eyes went to his shoeless feet, quickly looking away to avoid showing the shock on her face. She was certain he probably hadn't washed them for at least a week, if not longer! Maddie was still recovering from the surprise of seeing the state of his feet when, looking up at him, she noticed his teeth! They were so ill-fitting that every time he laughed or spluttered, the top ones would drop down, clasping onto the bottom set. Then he'd push them back up with the dirty, gnarled nails of his fingers!

Stepping aside, he gestured for them to enter and guided them to the kitchen. Jennifer, his wife, was a pleasant, plump woman. Although she looked harried, she was clean and tidy, unlike her husband. Alan and Bill discussed business, and before leaving, Alan struck a deal with Bill. They visited the solicitors to sign the necessary papers a couple of days later.

Peter was now attending a small local primary school. There were two rooms, two teachers, and a head teacher. Alan and Maddie joined the Parents and Citizens Association, and before long, Alan was asked to take on the position of Chairman. Maddie became friends with Sue, one of the teachers. She and her husband, Mark, owned a nearby chicken farm. Sue often invited Maddie to bring Peter over to play with their son, Edward. They knew she loved to ride and was welcome to come over sometime to ride their horses. Maddie jumped at the opportunity.

Sue was not interested in riding, as she was frightened of horses. However, she would look after the children while Mark and Maddie rode around the property. After they returned to the paddock, they would do a few rounds over the jumps.

The children loved spending time with their grandmother and were fond of Charles. He was always very kind to them, though not what you would call an affectionate person. It was always enjoyable when they were on outings together, such as picnics, drives to one of the dams, or trips into the hills.

Alan remained extremely possessive and distrustful, and it wasn't long before he ended his wife's visits after accusing her of having an affair with Mark. Maddie continued to take Peter to play with Edward, collecting him later in the day, but she never stayed. She knew Sue didn't understand why she didn't stop anymore to have a coffee with her, and Maddie was too embarrassed to tell her.

Sometimes, Alan would call his wife to tell her he was bringing someone home for tea. Other times, he'd show up with one or two friends. He knew that Maddie never minded and was always more than happy to welcome them into their home and put a meal together for them.

Then, it so happened that the HMS Hermes docked in Fremantle and anchored for two weeks. Alan met some of the officers in a local pub and invited all nine of them to his home.

They were a friendly bunch of guys, and despite the work involved in cooking and running around after them, Maddie enjoyed their company. Then one of the officers asked if some of their mates could come along, so Alan and Maddie decided to have a party. Several helped Maddie dish the food and clean up afterwards, while others played with the children. Maddie was sure they missed their own families. They played the fifty-year-old iron frame Pianola, which Alan had bought at one of the auctions, along with rolls of pre-programmed 1940s music. Everyone, including the children, loved it as they all took turns thumping away on the two-foot pedals, rolling out the music.

Alan, Maddie, and the children were invited on board the day before the HMS Hermes was due to leave. It was a memorable day – the children received a great deal of attention and were given many treats. They gifted Alan a couple of bottles of whisky, and Maddie was presented with several pairs of nylons and chocolates.

Bob, their main salesman, frequently visited their house. He was the same age as Maddie and was easy on the eyes, with his blonde, curly hair and tall, lanky physique. He had just come out of a long-term relationship and was living in lodgings, feeling sad and sorry for himself. Occasionally, Alan would bring him home to share a meal with them, and many times he would crash on the sofa, too drunk to drive home.

One day, Alan told Maddie that he had invited Bob to stay with them until he sorted himself out.

'Don't worry, love, it won't be for long. I'm sure he'll soon find somewhere of his own. He's going to give you something towards board and lodgings. Peter's room has a spare bed, so we can put James in there, and Bob can have James' room.'

'Ok, b-but you must make it clear to h-him that it is just for a short period and in the m-m-meantime he must look for somewhere. I've enough work to do with the children, and I bet your b-b-bottom dollar that he will expect me to wash and iron his clothes!'

Although Maddie welcomed him into their home, she was unhappy with the arrangement and hoped that Bob would soon get his affairs in order.
'
Four months later, Bob was still living with them. Several weeks after he had moved in, Maddie noticed that he was taking more than a friendly interest in her, which she initially dismissed. However, as time passed, she began to feel uncomfortable, especially when Alan wasn't around. He never made a move, but the way he looked at her and the insinuating remarks bothered her.

Maddie told Alan it was time for him to leave. He had been there too long and was starting to treat their home as his own. It was not until sometime later, after he had moved out, that Maddie realised just how much trouble he would cause.

They had found a reliable babysitter, a young teenager who lived with her parents just around the corner from their house. She was very good with the children, and with her parents close by, they had no qualms about leaving them in her care. It gave them the freedom to occasionally have an evening out.

Not long after Bob moved out, he submitted his notice at the factory, stating he was relocating to Sydney to stay with his sister and her husband. The last time they saw him, he was at the club, standing at the bar and drinking.

A few weeks later, Alan returned home in a horrendous mood.

'What happened between you and that bastard while he lived with us? You were sleeping with him, weren't you? You BITCH! I'll break his bloody neck when I see him next.'

Maddie couldn't believe what her husband was saying. She was horrified!

'I-I knew he had a c-c-crush on me. That was why I wanted him to leave. I've n-ever, ever, ch-cheated on you. W-why! How could he tell such terrible lies?'

'It is common knowledge up the club, he's told everyone that he slept with you. Why would he say that if he hadn't? You're a slut. How do you think I feel with everyone sniggering behind my back!'

Maddie was too upset to stay and argue with him; she couldn't understand why her husband didn't trust her. She felt like throwing it in his face that she knew about the many times when he was out late, that he wasn't always with his mates; it was with a woman. But that would only make matters worse.

Alan didn't speak to her for days. Maddie didn't know what to think or how she would face everyone. She couldn't stop thinking about it. Why would Bob tell such a horrific lie? Was it because she ignored his advances? Maddie knew that it was common knowledge her mother had slept with three or four of the club members, all of whom were married. Would they be thinking, 'like mother, like daughter?'

Eventually, Maddie approached her friends, worried that some might harbour doubts if she remained silent, but much to her relief, they assured her that they had never believed Bob for a second, and that they were not surprised, as they'd noticed the way he often looked at her. Having shunned him, of course, hurt his pride.

Daisy and Charles had been in their house for less than two years when they received an offer from the Western Power Company to buy their home. It was a state government-owned corporation responsible for building, maintaining, and operating the electricity network within the Southwest Interconnected System, which had merged with the regional electricity board. The general manager, Mr. Salmon, informed Charles that they wanted it for one of their caretakers and offered them a price that he and Daisy could not refuse, as it was far more than they had paid.

Daisy was eager to make one last trip back to the UK to see her mother before she passed away. She and Charles had also discussed buying a campervan and touring Europe. They left two months later.

Their business was expanding, so it was time to move to larger premises. They needed to purchase another printer, acquire more tables to work at, and hire additional staff to assist with compiling, among other tasks. Now that Bob had gone, Alan was left to deal with sales and secure new contracts, such as the Barman and Barmaids Union, Trotting Association, and many more.

In the meantime, Alan was drinking as much as ever, and even though Maddie pleaded with him to cut down, it made little difference. There were times when Maddie was convinced that he wanted to hit her, but at the last minute, he'd turn away and, picking up his keys, would walk back out of the house. She knew he would return to the pub or Bill's nightclub, where he would stay and gamble all night. She knew he had become more than friendly with one of the ladies there!

Maddie had been experiencing abdominal pains for the past couple of days, but kept it to herself, believing it might relate to the coil her doctor recommended instead of going back on the pill. She was not having regular periods, but she also attributed that to the coil.

Three days later, she was getting ready for bed when she experienced the most excruciating pain. Within seconds, blood was running down her legs. She was bleeding heavily, and there were bright red clots of blood. Maddie felt faint and was on the verge of collapsing as she screamed for Alan, who was in the next room.

As soon as he saw the state his wife was in, he immediately called the doctor at his home. The doctor instructed Alan to take his wife to the hospital as quickly as possible, emphasising that it would be faster than calling an ambulance. Alan made a quick call to the babysitter to ask her to come and look after the children.

When they arrived at the hospital, a nurse was waiting with a wheelchair to take Maddie to the wards. After stemming the haemorrhage, the doctor examined her. Alan waited on the other side of the curtains drawn around Maddie's bed. After the doctor left and the curtains were drawn back, Alan went to his wife's bedside, and she told him she was six and a half weeks pregnant!

A fat lot of good the coil did! Since her baby was still alive and they had stopped the haemorrhaging, they informed Maddie that they would be discharging her.

When they arrived home, Alan told his wife to go to bed, assuring her he would take care of everything. Maddie was too worried to fully rest, as her mind was in turmoil and uncertain about how she would cope with another child.

That night, she slept fitfully, and in the early hours of the morning, she was awakened by the most horrific pains in her lower abdomen, which were much worse than before. Then, her bed became soaked with blood, with large clots of blood far worse than before. She was terrified.

His wife's screams woke Alan, and sitting upright, he saw that she was trying to get out of bed before losing consciousness. Grabbing her dressing gown from the back of the bedroom door, he ran to the other side of the bed. Wrapping the gown around her, he lifted his wife into his arms and carried her out to the car. He then ran next door to ask again if they could take care of the children until he returned.

When they arrived at the hospital, a staff member called for a wheelchair. Alan stayed to fill out the personal details while Maddie was whisked away. The next thing Maddie knew, she was waking up in the recovery room, feeling cold and shivering violently. Two nurses stood by her bedside, anxiously waiting for her to regain consciousness. Then one of the women laid a hand on her arm and spoke to her.

'It's okay, Maddie, it's all over now. Doctor White will be with you soon.'

It was then that she noticed the tubes coming from every direction. One of the nurses was stroking her hair and telling her what a lucky young lady she was and fortunate to have reached them in time.

A few minutes later, the doctor entered the room and sat on the edge of the bed, taking her hand.

'I had to operate without getting your husband's consent. If I hadn't, you wouldn't be here now! You had what we call an ectopic pregnancy. The mass inside your fallopian tube was so large that it would have ruptured it. I had to remove the tube and ovary. Without the operation, your chances of survival would have been very, very slim. You will be staying with us for at least two weeks. It was a major operation, and you require much rest.'

Maddie was still very sleepy and unable to take it all in, but she knew that Dr. White had saved her life. She wanted to cry but didn't. Telling her to rest, he gently squeezed her hand, promising that he would come and check on her later that day. Overcome with emotion, Maddie was barely able to get the words out to thank him.

Maddie was shocked when she found out that the doctor who had previously discharged her would not terminate a pregnancy if the foetus was still alive because of his faith.

When Alan entered that evening, he told Maddie he had spoken to Doctor White, who informed him that she would be hospitalised for a while. He also suggested contacting the Home of the Good Shepherd, as they specialised in caring for children in such situations. Alan contacted them the following day and arranged for them to take James, Kim, and Joseph into their care. Unfortunately, they did not accept a child over the age of seven. As Peter was almost five, he remained at home with his father. Alan then went to the hospital, as Maddie was anxious to know how the children were. He told her that although the kids were pretty upset about being left, he was sure they would settle down, and having Peter in his care would leave little time to visit her.

Just as visiting hours were about to end, Alan ambled into the ward two days later. Maddie knew immediately that he had come from the pub because the smell of alcohol made her feel sick. She begged him to stay away from the pubs and to take care of their son. Alan told her that Peter was being looked after during the day by an aunt or an elderly couple who lived next door to the factory. Knowing that her child was being shuffled from one place to another so her husband could go to the pub made her even more anxious. She also became concerned about the younger children. Alan did not stay long.

It was nearly a week before he revisited her, and when he finally did, the staff had to ask him to go home and return once he had sobered up.

The next time he visited her, she asked if he could bring the children in to see her. He said he would arrange with the home to take them out for a couple of hours. True to his word, Alan collected James, Kim, and Joseph, and, along with Peter, took them all to the hospital. However, when he asked at the reception if he could take them to see their mother, he was told that it was the patients' afternoon nap time and to return in a couple of hours. Alan asked one of the nurses if they could tell his wife that he would take them outside the ward window so she could see them.

Maddie was on the third floor, which didn't make it easy, but at least they got to see one another. She waved to them through the window. Joseph started to cry, shouting, *'Mummy, mummy, I want my mummy!'* That started Kim off, but Peter and James just stood there, waving and blowing kisses, looking very sad. It broke Maddie's heart.

On the rare occasions when Alan visited her, he always had an excuse for not seeing her more often. He was either with the boxing troupe, earning money, had a customer to attend to, or was tired.

Maddie became so depressed that Dr. White prescribed her medication because her state of mind was hindering her recovery. He would not discharge her until he was sure she was mentally and physically strong enough.

She was anxious to go home because she wanted to be with her children. They needed her. Early one evening, the screen was pulled around her bed, and she was chatting away with another patient.

'When I see my doctor, I'm going to tell him I'm going home, and if he doesn't let me, I w....!'

The curtain opened before she could finish her sentence, revealing Dr. White standing there.

'Yes? You were saying?'

Her hand flew to her mouth in mock shock as he, with a huge grin, wagged his finger at her.

'If you promise to be good and do what you are told, I'll let you out tomorrow afternoon.'

Maddie was ecstatic.

'Of course I will. Thank you so much.'

Bursting into a laugh, he turned to walk away, pulling the curtain behind him. Then he stopped and, peering around the curtain, asked:

'So, tell me, young lady, pray tell me, what would you do if I said you couldn't go out?'

The day after Maddie returned home, they collected the children. Peter was pleased to see his brothers and sister, even though he was not one to say much. He was a deep thinker and kept much to himself.

Maddie noticed many changes in the children, especially Joseph. They had always loved bath times, starting with Peter and James and then topping up the water for Kim and Joseph. It was always a fun time. But now, it wasn't fun for Joseph anymore. The moment she placed him in the tub, he screamed, clinging to her arms and begging to be lifted out. It took weeks of patience and coaxing before he settled down. Maddie's instincts told her that something had happened at the home that had changed her son so much.

Life went on as before. There was always something to worry about, such as when Alan took Joseph with him one afternoon while visiting one of his friends, without letting his wife know. She had the whole neighbourhood out looking for her son and was on the verge of calling the police when he arrived home. Alan couldn't understand what all the fuss was about and kept assuring her that the other children knew.

Maddie used to take the children to the nearby little beach. Occasionally, they would ask if the two boys next door could come. She would sit with her eyes focused on them as she watched them play in the sand or paddle at the water's edge, counting one, two, three, four, five, six, and seven—the number of children in her care.

One day, she must have looked away for a second, possibly at a dog or a person walking on the beach. When she turned to count the children, she immediately saw Kim floundering face down at the water's edge, deep enough to submerge her face! She ran as fast as she could, shouting to the other children to immediately get out of the water and sit on the beach. Upon reaching her daughter, she quickly turned her over, and almost instantly, Kim began coughing and spluttering, with some colour returning to her face, which had been deathly white. Maddie was so shaken that she gathered the children and took them home.

Alan still attended many lodge meetings and often came home drunk. Sometimes he drove home, while other times he got a lift, returning to collect his car the following day.

On one particular occasion, Maddie had only just gone to bed when she heard someone knocking. Putting on her dressing gown, she made her way to the front door and opened it a crack to see who it was. It was Alan's friends, Harry and Reg.

'Sorry to wake you, Maddie, but we've brought Alan home because he got very drunk. We've tried to wake him, but he's completely out of it. We decided it would be better to leave him in the car and let him sleep it off.'

'Thank you, Harry, it's very kind of you both. I'm used to it. Normally, he drives home anyway. It's a wonder the cops have never picked him up.'

Harry nodded in agreement with her.

'It's a pretty cold night, so I think throwing a blanket over him would be a good idea.'

'Ok. Good night, guys, and thanks for bringing him home.'

As soon as they drove away, Maddie went to the car, rolled down the two front windows, and returned inside the house. She had had enough of his late nights, early mornings, drunkenness, and playing around. It might not have been nice to leave him out in the cold, but at that moment, she could not care less.

One day, when Alan was in a particularly foul mood, he swung an axe straight into the asbestos wall in the kitchen, leaving a gaping hole. Thankfully, the children were at their grandmothers' playing in the little paddling pool. They couldn't play in their backyard, as a garden did not exist – they had a junkyard. The only stretch of grass was the one that led down to her mother's.'

s.

Maddie constantly rearranged the furniture because she grew tired of seeing it the same way. One day, she changed everything in their bedroom, moving the bed to the opposite side of the room. Alan arrived home in the early hours of the morning, creeping into the room as quietly as he could so as not to wake her. He then began getting undressed. She could hear him cursing as he fumbled around the room, trying to find the bed.

Twelve months after Charles and Daisy sold their house to Western Power, Mr. Salmon approached Alan and Maddie with an offer to buy their home and the adjacent land for $13,500, more than double what they had paid. He informed them that they could stay until they found another place, explaining that they only wanted it for the land and had no need for the house, so they could take whatever they needed.

Maddie was not keen on moving as the house was renovated just as they wanted it, and the children were now settled into their new home and school. However, she knew it was too good an offer to refuse. Even after purchasing another place, they would still have enough left to pay off their debts, and they'd have some ready money for the printing business, as most of her grandfather's inheritance had been spent.

Peaks and Valleys

Driving home from work one day, Alan passed a 'for sale' sign that he hadn't noticed the day before. Pulling up alongside the curb, he got out of the car to take a closer look. As he walked up to the front door, he was not surprised to see a notice warning that the building had been condemned.

Maddie was less than enthusiastic when her husband told her about the house, arguing that buying a condemned place was ridiculous. Despite her lack of enthusiasm, Alan was determined to find out more. The following morning, he reached out to the agent without mentioning anything to his wife and was informed that the owner's asking price was $3,500. However, it was in a prime location, with a primary school within walking distance. He eventually convinced Maddie to agree to at least look at it, stating that it made sense to find a place where they could utilise the fittings and fixtures from the house they had just sold. Ultimately, as always, Maddie gave in to her husband's persistent badgering.

Alan arranged for them to meet with the agent that same weekend. After showing them into the house, the agent left them to look around and discuss among themselves, asking them to lock up when finished and return the keys to the office. They spent a considerable amount of time exploring the building. Alan pointed out to Maddie what could be done to the place, and most importantly, how it could be improved to meet the council's standards. Then, upon returning the keys, he shook hands on a deal of $3,250.

Several friends rallied to help with the renovations. Don, the electrician, renewed the antiquated electrical wiring at the printing works; Mark, the plumber, and Dominique, a jack-of-all-trades, collaborated on the project. They knocked down an internal wall that separated two small rooms, creating a decent-sized sitting room. They also replaced the rotten windows and doors. By enclosing the back veranda, they could construct two more bedrooms. Maddie was often found on the top rung of a ladder, holding sheets of plasterboard over her head to enable Alan to secure them to the ceiling joists. She painted the rooms, cleaned up after the workmen, and supplied endless cups of tea, sandwiches, and a beer or two near the end of the day.

One day, when Maddie was pulling up some of the old linoleum, she found several ancient newspapers and a Grammar School yearbook. Carefully turning the pages of the tabloids, she came across photos of the first settlers taken around 1869, who were camping on the edge of the Swan River in Perth. Despite being laid under the floor covering for the past thirty-four years, they were remarkably undamaged.

Maddie was still recovering from the near-fatal ectopic pregnancy. She was worried as she had lost quite a lot of weight, but she attributed it to the extra burden of renovating the house, caring for her family, and dealing with Alan's drinking. Not to mention his relatives, who would always turn up unannounced and expect to be given shelter and sustenance.

She then developed an irritating cough but was not overly worried, thinking she had probably picked up the latest germ circulating, so she took elixirs. However, it worsened within the week, to the point where she couldn't speak without violent coughing. Her chest felt heavy and hurt when she breathed. Alan insisted on taking her to the doctor, who, without delay, admitted Maddie to the palliative care ward at the Fremantle hospital, where she was diagnosed with a severe case of bronchial pneumonia.

Peter, James, and Kim were now attending school. Alan suggested to Maddie that she might enjoy working part-time at the factory, and she readily agreed. She spent much of the week on the road, collecting advertising copy from their customers and returning to the office with material for the typesetters. She sorted payments and dealt with bad debts. For those who were genuinely struggling, Maddie arranged for them to pay their tab in instalments. She understood what it was like to struggle and live hand to mouth!

Joseph was not due to start school for another six months, so Maddie took him to work with her. He loved being with his mother, especially in the car, as he looked out the window, learning the names of all the cars and petrol stations. While driving around, Maddie taught him the numbers and the alphabet to prepare him for when he started school the following year. It was a special time for just the two of them. Maddie sometimes felt sad that her children were close in age, as it meant she didn't get to spend special time alone with each of them.

She experienced a thought-provoking day when she was sent to a company in Perth to pick up a cheque and deliver advertising copy for their next advert. Parking outside a large, impressive Victorian residence, she made her way up several steps and rang the large brass bell on the wall next to the door. She was taken aback when a very attractive, somewhat scantily dressed young lady opened the door.

Following her down the long, wide hallway, Maddie noticed several rooms on either side. Except for one, all the doors were closed. Maddie slowed her pace, taking a moment to glance inside the room. She was amazed to see an enormous bed adorned with pillows and dim lights illuminating the chamber. There were whips, little feather dusters, and many other items she could not make out on a table beside the bed! As Maddie quickened her pace to catch up with the young woman, she suddenly realised what she had seen… She was in a high-class brothel!

'Interesting,' thought Maddie. '*Is this what they were advertising*?'

After receiving the editorial, Maddie walked down the passageway towards the front door when she heard intimate sounds from one of the bedrooms! Hurrying on, she left the building, jumped in her car, and drove back to the office.

While driving home, Maddie reflected on the time she and Alan had spent in the northwest town of Kalgoorlie. Alan had visited the town before and took Maddie to show her the sights. She remembered driving past the Hay Street brothels and imagining them all lit up at night, ladies sitting in chairs outside, waiting for the next client! Later that evening, as she related her day to Alan, he told her that the brothels had been established during Kalgoorlie's gold rush era, in the 1890s, and were still operating, catering to the needs of lonely miners and others who chose to visit the cramped rooms. They traded illegally under the Criminal Code but were allowed to remain under the state government's unofficial 'containment policy.' The police chose to look the other way.

The business was thriving, and Alan was becoming a well-known figure around town. He was coming home late more frequently now and spending many nights at Bill's nightclub in Fremantle. One time, when he arrived home in the early hours of the morning, he woke Maddie up, and throwing a wad of notes on the bed, he told her he had been paid to guard a couple of wealthy Chinese businessmen, both with a serious gambling habit. He went on to say to her that it was the intoxicating mix of chance, risk, opportunity, reward, and luck, along with the buzz of alcohol, the nonstop, hypnotising spin of the reels, and, of course, the chance to win. All of this spurred them to feel like winners, to *be* winners! If they won, they gave Alan a percentage of their winnings. Occasionally, when things got out of hand, there would be a brawl!

Life with Alan was becoming unbearable. Maddie was aware that the office girl, Lana, and her husband were spending more and more time together, but she never said anything. After all, what would be the use? Alan would, of course, deny it. She knew this was not the first time he had cheated on her.

Daisy and Charles had recently returned from their adventures around the UK and Europe. They joined together once again, enjoying Sunday drives into the hills. It was the children's chore to gather kindling for the barbecue while Maddie and Daisy unpacked all the food onto one of the picnic tables—bowls of salad and fresh rolls kept in the cool box until the cooked food was ready. Once the embers settled, it was Alan and Charles' job to cook the sausages and chops on the grill, finishing with the aroma of onions and pineapple slowly browning.

One bank holiday, they drove to Horricks Beach, a small fishing settlement two hours north of Perth. Several fishermen's huts were scattered along the beach, and a tiny camping area was nearby. Alan had recently bought a little trailer camper, which they towed up to the commune. Charles and Daisy drove in their car with a small tent. They all arrived around four o'clock in the afternoon. The children knew well enough to keep out of the way when their father was unloading or loading, fully aware that he had a very short fuse, especially if things did not go as planned.

When Alan opened the camper, there was a large bed on either side – one for Maddie and Alan, and the other for the younger children to share. Packed on the floor were two camper beds and a canvas annexe.

Daisy took the children to the beach, leaving Maddie and Charles to help Alan erect the annexe. Alan told them that the person who sold him the camper said that it would be up in no time because there were only six poles.

Maddie and Charles held a pole at either end of the awning, supporting the canvas as they waited for further instructions from Alan. Only four poles remained. Alan was struggling to determine where they should go. He was getting upset and beginning to lose his temper, snapping at Maddie and Charles, who were offering suggestions, of which Alan took no notice, insisting that he knew what he was doing. Meanwhile, Daisy and the children had returned from the beach and sat to watch the antics, trying to suppress their giggles. This made Alan even madder. The light was fading. Charles lit some lamps so Alan could see what he was doing. Thankfully, the tent was erected shortly thereafter! In the meantime, the children had been fed, and the adults now enjoyed a well-earned drink, or two!

Despite Alan's lack of patience, these were fun times spent as a family. Maddie knew she was not in love with him but cared for him in many ways, especially when they were all together as a family. She was aware that Alan had a severe alcohol-related problem that he could not control. Maddie could never completely relax, as she never knew whether he would be home with them or out drinking with his pub mates and whatever else he did in the early hours of the morning!

He'd fly off the handle if she questioned him, blaming Maddie for his drinking and, in the same breath, saying that she would not be able to live without him. She was sure that the children had heard their raised voices and would plead with him to stop, sometimes even begging him to forget it, and going so far as to say *she* was sorry.

Then, one time, when he arrived home so paralytic, she threatened to leave him, taking the children with her. She realised it was foolish to say because *'where would I go?'* There was no chance she would run to her mother's, and she had no money to live elsewhere. Alan had had a skin full that night and was in a strange mood. Then, suddenly, he made his way to the front door, flung it open, and turning back to look at Maddie, warned her that she would regret it if she ever thought of leaving him. He opened the door, and Maddie watched as he veered toward the garage.

Maddie ran after him, her heart pounding in her chest, hoping he wouldn't drive the car in his current state. However, as she entered the garage, she was shocked to see him slinging the tow rope over one of the rafters. It wasn't until she saw him tying a noose in the end of the rope that she realised what he was doing.

Maddie couldn't endure it any longer. She had to risk that it was yet another of his manipulative tactics. She called his bluff and walked out of the garage into the house.

Maddie contemplated leaving him, but realised she could never separate the children from their father. She needed to cling to the hope that one day things would change.

She knew she needed help but had no one to turn to. All their friends thought they were a very happily married couple. The last person she would confide in was her mother – she had always sided with Alan. Alan had once called Maddie a *'wowser'* in front of Daisy and Charles, inferring that she was a prude because she drank very little, if anything. Her mother had not defended her. In her eyes, Alan was the *bee's knees*! Maddie had made her bed, and she had to live with that.

Ultimately, she visited their doctor, hoping he would be able to give her advice. He was a kindly man who knew them both well and was aware that Alan had a drinking problem, but had no idea how serious the situation was. He was very concerned for Maddie's welfare and suggested that perhaps she could recommend that he attend an Alcoholics Anonymous meeting. Maddie knew that unless Alan accepted, he had a problem and needed help, he would never approach them.

Maddie decided to quit her job at the printers. She had enjoyed working and could get home in time for the children when they returned from school. She realised that Alan arranged to meet prospective clients at their local hotel or pub, where he would charm them by buying lunch and a round of drinks or more, helping to seal a deal.

One night, Alan and Maddie were fast asleep in bed when they were awakened by the ringing telephone. Alan glanced at the clock next to his bed—it was just after 2 a.m. He hauled himself out of bed and swiftly made his way to the hallway, snatching the receiver off the hook and wondering who on earth was calling at that ungodly hour!

It was his sister Rita calling from Sydney to inform him that their eldest daughter, Lucy, had been killed in a car accident. She was too upset to provide him with the full details, but assured him they would be in touch soon.

Rita's husband, Frank, called the following morning. It was the end-of-year dance at school, and it was also Lucy's first date. The boy had been driving too fast and hit a light pole. Their daughter took the full force, and the impact was so brutally strong that she was almost beyond recognition. Lucy was eighteen years old, a beautiful young lady with a brilliant future ahead of her. One of the statements on the day of her funeral was: *'God only takes the best.'*

Alan and Bill decided it was time to sell the business. Although they had some excellent contracts and everything was going well, they were always short of money, spending considerably more than they were making. The business was in the process of being sold to Frank, one of Alan's associates, but at the last minute, he withdrew from the deal. Consequently, the business went into liquidation. Alan's car was returned to the finance company, and he traded in Maddie's little runabout for an old Rambler that looked good but turned out to be a heap of rubbish.

With the children now all at school, Maddie was working in a large store's 'Home Cookery' department. She had not been there long before she was promoted to department manager. She was the youngest supervisor there. After school, the children went to stay with one of Maddie's friends who lived across the road. It was a suitable arrangement for them both, as Maddie often looked out for Mary's children when she and her husband went out for the evening.

Maddie loved her work and got along well with the two young girls who worked with her, especially seventeen-year-old Leonita, whose family had emigrated from southern Italy several years earlier. Leonita was a lovely girl, very pretty with her dark brown eyes and hair the colour of chestnuts that fell well below her shoulders. She became attached to Maddie and always confided in her. Leonita had an older sister who attended a local workshop for people with disabilities. Her parents once invited Maddie, Alan, and the children to their home to share a meal. It was a delightful evening. It was the first time they tasted authentic Italian fare and enjoyed the wine produced by her father, Jacopo. Leonita's mother, Giulia, showed Maddie how they made the rich tomato sauce and insisted on giving her some to take home. The smell, taste, and flavour of the sauce were perfect.

Maddie was given a two-year-old Boxer dog named Sheba. The family that owned her was moving away and could not take her with them. She was gentle and very good with the children, quickly becoming part of the family. They contacted a local breeder, believing it would be nice for Sheba to have one litter of pups. No money changed hands, as the owner requested the first pick of the litter.

It was a Sunday when Maddie noticed that Sheba was becoming restless and secreting a mucous-like fluid. Maddie encouraged her to lie on an old candlewick bedspread, which she covered with newspapers. The children came and sat next to her, waiting anxiously. Maddie encouraged them to go and play, promising she would call them when Sheba started giving birth. They didn't have to wait long – one after another, a tiny creature slipped and squirmed into the world. The children watched as she tore open the sack, clearing the fluids away from their little faces. They were still sitting and watching as Sheba, totally exhausted, produced one baby after another until there were ten tiny babies, crying and crawling in circles around their mother, feeling her smell. It wasn't long before they all found a teat and were contentedly suckling at their mother.

When the puppies were weaned, Maddie would place five dishes of cooked mince and rice on the back patio. More often than not, they played with their mother at the bottom of the garden, and Maddie called them: *'Pup, pup, come on, pup, pup, pup,'* and they would all come running up to the house as fast as their little legs could carry them.

One afternoon, when Alan was working in the garden, he thought he heard Maddie calling the puppies for their feed. He was mystified, as it was much earlier than usual, but then, seconds later, they came tearing up to the patio, expecting to see their food dishes, only to be disappointed when they found nothing waiting for them. When he mentioned it to Maddie, she told him it was their pink and grey Galah cockatoo that mimicked her voice and brought the pups running several times a day, confusing Sheba and her babies!

Since selling the printing works, Alan had taken on odd jobs, but he wasn't happy and told Maddie he wanted to start another septic business. They didn't have the funds since Maddie's inheritance had been spent some time ago. Alan reached out to one of his former business associates, Cyril Brown, who had recently purchased a small private hospital. They decided that going into business together would benefit them both.

Alan met with Cyril and his partner, David, and after a lengthy discussion, they agreed to finance the business. As part of the deal, Alan would maintain the tanks and address plumbing issues at the hospital. In return, the truck would be at Alan's disposal, and he would retain all the profits.

Peter had recently turned ten, and his brother James was eight and a half when they joined the local Church of England Boys' Club. Peter decided it was not for him. Instead, he joined the local under-11 rugby league team. The family attended a couple of matches, but Peter told them that he wasn't ready for them to come and watch him play. At the end of the season, Peter was presented with a trophy for the most improved player. His parents were very proud, and his younger brother, Joseph, told them he wanted to play rugby when he was older!

Joseph was the quietest of them all, keeping many of his thoughts to himself. He was very independent. When his siblings started their first day at school, Maddie walked with them, but Joseph boldly told his mother that he did not want her to take him, that he would walk with his brothers and sister. When Maddie was sure the children would be in their classrooms, she walked up to the school and, seeking out one of the teachers, enquired if her son had settled in. She didn't want the school to think she was a neglectful parent.

Maddie was strict with the children—manners were essential. She took pride in how they conducted themselves when out and about, but she was happy they were typical youngsters, filled with mischief and adventure. Peter was the studious one among the boys, and at times, he was reserved, while James and Kim bumbled along at school and often engaged in shenanigans. Joseph was, in many ways, like Peter, a thinker, and spent time tinkering with things from a young age.

A few doors down from where they lived, there was a delicatessen where Maddie bought a few everyday essentials. Occasionally, she would send one of the older children to buy a bottle of milk or a loaf of bread. Maddie and Alan were unaware that when going on an errand for their mother, James, Kim, and Joseph dawdled for a while around the back of the shop. One would climb over the fence and into the deli yard, then pass some empty cool-drink bottles to one of the others. Afterwards, the three would return to the shop and cash them in for lollies! One day, Peter saw what they were doing and dobbed them in to their mother. When Alan found out, he took the three scallywags back to the shop and made them apologise to the storekeeper. He also stopped their pocket money for the next two weeks. They were not very happy when they found out that their brother had snitched on them!

Another time, James and Kim pinched one of their father's fags and a box of matches. Then, scurrying across to the vacant block opposite the house, they crouched down behind a bush and lit one of the cigarettes. No one would have known, except that somehow the bush caught fire as the dry leaves and twigs started to burn. Smoke rose, and there were flames! It was not until Maddie and Alan heard the fire engine arrive that they realised what had happened. By this time, James and Kim had scarpered!

Christmas was only a few weeks away. It was time to go shopping for presents. This was a special time for Maddie and the children as she took them all on the bus to Perth for the day so they could shop for gifts for the rest of the family. They had all managed to save some of their pocket money for the occasion, and their father always ensured they had a little extra. While they made their way around the shops, Peter kept hold of Joseph, while James looked after his little sister. They wandered through the large stores looking for something to spend their money on, each ensuring that their sibling's prying eyes could not see their purchases. After they had bought all their gifts, they felt hungry, so Maddie took them to the store's cafeteria, where she let them choose their meals—within reason, of course!

It was a very special day for all of them.

Maddie enjoyed her work at the department store. She was, however, becoming increasingly perturbed at being told that everything baked the previous day was to be sold as fresh at the same price! Every morning, Maddie and her staff of two displayed everything on large trays underneath a glass partition on the counter. Fresh items were placed at the front, while those from the previous day were positioned at the back of the tray. The items from the back were to be sold first. If, as had happened on a couple of occasions, a customer returned complaining that the cakes were not fresh, Maddie would replace them with ones from the front of the tray!

Maddie voiced her concern to the floor supervisor, who assured her that he would bring it to the manager's attention. Several days later, Maddie was summoned to the main office upstairs. She explained her concern, stating that it was against her principles to deceive their customers. She suggested that they might sell the older items at a reduced price. After a brief discussion, Maddie was informed that it was not their policy to do that. The following morning, she handed in her resignation.

Alan was still drinking heavily, but what was more worrying were his mood swings, which were becoming worse. She never knew if he was happy with the way his life was or if it was that he was unable to get off the roller coaster he had created. She knew there was little she could do to help him, besides being a good wife and mother.

One evening, when the children were in bed and Maddie was alone watching television, she received a phone call from the inspector at their local police station, who informed her that her husband had been detained for driving while drunk. He told Maddie that Alan had used the one phone call he was permitted to make to contact a mate to come and bail him out.

Arriving home, he barely acknowledged his wife and remained distant for several days. Then, out of the blue, when they were sitting and watching television and Alan had downed a few cans of lager and had just poured himself a glass of whisky, he looked up at Maddie, his facial muscles tensed, lips pressed together in a thin line. He set the tumbler down on the coffee table next to him.

'You told them where I would be drinking, didn't you? It could only have been you who dobbed me in to the cops. How many times have you said I hope you get picked up for drinking and driving before you kill someone! I know you did, so don't even bother denying it. Why else would they have stopped me? Answer me that!'

Maddie was astonished by his outburst and shocked to consider that he would accuse her of such a thing. Even if she had known his whereabouts at any given time, she would never have alerted the police.

Yes! She was pleased that he had been picked up! Perhaps now he would do something regarding his excessive drinking.

'Of course, I didn't! Why would you think such a thing? I wouldn't have the faintest idea of what time you would be leaving the pub, or, for that matter, which one you would be drinking in. Or, for that matter, what time would be on your way home? You are being ridiculous!'

Alan flung himself out of the chair and, marching over to Maddie, continued to abuse her.

'You're a wowser, little Miss Goody Two-Shoes, who is so careful not to drink too much. Well, I enjoy my drink, and I'm not, as you seem to think, an alcoholic. I like a drink; so is that a crime?'

Maddie had had enough; she was sick of his drinking, his constant moods, and fits of abuse. She pushed herself out of the chair, stood close to him, and started pounding on his chest, wanting to hurt him as much as he had always been hurting her. Grabbing her arms, he shoved her against the wall. Then, he hit her across the face with such force that she fell to the ground. Without a backwards glance, he walked out of the room. The next thing Maddie heard was the front door opening and then slamming shut.

The following morning, she tried to conceal her bruised cheek and swollen mouth as much as she could, hoping that the children wouldn't notice, and that the outburst of anger had not awakened them.

Maddie was becoming increasingly depressed, to the point that she felt she couldn't handle her life anymore. It would be much easier to slip into a deep sleep and have no more worries. Instead, she prayed, although not quite sure to whom, but she knew there had to be a Higher Power guiding her.

After that incident, Maddie noticed a slight change in him. He started coming home earlier and, some nights, hardly had a drink. One evening, a few weeks later, Maddie was preparing the evening meal while Alan was in the sitting room speaking with someone on the phone. Minutes after they finished their tea, someone knocked at the door. Alan told Maddie he would answer it.

He returned to the kitchen, accompanied by a man whom Maddie estimated to be around forty. Alan informed his wife that they would go into the living room. Sometime later, they both came into the kitchen, and Alan introduced her to Cliff, telling her he would return later that evening to take him to an A.A. meeting.

Alan reached out to Alcoholics Anonymous, and that very day, a recovering alcoholic was there to support him. Maddie's prayers had been answered!

Unsettling changes

Although she was no longer working at the department store, Maddie kept in touch with Leonita and her family. She became part of the family and, in turn, embraced the Italian way of life. When taking the children with her, Grandma hugged them tightly while showering them with kisses. Leonita's mother's famous sauce and meatballs had a smell, taste, and flavour that embodied perfection and deliciousness. The family's love for one another was boundless.

Leonita was in love. For the past year or so, she had been dating a young English lad who worked in the department store's grocery department. Then the inevitable happened: she became pregnant. As a good Italian girl, she knew that they would be devastated if she told her family, and her father would probably ban her from their home. There was only one person to whom she could turn, knowing she would understand.

Maddie felt so sorry for Leonita, knowing how hard it would be for her to tell her parents, especially her beloved Papa, because as much as he loved his daughter, he would never accept the disgrace it would bring them.

Maddie eventually convinced Leonita to tell her mother. Giulia was shocked at the thought that one of her daughters could bring such shame to the family and realised she couldn't tell Giovani, as he would throw their daughter out of the house and forbid Giulia from contacting her.

Alan was still attending AA and had become much easier to live with. They were a proper family. Maddie told him about Leonita and asked if he would mind if she came to live with them until her baby was born. Leonita approached her father and told him she wanted to move out to share a flat with a girlfriend. She was relieved when he, albeit reluctantly, consented to her decision. A week later, she moved in with Alan and Maddie, settling in very well, and the children took to her immediately. Leonita continued working until she realised that her belly was becoming too large to hide under her ill-fitting clothes. Tony left the store and stopped seeing Leonita, whom he had professed to love, saying he was not ready to become a father. Leonita, although devastated, realised that it was probably for the best, as he did not love her as she had loved him.

She constantly worried about her unborn child. What was she going to do? Adopt or keep the baby? She knew that if she decided to keep her unborn child, it would not be easy. She needed Maddie to tell her what she should do. Maddie refused to do so, telling Leonita that no one could make such a huge decision that could, in the future, affect the rest of her life. However, she explained the pros and cons of adopting or raising a child on her own.

A couple of months before her child was due, Maddie contacted Leonita's mother, suggesting it might be the right time for her daughter to tell her papa. Although apprehensive about the outcome, Giulia agreed that her husband must be told. As they expected, he was furious and refused to discuss it with them. Her mother advised Leonita to stay away for a while and let him come to terms with what had happened, hoping that, in time, he would forgive her. Not long after, Giulia contacted her daughter, telling her that her father requested to see her. She mentioned that he had mellowed and was angrier with the bastard who had got his daughter pregnant and then deserted her. Additionally, he was not Italian!

Leonita continued to live with Maddie, and when her time came, she and Giulia attended the birth. Cradling her baby in her arms, Leonita agonised over the future of her baby girl, whom she wanted to raise herself. However, understanding how her father felt, she reluctantly gave her up for adoption. Although Maddie never wanted to sway her decision, she had hoped, with all her heart, that Leonita would keep her beautiful baby girl. She worried that in the future, when she married and started a family, she would regret it.

When the day came for Leonita to give up her baby, she did so reluctantly and then retreated to a private room where, distraught, tears flowed uncontrollably as she sat staring at the ceiling, not wanting to see anyone. She knew that her life would never be the same again. Two days later, she returned home to her family. Her loving father eventually forgave her.

A local council published a notice in the paper requesting tenders for the town's sanitary services and septic tank cleaning. After submitting his application, Alan was relieved when he was told he had won the contract. Having already approached the bank for a loan in anticipation of being awarded the contract, he could now purchase two trucks: one for disposing of waste from underground tanks and the other, a two-ton flatbed, to remove sanitary pans from residential homes. They rented out their house and relocated to Stirling, as a nearly new council house was included in the contract. It was situated in the light industrial area, directly opposite where the trucks would be parked when not in use.

Alan was always up by four o'clock for the sanitary run, as he had to be off the road by eight thirty, nine at the latest. It was hectic during the summer months, when tourists arrived, staying in rented accommodations that were often vacant for the rest of the year. Maddie sometimes went to the wasteland where the sewage was emptied to help unload the pans, and then they would return for breakfast. Alan inherited Alex Schmidt, who the previous contractor had employed.

Alex, to say the least, was quite a character. He was a scrawny little guy with a slight stoop. With his sharp features, he gave the impression of being older than his mid-fifties. Many times, he would turn up for work still drunk from the night before. He told them he was married and had eighteen children ranging from young adults to primary school age.

Maddie burst out laughing the first time he shared his jokes.

'What is the most powerful truck in town? A shit truck as it has four cylinders and flies!' The other was: *'What's a humdinger? A shit truck with bells!'*

Alan was tired of getting up so early in the morning. He took on Jack, whom everyone called Bluey because of his red hair, and had also worked for the previous contractor. Maddie often felt guilty, especially during the winter months when Alan headed off to work in the dark while she stayed snuggled up in bed. Alan drove the truck loaded with clean pans while Alex, armed with a torch, went into the backyards to collect the full ones from the dunnies, as they called the outside toilets. Then, regardless of whether anyone was inside the outhouse, he'd pull the full pan out from under the seat and shove in a new one, ready to be used. If someone were in there, he would say a cheery. *'Good morn'n!'* Or if he knew the person perched on the dunny, he would have a conversation with them as they got on with their 'business! *'Morn'n Mrs Jones, ow's th' ol' man? See ya next week.'* Then off he'd go.

Once, he plucked a couple of bunches of grapes from a vine in someone's garden, placed them on the upturned lid of the full pan, and then offered to share them with Alan, who, needless to say, declined. Alex's humour was so dry that many believed the tales he told. Occasionally, when he worked on the septic tanker with Alan, he and Bluey would stop by the pub for a quick drink before heading home, and most times, they had the bar all to themselves, as no one could stand the stench of them!

Another time, while they were drinking at the local pub, they overheard the publican mention that he was looking for a kitchen hand to cover the evening shift. Alex approached him, claiming he had all the qualifications, necessary brushes, and equipment. What the publican did not realise was that, first, Alex was joking with him, and second, the brushes he owned were used for scrubbing down the shit truck!

There was a time when Alex received a summons from the courts. He had recently separated from his wife, and she had taken him to task for not keeping up with her maintenance payments. Alex asked Alan if he would accompany him as a character witness. Alan came home that evening and told Maddie that it had been hilarious and entertaining. As Alex only paid his wife ten dollars a week, the judge ordered him to pay her thirty dollars a week. Alex was indignant, telling the judge that it was unfair.

'What about the fuckin pig I kill every week, the fuckin honey and the truck load of fuckin bread I give them?' Without giving the judge time to reply or shut him up, he went on: 'And the fuckin eggs and th…'

Finally, the judge succeeded in silencing him.

Under the circumstances, I'm afraid the order stands, and you will pay your wife thirty dollars a week. You are fortunate I am not holding you for contempt of court!

Alex refused to give up until he had the last word.

'Well, I'm not fuckin' well pay'n it!'

He was then escorted out of the room and to Alan's car. As they drove away, Alex leaned out of the car window, shouting:

'And I'm not fuckin' paying it!'

Alan knew that the truckload of bread, which Alex had referred to, was what he had collected from the back of the supermarket to feed his pigs.

Maddie had attended AA meetings with Alan, hoping her support would help her gain a better understanding. Then, one day, he told her he would not be attending any meetings, as he didn't need their help. He started going to the pub more often and was drinking light ale. As far as Maddie was concerned, that was okay, as he was not staying out all hours and seemed to be coping well.

At the back of their house was a large block of vacant land, and besides the local dog pound, there were no other buildings. The local ranger, who lived next door, also served as the catcher of stray dogs. One day, Maddie and Joseph were outside in the garden when they heard a shot from the compound. They peered over the fence and saw that the ranger had one of the dogs tied to a post. It was likely a stray that had not been claimed. He shot at it a second time, still failing to kill it, and finally, the last shot ended the poor beast's misery. Maddie and her son were distraught to witness his cruelty, so they vowed to act. Later that evening, as darkness began to fall, they went down to the compound. Joseph climbed over the low fence and discovered that the pens, where some of the dogs were kept, were unlocked. They let the dogs out and then went to the gate, which had a sliding latch, and opened it. The very happy animals scattered in all directions. Freedom!

Peter was still attending the rugby team from their previous home. He loved it and was doing well, but it was challenging having to travel the long distance, at night, twice a week and on weekends. Alan suggested that Maddie advertise in the local paper, inviting anyone willing to coach a junior rugby league team to meet them at the local sports ground. They also contacted both schools, inviting any interested boys to attend. They were quite surprised when, at that first meeting, several boys and their parents showed up, and two fathers, retired rugby players, offered their services as coaches. It was a promising start, as they had the makings of under-twelves and under-fourteen teams. Some boys were eager to try rugby, but since their fathers were staunch Aussie Rules players, they had been forbidden from playing football. With nearly forty young lads to transport to away games, Alan, Maddie, the coaches, and a handful of parents loaded them into their cars. Peter and James loved the game and both performed very well.

Then a tragedy occurred in the town. The fourteen-year-old sister of one of the boys on Peter's team went into town with friends on a Saturday and did not return home. After the initial searches proved fruitless in locating her, she was believed to have been kidnapped. Despite numerous reported sightings, her whereabouts remained unknown. The family was distraught, and eventually, the parents divorced. Several months later, the father drove to a north-west town and, heading into the bush, doused the inside of his car with petrol, setting fire to himself. Her body was never found, but they kept the case open for many years.

Alan and Maddie, along with the help of two or three dedicated parents and the coaches, arranged camping trips and played against the local league teams on many occasions. As the club grew, it became increasingly complex to transport everyone to the away games. After much discussion, they decided to try to buy a second-hand bus! Alan contacted the Metropolitan Transport Trust to inquire whether they had any old buses for sale. It just so happened that they had an old 42-seater available. The quoted price was reasonable, as it was for a good cause. One snag – they did not have the funds! A committee meeting was held, and a plan was formulated. Alan reached out to a couple of businesses, and Maddie spent days visiting local establishments to sell advertising space on the side of the bus, which they divided into panels. Within a few months, they had met their target, and shortly after, the club acquired a bus, enabling them to transport their teams in comfort and safety to away games. The next step was for Maddie to apply for her bus license, as they would need more than one driver.

A senior Rugby team from the UK got in touch, saying they were coming to Perth for one week and were wondering if they would be willing to host them. They, of course, accepted, as it was a great honour, but this also meant that a lot of organising needed to be done.

As the team wanted to attend the Ascot races, Alan agreed to take them. Maddie had only recently obtained her bus licence and did not feel confident in transporting a team of rugby players through the busy streets of Perth city.

Everyone had a great time, especially those who selected several winners. Alan spent most of the time with the guys, making Maddie extremely anxious as she knew he was downing quite a few pints. Shortly before they were ready to leave the racetrack, she overheard one of the rugby guys asking her husband, in a somewhat concerned voice, if he would be okay to drive them back. He assured him it would be fine since Maddie would be driving home! That was the moment Maddie realised he had no intention of making the return journey. He was out to enjoy himself! She could have happily walked away at that moment, leaving him to sort it out.

As everyone gathered around the bus door, Maddie made her way up the steps and, sitting in the driver's seat, appeared calm and unperturbed by the circumstances, but her insides were churning! Starting the bus, she watched as they began boarding one by one. As they made their way down the aisle, they stopped and, turning to look at Maddie, made a cross motion! She realised then that they knew this was her first time with a load of passengers. They were a wonderful group who made her laugh, especially since they knew she could take their teasing in good spirits. Her nervous breakdown would come later!

It was peak time, and the roads were jammed full of cars leaving the racecourse. With everyone on board, Maddie slowly moved into the traffic and took the bull by the horns as she overtook a car, praying she would not sideswipe it. Once out of the main bulk of the traffic, she began to relax, and when at last she delivered everyone to their hotel, she was surprised when they all clapped and cheered. Before leaving to return to the UK, the team members gave Maddie a signed photo of all the players.

'To the best driveress in Australia.'

As 1974 drew to a close, the shire council notified Alan and the tenants on either side that they were auctioning the houses. Only a small crowd attended, as most knew that the current occupants planned to bid on the property. Alan purchased his for the bargain price of $3,000.

A year later, they sold it for a substantial profit of $12,000, allowing them to purchase a place near the estuary. The house had functioned as a holiday home, so it was in good condition, but there was potential for improvement. After demolishing walls and adding an extension, they converted it into a spacious family home.

Peter and James were continuing to play rugby. Joseph had joined the Police and Citizens Club and reluctantly taken up boxing. Maddie knew that he wanted to impress his father, who, many years ago, had received the Golden Gloves as a heavyweight. There was a match at the Football Club, and his trainer overmatched him. James was getting a hiding, but he would not give up. He kept going back for more. Maddie cried and kept looking away, unable to bear seeing her son repeatedly knocked to the ground. All that was because he wanted to win his father's admiration and love.

The children were encouraged to bring home friends, and consequently, more often than not, they ended up with a house full of boys and girls of all ages. There had to be strict house rules, especially when some camped overnight in the backyard and became too noisy. Maddie or Alan would then reprimand and threaten to send them all home. That usually did the trick.

Maddie took care of the books—paying the never-ending bills and wages and, when necessary, visiting the bank manager. Alan still had a chequebook, making it impossible for Maddie to keep track of the amounts going out each month.

The local magistrate, Duncan, a friend of Maddie's, happened to mention to her that a shop opposite the post office had been empty for some time and would be ideal for a second-hand project. After discussing it with Alan, she decided to go ahead, and with Duncan's excellent reference, her application was approved within days. Alan and Maddie made early morning trips to the auctions, bidding on and successfully purchasing some quality stock for the shop. Not long after they had opened,

Maddie secured a franchise with one of the electrical companies and was now selling new fridges and freezers.

For some time, Maddie had been suffering from abdominal pains, which became so intense that she made an appointment with their local doctor, who told her that he was unable to find anything wrong with her. She went to another surgery for a second opinion, and after having an X-ray, she was once again told everything appeared normal and that her problem was most probably caused by stress. Over the next couple of weeks, the pain intensified, so much so that she could hardly stand. Desperate, she travelled to a nearby town to seek another opinion.

After managing to secure an appointment, she sat in the waiting room until she was called into the practitioner's room. Once seated, he inquired about her problem. Maddie immediately broke down as she could tell he was very kind. When she explained her issue, he informed her that he needed to conduct an internal examination. Although he found no obvious signs of her discomfort, he acknowledged that she was experiencing significant pain and that there was something seriously wrong. He provided her with a referral to see a gynaecologist, who then arranged for her to go to the hospital for an internal examination.

Maddie awoke in the recovery room feeling very sore and sorry for herself. Before being transferred to a ward, the surgeon came and told Maddie that they had removed a large fluid-filled ovarian cyst, telling her that they had thought it wise to do a total hysterectomy.

Rather than being upset, Maddie was delighted! No more babies!

The second-hand shop was still doing well. Another year had passed, and the children were now teenagers. Peter, now seventeen, had secured a position with one of the major fuel companies. Jason, Kim, and Joseph were all in high school.

The sanitary contract was nearing its end, and the council had issued an advertisement for tenders. Alan was undercut. No longer employed by the local council, he needed to work out his next move. Eventually, he conceived the idea of starting a furniture removal business. Convincing Maddie that it would be perfect timing, as they would be the only ones in the immediate area.

Since the previous bank loan had been paid, Alan succeeded in securing another and purchased a six-year-old Pentec removal van with the capacity to transport the contents of a large house. It came with all the necessary equipment for packing and carting. He then employed a sign writer to put advertising on both sides of the vehicle. All that was left was to advertise the business and secure customers.

It was not long before they were up and running. Alan employed a couple of local lads to help him with the removals. Maddie saw the bookings, the delivery of the packing boxes, and anything else that needed doing.

In addition to relocating clients, they packed and boxed all their household items. Maddie had two, sometimes three, ladies working with her as they worked through the day until every item had been boxed. It was backbreaking work.

People came from as far as Fremantle and Perth to buy from *Maddie's Corner*. The business was going so well that Maddie employed a young girl, Fee, the sister of one of the young rugby boys. Her mother was a friend of Maddie's. Fee was a tremendous help, quick to learn and willing to please. One day, Maddie asked her to run to the shops and get something for their lunch. Fee ran all the way there and back as fast as she could! Although perturbed that Fee had taken what she said literally, Maddie dissolved into laughter.

'I didn't mean you had to actually. It was just a figure of speech!'

Alan had built a high fence around their backyard, mainly to keep the animals in. He was also in the middle of building a substantial garage.

One evening, they attended a very boring event in the company of stuffy politicians and their wives. Next to Alan sat a rather stuffy lady. Alan was bored and was about to ask Maddie if they could escape and go home when the woman decided to acknowledge him. They chatted for a few moments, mainly about things of very little interest to Alan, so he decided to spice up the conversation.

'Do you know how you tell the age of an elephant?' he asked.
'No,' she replied.
'You count the rings on his trunk, and however many there are, that will tell you how old it is.'
'Oh!' she said, 'That is very interesting, how do you know that?'
Alan went on to tell her much more about elephants, none of which he knew was factual. He and Maddie ended up staying for most of the night.
A few weeks later, a circus came to town along with all the usual animals, including two elephants, mother and her half-grown calf. Maddie decided to cause a bit of mischief, and after telling Alan about it, they placed an advert for an elephant trainer in the local paper. The next day, Maddie took a call from a man who spoke with a strong Indian accent.
'You advertise for an elephant trainer, yes?'
Maddie hesitated, not quite sure what to say.
'Y-yes!' she replied.
The man went on to say:
'I have qualifications, I am an excellent elephant trainer.'
Maddie interrupted:
'I am not sure tha...'
Not giving Maddie a chance to continue, he kept talking:
'I am an expert, ma'am, as I've been playing with my trunk for many years!' He then hung up, leaving Maddie unsure whether to laugh or panic!
Unbeknownst to Maddie, her husband had spoken with the circus, asking them about their elephants. It was not until she started receiving calls from the major newspapers wanting to interview them about their elephant, that she found out that Alan had paid the circus owner money to load the younger elephant into a horse box and park it outside the shire council and then, to go inside and enquire where she and Alan lived as they had an elephant to deliver! One of the council officers, who was a friend of Alan's, knew that a large fence had been built on their property, so, although disbelieving that they would be buying an elephant, he directed the man to where they lived!
Alan and Maddie decided that they had better try to put an end to their mischief. The children were getting upset with them

because everyone, including their friends at school, kept asking about the elephant! One local estate agent had even wondered if their elephant could parade around the town advertising their business!

APRIL 1979

It was a freezing autumn day, and Maddie was looking forward to being home in the warmth of the kitchen, preparing the evening meal. Upon opening the front door, Maddie heard voices coming from the kitchen and was surprised to see Alan sitting at the table talking to young Jo, who helped out with the removals when it was really busy. Jo's parents owned a service station a couple of miles outside of town, which, besides selling fuel, stocked fresh fruit and vegetables, a few everyday essentials, hot chicken, meat pies, and pasties. Maddie didn't have a chance to acknowledge either of them as Alan was the first one to speak.

'Good, you're home nice and early. Jo and I have been discussing a business situation which sounds like an exciting venture for us.'

Maddie's euphoria at having such an excellent day at the shop faded. She had been looking forward to telling her husband that she had had two or three large sales that morning and was feeling upbeat. She knew that this would be another one of his schemes and dreaded hearing what he had to say. Ignoring Alan for the moment, she turned to Jo.

'Hi, Jo, nice to see you. What is this business that you two have been discussing?'

Jo glanced at Alan, not responding to Maddie's question, but she could sense his embarrassment.

'I think I will leave you two to talk. Alan, if you're interested, you'll need to discuss it with my parents. I'll find my way out. See you tomorrow. Bye, Maddie.'

As soon as the door closed behind him, Alan turned to Maddie.

'Why don't you pour yourself a cuppa, luv, the tea hasn't been brewing that long, and while the children aren't here, it's a good time to discuss what I feel would be a great opportunity for us.'

Maddie knew that Peter, James, and Joseph were at rugby training, and Kim, who had just celebrated her fifteenth birthday, would be next door with her best friend Janelle. So, if there were to be a discussion, it would certainly be easier without them.

Alan explained that Jo's parents, Brian and Betty, were selling the service station because they had run out of capital to keep it going. Also, the long hours, working from early morning until late at night, were too much for them. The purchase price was significantly less than the property's value. Alan convinced her that it would be an excellent investment, as the land and the house were freehold, meaning they could use it for any purpose as long as they followed local regulations.

Maddie was confused.

'We can't possibly buy it. We haven't got the money and most of the time we barely keep our heads above water!'

There's a dwelling attached to the shop, so when we sell our house, we can live there. I haven't seen the place inside yet, but I am sure it will be okay, as Jo, his young brother, and his parents have lived there for a few years. We will need to take out a Bridging Loan, and once our place sells, we can repay it. The debt will then be cleared. People are doing this all the time. It's designed to help complete the purchase of a property before selling the existing home. It will be a high interest rate, but trust me, this will be a good move.'

Alan, eyebrows raised, was looking quizzically at his wife, waiting for her to say something. Meanwhile, Maddie, deep in thought and with hands clasped tightly round the rim of her mug of tea, was still trying to take it all in. He made it sound so simple.

Maddie was still struggling to keep up with the bills. She had, once again, gone to the bank to ask for an increase in the overdraft facility, contacted utility companies such as the water, electricity, and phone departments, and requested an extension of time to make the payments.

'Well?' Alan was becoming impatient. 'I can phone them now and say we'd like to call and see them. Ask the questions and determine exactly how much they would take. Okay?'

Reluctantly, Maddie agreed that it would not hurt to meet them, learn more about the business, and, more importantly, view the house where they might live.

Shortly after putting their house in the hands of a local estate agent, Alan applied for a Bridging Loan from their bank, facilitating the purchase of the service station. While the exchange was in progress, they often worked alongside Jo's parents, learning as much as possible about the business. The family had already found somewhere else to stay, leaving the accommodation at the back of the shop empty, which allowed Maddie to get rid of all the junk they had annoyingly left behind and give it a thorough clean. It had to be habitable for when they sold their house. There were three small bedrooms, and the bathroom and toilet were in the partially enclosed veranda. The kitchen was the largest room of all and the dirtiest. All the equipment was from the late 1960s. A New World gas stove sat next to a kitchenette, and alongside that was a Kelvinator refrigerator, a futuristic fridge with soft curves which, much to Maddie's relief, included a freezer compartment. Everything, including the fridge and the stove, was a shade of olive green. A benchtop and half a dozen small cupboards lined the wall, and under a small window that overlooked a wasteland, a small sink was located.

Immediately after the loan was approved, the previous owners vacated, and Alan and his family moved in. The linoleum was ripped in places and needed replacing, the walls required a fresh paint job, and the fridges and freezers needed to be replaced. They spent the next few weeks scrubbing and cleaning everything while operating the business seven days a week from early morning to late at night. The weekday started at six in the morning, with commuters already making their way to work. On Sundays, they had a sleep-in until 8 am. Most evenings, they turned off the pumps and shut the door around nine o'clock.

Alan worked hard and continued to run the removal business, leaving Maddie to manage the shop, operate the fuel pumps, and sell groceries, fruit and vegetables. During the Christmas Holiday, when all the tourists were down, Maddie employed a young lad to assist her as they were now making sandwiches, cooking burgers and selling hot chicken. Alan approached a local fisherman who supplied them with fresh Tailor and River Cobbler. After filleting the Taylor, Maddie stripped the tough skin from the cobbler with a pair of pliers. Two or three times a week, at four o'clock in the morning, Alan drove forty kilometres to the wholesale markets in Perth where he bartered with everyone else for crates of fruit and vegetables. On a good day, he was fortunate enough to buy high-quality items at a very low price. Occasionally, Maddie would accompany her husband to the market and leave one of the children to watch the store until they returned, just in time for them to go to school.

One afternoon, when Kim and Joseph had returned from school, Maddie took them for a walk in the bushland across the road because she wanted to photograph the masses of Kangaroo Paws – one of the many beautiful Australian wildflowers. The red and black colours were amazing. When Maddie stopped to take photos, the children wandered off to explore. A few minutes later, they came running back, giggling with excitement.

'Mummy, mummy, look what we found. Someone must live here as they have made themselves a bed.'

Maddie took a closer look and then burst out laughing!

'Hmm, yes, my dears, it is a bed, but not the sort you might like to spend the night on. It's an Aboriginal deathbed!'

Before Maddie had time to tell them more, Kim and Joseph had dropped the stretcher like a hot potato, sending it crashing to the ground. The two children ran off screaming! Maddie called them back and explained.

'It hasn't been used. They have it ready for when one of their tribe dies. They put the deceased on the stretcher and built a fire underneath, and, as soon as it was lit, they danced around it, celebrating the death of a member of their tribe. They believe that they will then go to the Land of the Dead, and some are convinced that death is seen as a rebirth from their previous life.'

Joseph grabbed his mother's hand.

'Mum, can we go home now? It's spooky, and I don't want to come here again.'

They made their way back home just in time for Maddie to take over from Peter, who had offered to look after the shop while they went for their walk.

Early one morning, not long after they had moved in, Alan was browsing through the local paper when he spotted an advertisement for anyone interested in giving a mare and her young foal a good home. He promptly showed it to Maddie, asking for her opinion, and they both agreed that, as they had just over an acre of land in the back, it would be ideal for a couple of horses. Like her mother, Kim was a keen rider, spending much of her free time at the local riding school, where she groomed and exercised the horses. By that evening, Poppy and Stormy, the foal, were ambling around the field. Kim was ecstatic and wanted to ride the mare straight away, but was told she had to wait until the weekend to give Poppy time to get used to everyone. Stormy was extremely skittish but seemed very happy in his new home.

Kim had not yet gained enough experience, so she was mostly confined to riding around the property. Occasionally, though, as long as someone was with her, she was allowed across the road onto a vacant plot of land surrounded by gum trees.

In time, Kim began getting bored riding Poppy around the field, wanting more freedom to put the mare through her paces. So, one Saturday morning after finishing all her chores, she decided it would be a good time to ask her father. As she suspected, he said.

'Ask your mother.'

Kim knew her mother was busy serving in the shop, so she hoped that would be a distraction and Maddie would agree. Especially if she told her that her father had said it was okay! Kim could hardly contain herself when Maddie said yes – she hardly listened to all her nagging about what she should and shouldn't do, other than saying she had to take one of her brothers with her.

James, working outside with his dad, jumped at the opportunity as it would get him out of work. After carefully crossing the road and making their way through the trees, Kim mounted Poppy. After about twenty minutes, having let Jason have a couple of goes, Kim was astride for the final time and was determined to see if Poppy would go into a canter for her. James was not happy and warned his sister that their parents would be angry if they found out.

Kim ignored him and, giving the mare a couple of kicks with the stirrups, urged the mare into a trot. Then, shaking the reins and giving her a few more kicks, Poppy took off at a fast canter. James was shouting out to his sister, telling her to rein in, but her mount was not responding, and then suddenly, when she broke into a gallop. Kim tried to turn her around, but in doing so, lost her balance and tumbled off the horse, landing on the ground. Her body smashed against a large tree. She was screaming in pain!

James quickly went over to her, but he knew he could do nothing, so he ran back home as fast as he could. He found his mother serving petrol at one of the petrol bowsers and, grabbing her by the arm, told her to come quickly as Kim had been thrown off the horse.

The gentleman she was serving told Maddie to call the ambulance, then, sprinting across the road, he went to help her daughter. Hearing the commotion, Alan came running across the yard to see what the problem was. He immediately instructed Maddie to go to Kim while he was getting help.

When the ambulance arrived half an hour later, it took the responders quite a while as they had to remove Kim from the tree very carefully. Every little movement was making her scream out in pain. Eventually, they got her safely onto the stretcher and into the ambulance, with Maddie insisting that she go with her. Alan told James he was going to drive to the hospital and asked him to stay and look after the shop, letting his brothers know what had happened.

Once at the hospital, Kim was rushed to the x-ray department—the doctors were fearful that she might have broken her back. Alan and Maddie sat fitfully for what seemed like hours, waiting for the results. Thankfully, her back had not suffered any damage, but she did have a very nasty fracture of her femur. They scheduled her to be operated on the following morning, and the insertion of a twelve-inch metal pin meant that their daughter would be out of action for some time.

Six months later, their house had still not sold, meaning they continued to pay the bridging finance. Then, a price war broke out over fuel, with all garages in the area competing to undercut one another. Maddie and Alan had no option but to battle on. At the best of times, the profit they received on a gallon of petrol was one cent. They were now down to virtually nothing. They could not keep going – much of what they earned from the furniture removals supported the garage. Bills were coming in from left, right and centre. They were struggling to pay any of them.

In desperation, they sold to a major fuel company that took advantage of them, leaving them still in debt. They did, however, let them off for the amount they owed for the last fuel load. Meanwhile, Maddie had secured a position working in the kitchen of a local hotel. Alan continued with the removals, bringing in just enough to cover their living expenses and the outstanding bills.

They had no other option but to file for bankruptcy. Yet, before doing so, Alan signed over fifty percent of the ownership of the removal truck to James, as this meant the courts could not seize it. The bank now owned the house and had informed them that the balance would come to them if it were sold for more than the valuation. They were given a month to vacate.

Peter was doing very well, having secured a job at one of the major fuel companies. James, Joseph and Kim were all at the grammar school. Meanwhile, Alan once again visited the Pastoral office, hoping that something would come up with one of the sheep or cattle stations up north.

Alan and Maddie had been anxiously waiting to hear from the bank, hoping that the sale of their house would wipe out the bridging loan on the garage. A week before they were to move out, the bank contacted them. It was not good news. They had sold it for far less than the valuation. Sometime later, they discovered that it had been sold to a local bank manager.

When Alan received a phone call from the Pastoral Company, saying that an appointment had been made for him and his wife to present themselves at their office the following morning. The station owner, usually referred to as the grazier, George, had driven down to interview Alan and Maddie personally. Explaining their chores, he said that the property comprised 115,000 hectares of high-quality rangelands near Carnarvon, with 1,000 head of cattle and 4,000 sheep. Maddie's duties were to take care of the six-bedroom homestead and cook the meals, which included the Jackaroo and the stockman who lived in the shearing quarters. They were hired and told to be ready to start work by the end of the following week.

At the time, Peter worked in Fremantle and stayed with his father's aunt. James had left school and was working at McDonald's Burger Bar. Kim still had one year at school. Joseph was in his final year of high school, and although he wanted to be with his family, he decided to stay with his grandmother and

Charles until the end of the term. Maddie was devastated. Yet, she had to put on a brave face for Joseph's sake, but the thought of leaving him behind was too much. He was her baby. She knew he felt the same, but he wanted to spend the rest of the year with his friends. He was never one to share his feelings, but she sensed his pain in having to make such a huge decision.

Alan did an excellent deal with one of his mates, buying a 1970s Ford Transit van, as their car had been repossessed. With the help of a couple of friends, the removal van was loaded with all their belongings, ready to make the journey. James travelled in the truck with his father, while Maddie drove the van, which they named Ambrose. They took Kim, their three dogs — Candy, the Retriever, and the toy Poodles, Monkey and Fluffy, as well as Snibbles the cat, and their very talkative pink and grey cockatoo.

They were about three hours away from their destination, and it was starting to get dark, so they pulled up in a parking bay alongside a large road train taking goods up to Darwin. Alan told James and Kim to go and find some wood. Whilst they were away, he formed a small circle from some large stones, and when the children came back, he placed the kindling at the bottom and then layered the larger branches on top. Then, setting it alight, he poured a small amount of kerosene to get it burning more rapidly. They all watched as the flames flickered and set the small branches alight. Maddie retrieved a small iron sheet from the Ford, and Alan laid it across the top. They could cook on it once the fire had heated up enough, and the flames died down.

It was the height of summer when the evenings were hot and sticky, so they sat outside eating well-cooked sausages, bread and fruit. Alan chased it down with a beer, and Maddie and the children drank Coke. After cleaning up the campsite, everyone kipped down in Ambrose. It was not the most comfortable of nights since much of the room was taken up by the dogs, the cat, and a squawking Galagh!

Early the next morning, they continued to the town of Carnarvon and then another twenty kilometres towards Coorayla Station. Arriving at the turn off, they had to travel another three kilometres along a dusty, barren track. Either side was mostly low scrub with random mulga and gum trees. They encountered a couple of kangaroos, goats, and snakes that slithered into the scrub. Eventually, they came to a wire fence with a large timber gate, which Alan opened and drove through. Maddie followed, and Kim jumped out of the van, closing it behind them. Besides a couple of very old, large timber and corrugated sheds, the land remained barren. Driving for a further half a kilometre, they were relieved to see the homestead.

Alan parked the truck outside a large open shed opposite the house and beckoned for Maddie to park in the same place. Meanwhile, James and Kim looked around in awe at the vastness and wondered what they were doing in such a desolate place. They stared at the sprawling colonial brick and iron homestead that was to become their home. James gazed around the place, not believing that this was where they would be living.

'Dad, Mum, you must be joking! What will Kim and I do all day in this God forsaken place?'

'Son,' started Alan, 'when we go into town, you can go to the employment agency and put your name down, but until then, you will be helping me to fix windmills, fences and whatever else is needed. There will be no slackers here.'

'What about me, Dad!' exclaimed Kim.

'You, Kim, will be doing your lessons via the School of the Air. All of your classes will be conducted by radio with the help of your mother.'

Just as Kim was going to speak, they were aware of a full-bodied, middle-aged woman dressed in faded and well-worn dungarees striding towards them.

'G'day, I'm George's sister, Bernie. Welcome. My brother phoned to say that you would be arriving sometime today. Certainly not the best time of the year to be landed in this God forsaken country.'

Alan smiled as he shook the strong, work-worn hand thrust at him.

'My wife, Maddie, and I know how hot it can get, but it is all new to the kids. I'm sure they will soon get used to it, and having worked in the bush before, we are both aware of how harsh and isolated the environment can be.'

'Well, we can't stand around in this heat, so let's get into the house, as you'll all be dying of thirst. I've made a large plateful of lamb and chutney sandwiches.'

While the adults sat around the solid, but very old, kitchen table, which took up most of the room, James and Kim were given a handful of sandwiches each, as Bernie knew they were anxious to go outside and explore. While talking to Alan, Maddie glanced around the kitchen and was relieved to see an Aga stove, as she had got used to one when they worked on the sheep station when Peter was a young baby. She was eager to explore the rest of the house and see where they would be living.

Bernie had spread a map of the station out on one end of the table and pointed out to Alan where all the boundaries were. She went on to explain that there were fourteen wells and bores, 12–15 windmills, a large workshop, an iron shearing shed and nine room shearer's quarters, with two rooms occupied by the stockman and the young Jackaroo.

Then Bernie turned her attention to Maddie.

'I'm sure you want to settle in as quickly as possible. So, come with me, I'll show you where your living quarters are and then, Alan, we will go and find Ginger and Kirra.'

Alan nodded, and Maddie rose from the table, making her way to the door. She called out for the children, as she was sure they would want to see their rooms. Bernie laughed.

'Don't worry, when they see us walking up to the quarters, they'll come running!'

Maddie was taken aback, as she had assumed, they would be living in the main house. They followed Bernie about two hundred yards across the dusty soil to a prefab building with a wide veranda running across the front and sides. When they were shown inside, Maddie was pleasantly surprised to see that there were three bedrooms and everything, although very basic, was far better than some places they had lived in over the past few years. It was also completely furnished, meaning they only had to unload their belongings. Bernie returned to the homestead, and Alan fetched the truck up to the cottage.

In the morning, Bernie introduced Alan to eighteen-year-old Ginger, explaining that he had joined them as a ringer about a year ago and was an excellent worker with a positive attitude.

Alan knew that the job of a ringer was not for the faint-hearted as they were responsible for the care of livestock and the treatment of their injuries and illnesses, including feeding, watering, mustering, droving, branding, castrating, ear tagging, weighing, vaccinating livestock and dealing with their predators. The days were long, and the work was physically draining.

After that, Bernie drove a short distance to the stockyards, where they found Kirra repairing one of the fences. Alan was pleased to know that he would be working alongside Aboriginal people, as they had played a significant role in developing the cattle industry in the North-West of Australia and were highly valued and respected workers.

Later that day, Alan took the time to explain to James and Kim what to expect while living at Coorayla.

'Do not wander away from the homestead area because it is vast. Australian sheep and cattle stations can be thousands of square kilometres in area, with the nearest neighbour being hundreds of kilometres away. We are lucky as we are less than an hour away from the nearest property. Kim, most of your time will be spent on schoolwork and helping your mother around the house. James...'

James interrupted his father.

'Dad, can I hang out with Ginger while he is working around the place or... maybe go with you and Kirra to check the windmills, please?'

Alan pondered for a moment. He knew how much his son wanted to please him, so letting him watch and learn from the ringer would give him more confidence in himself.

'Okay, son, but don't get in his way and don't stop him from working with your idle chatter. He'll be going out to get a killer when the sun has gone down, and if he doesn't mind, you can go with him. He will then bring it back, cut its throat and hang it in the cool room to let the blood drain for a couple of days. Seeing an animal slaughtered is not the best of sights, so I will leave that up to you to decide.'

Around midday the following morning, Maddie heard the whirring sound of a flying helicopter. Looking up, she was startled to see it hovering while slowly lowering to the ground just a few yards from the homestead. She was even more surprised to see George climbing out of the cockpit and walking towards the house under the slowly rotating blades. He said he'd come to take Bernie home to Perth.

They were now able to get into their routine. Maddie was aware that station cooks had the unenviable and often thankless task of being the first up and the last to bed, so she was already dressed and ready for work at five o'clock in the morning. Then, after checking her husband and son were fully awake, she'd go over to the homestead as the men would soon be arriving for their breakfast. Shortly after, everyone sauntered into the kitchen and, after eating heartily and downing several cups of tea, they'd be off.

About nine thirty, Maddie or Kim would strike the large brass bell that hung from the veranda, calling them in for smoko, which was a welcome break from a long morning. They'd drink their coffee and knock back some freshly baked scones or wholesome fruit cake, and off they'd go again. After lunch, everyone rested until the heat of the midday sun had cooled down. Dinner was anytime between eight and nine, depending on what everyone was doing. If they were moving cattle, it could be a bit later. Even with the little help that Kim gave her, Maddie seldom finished her day until late in the night.

Most provisions were either canned or dried, and more importantly, they maintained a good stock of flour and eggs. The primary source of meat was goat, and there was always a large supply of tinned spam. Maddie was running out of different ways to cook goat! Roast, casserole, stew, mince dishes, and thin slices of the meat cooked in batter.

Alan found a clapped-out Ford Ute in the barn and spent a few days repairing it. A 1965 Honda motorbike was lying on its side among some old machinery. He was preparing to spend a day out in the paddocks with James so that his son could get a feel for the place. Meanwhile, Kim, although happy hanging around with Ginger, would not settle down to her schoolwork, and Maddie was finding it increasingly hard to spare time to help her while keeping up with her chores. Her daughter rebelled against everything, and Maddie began feeling the strain.

The days were becoming unbearable with temperatures rising as high as 46 degrees. James was suffering from heatstroke and hated living there, so they took a morning off and went into town so that he could put his name down at the job centre. Two days later, they contacted him about a vacancy for a butcher's apprentice. Although not a job he would have chosen, he jumped at the chance and was invited to live in town with the family. Maddie was calmer now, knowing that he was away from the station – she knew how unhappy he had been, but she was also worried that he would end up slicing his fingers off with one of the sharp instruments.

They had been there just over a month when Alan rang the bank, which confirmed that $300 had been deposited into their account. Station workers were lowly paid, even considering that they were given food and accommodation, but between the two of them, working a seven-day week, a total of eighty-four hours, $300 for the two of them was hard to stomach.

As much as Maddie tried, Kim would not settle down to her studies and was slowly falling behind. She still had another year to go before leaving school, but Kim had had enough. Kim hated having to help around the homestead, and her mother realised that her daughter was isolated living so far away from the town and not getting the chance to make new friends.

Although the hours were long and the pay was inadequate, they had a roof over their heads and food in their bellies. Yet, in her heart, Maddie knew that they would soon, once again, be moving on.

Carnarvon

George was having a difficult time finding a suitable replacement. Although dissatisfied, Alan had agreed to remain until a replacement was found.

A month after giving their notice, George contacted Alan to inform him that the new manager would arrive that weekend. The following day, Alan loaded the previously packed boxes into the van. After verifying that everything was in order, they facilitated a smooth transition for the next Overseer and departed the property to drive the short distance to the town of Carnarvon. Kim rode in the van, following Alan, who was driving the furniture removal truck.

Alan had driven into town the week before, hoping to find a place for them to stay. It had not been easy, as they needed space to park their vehicles. Maddie had no idea where they were going and was surprised when, about a kilometre out of town, her husband turned onto a short track leading to a banana plantation. Then, parking the truck in front of a large shed, he motioned for his wife and daughter to get out. As Maddie opened the truck door and was about to jump out, a stocky young man emerged from the shed and walked towards Alan, holding out his hand.

'G'day mate.'

Taking his hand, Alan responded.

'G'day, Tom. Nice to see you again. This is my wife, Maddie, and my daughter, Kim.'

Shaking Maddie's hand and acknowledging Kim, Tom beckoned them to follow him into the large shed. Long, wide benches surrounded three sides of the room, and every inch of space was piled high with bananas.

Maddie grabbed hold of the sleeve of her husband's shirt.

'Why are we going into the shed? I'd like to see the accommodation?'

Alan pulled his arm away and, walking nearer to Tom, he listened as he explained the process of storing the fruit.

'When we pick each bunch of bananas, they are individually placed upright onto the trailer, which is padded on each side to prevent any rubbing between the bunches. Then, we bring them into the packing shed, hang them, wash them, and pack them into those crates. These will be boxed sometime today and ready to be sent to Perth's fruit and vegetable market tomorrow. Retailers will bid for them.' Tom hesitated a moment before continuing. 'Come, I will show you the accommodation.'

'C'mon Mum, I don't like it in here, it's spooky. And I've seen a couple of rats running around the top of the walls! I'm going outside.' Without waiting for a reply, Kim scampered back out into the yard.

Maddie turned to follow her when Alan called her back.

'Where are you going? It's this way. C'mon.'

Then, she noticed Tom had entered a door at the back of the shed and was waiting for them to join him. Following her husband into the small room, she suddenly realised that this was it - this was where they were going to live.

The first thing she noticed was that there were no windows. An old gas stove sat next to a couple of cupboards, alongside a ceramic sink that had seen better days and needed a good cleaning. The kitchen was dark green and featured a larder, an ancient wooden table, four chairs, and a kerosene refrigerator. He then showed them two small bedrooms and a tiny washroom. Before Maddie could speak, Tom continued.

The toilet's outside at the back of the shed. You'll need a torchlight at night as you'd break a leg falling over the boxes scattered about the barn.' Then, turning to leave the room, he paused.

'Well, folks, I'll love ya and leave ya to settle in. When you're ready, come to the house and the missus will have a cuppa ready for you, and if you're lucky, some of the cake she baked earlier. In the meantime, if you need anything, give me a yell.'

'Thanks, mate. We'll see you soon. I'm sure a cuppa will go down well with all of us.'

Then, turning to Maddie.

'Best we get some of our things out of the van, and then we'll pop over to the house as I want to pick Tom's brains. He may know of someone who's looking for a good worker.'

Over the next few days, Maddie made the place as comfortable as possible, hoping it would not be too long before Alan found a job and they could move into town. A few Aboriginals came into the town most days, and an elderly woman called 'Mad Molly' was quite a handful. If someone upset her, she would become violent, spouting mouthfuls of expletives for all to hear! Occasionally, she would be carted off in the paddy wagon.

Maddie wanted to know more about her neighbour's culture, so she visited the small museum in town and came across the following, which she found very interesting.

The Inggarda people were traditional owners of the region around Carnarvon. Before European settlement, the place, now called Carnarvon, located at the mouth of the Gascoyne River, was known as Kuwinywardu, which means 'neck of water'. Aboriginals associated with the Carnarvon area, typically considered to be traditional speakers of the Wajarri language. During the 1960s, NASA set up a tracking station nearby to support the Gemini and Apollo space programs. The tracking station was closed in the mid-1970s. Only the foundations of the historical site remained. It is adjacent to the OTC Satellite Earth Station Carnarvon.

The Gascoyne had not experienced rain for the past three years, and the entire area was suffering from drought. Within days of moving onto the plantation, the town was placed under a flood alert as a large cyclone that had hit the far north was causing major flooding all along the west coast and making its way south. The town was on emergency alert. About 7,000 sandbags had been flown into the area the previous day in preparation for the floods. An Aboriginal reserve near Carnarvon, 920 kilometres north of Perth, had been evacuated. The Acting Premier of Western Australia, Mr O'Connor, ordered emergency measures and stated that he expected the floods to be worse than the 1974 flooding of Carnarvon, when more than 200 people were evacuated from their homes. The Gascoyne River had already burst its banks overnight after the heavy rain. Mr O'Connor indicated that the flooding would reach Carnarvon by about 7:30 am.

Concerned about the possibility of being homeless again, Alan went to the Banana Plantation Caravan Park across the road from where they lived. He hoped to move themselves, the vehicles, and the animals there, as he knew the plantation would be flooded within the next twenty-four hours or so.

The park was located on a high mound, so he knew they would be safe from the flood. The manager kindly allowed them to bring the two vehicles and animals onto the site and use one of the cabins. The dogs had to be tied up, while Mustard, the cat, stayed around the site.

Maddie and Alan drove to the small riverbed on the outskirts of town, just before the bridge spanning the Gascoyne River. They watched for quite a while as the water slowly began to ooze along the dry bed, and soon, as the volume started to build, they made their way back. They knew that once the river overflowed its banks, the floodwaters would spread through the vast agricultural and grazing areas, severely damaging crops and killing cattle. Hopefully, the main centre of town would remain untouched due to the levees constructed in 1960.

Residents of the park stood along the bank, watching as the water trickled down the road below them. However, it was not until the following morning that the river eventually exceeded its banks, and the flow, as it made its way down the road, rose higher and higher until it was almost at the top of the telephone box at the service station below them. They knew it would not be long before the entire town would be isolated from the surrounding areas as the floodwaters cut off all roads. The water line on the shed, where they had been staying at the plantations, was several feet high. Hopefully, all the bananas stacked along the benches would remain untouched. Then came the debris of uprooted bushes and piles of rubbish that had caught up in the branches. Maddie cried when she saw a small dog trapped in one of them, knowing she could do nothing to save it.

Men arrived in their dinghies, transporting people into town and delivering supplies to those stranded. By the third day, the water had receded enough for many to wade two kilometres into town. Alan knew it was an opportune time to visit the State Housing Office to apply for a house, confident that they would have a better chance of being placed on the emergency list due to their circumstances.

Before leaving Perth, Alan took their small camper trailer to Charles. At that time, he didn't think there would be any need for it where they were going. However, he realised they could not stay in the cabin much longer, especially since they hadn't been paying any rent. He called Charles and asked if he could bring it to the caravan park.

Charles and Daisy arrived a few days later with their trailer in tow and checked into one of the onsite caravans to spend the week with them. Their new 'home,' measuring four feet wide, featured a hinged wing on either side, which opened into two small double beds. Packed inside were a small folding table and four collapsible chairs. They attached the ten-foot square annexe, and after rummaging around in the removal van, they managed to furnish the tent with everything needed for their daily lives. Maddie and Daisy made the most of the short time they had together.

Six weeks later, they received a telegram informing them that they had been allocated a council house. They needed to collect the keys and move in immediately; otherwise, the house would be given to someone else. Alan wasted no time getting the keys, went straight to the house, and took possession of it. The following morning, they dismantled the tent and the trailer, hitched it to the van, and drove to the house. Alan hitched a lift back to the park and collected the truck that held all their possessions.

It was a brand-new house within walking distance of the town. They quickly discovered that Aboriginals occupied every other home, as the authorities hoped to integrate the two races and have them live together. They didn't have a problem with this as they had happily worked and lived alongside them when on the sheep and cattle stations.

Maddie was relieved and very happy that Joseph was back living with them. He had finished his term exams and wanted to be with his family again. Daisy and Charles drove to Carnarvon with him and stayed for the week. Maddie was much happier because she finally had three of her children with her. She, of course, missed her eldest son, Peter, but was pleased that he had an excellent job as a welder for a large oil company.

Alan was becoming increasingly frustrated because he had not found work. He spent a few hours helping out at one of the caravan parks, but that was all. Most days, Maddie went into town, trawling around the shops and hotels, hoping to eventually secure a job. In the meantime, she got up every morning at five to clean the ablution blocks at one of the caravan parks.

When she was about to give up hope, the owner of the local supermarket called her in and remarked that her persistence was wearing him down, so he offered her a job at his newsagent, working a four-day week. Then, James's boss at the butcher shop inquired if she could work afternoons. At last, a decent wage was coming in.

Alan was now working after receiving a call for an interview with the Dampier Salt mine at Lake McCloud. Maddie felt relieved, as he had been spending too much time at the local pub and returning home drunk. Most of the money he received from the dole went toward alcohol. Since he was an experienced operator, they assigned him to the large Skid Steel Loaders.

One day, as he was slowly navigating an enormous mountain of salt, a giant tarantula crawled out from under his seat, crept up his torso, and eventually covered most of his face before climbing onto his head. He was petrified, but he knew it would have been too dangerous to let go of the steering wheel to brush it off! By the time he reached the bottom of the incline, he was a quivering wreck!

Every morning at seven-thirty, the mining bus collected its workers from the town centre, taking them on the hour-long journey to the mine. One particular morning, Alan was running late, and Maddie, still in her pyjamas, drove him, hoping they would arrive before the bus. Unfortunately, that did not happen, and to make matters worse, he forgot to take his lunch from the car, which meant she had to run to the bus and pass it through the window to him. Meanwhile, she was met with a barrage of wolf whistles!

Kim was unhappy at school and often got into trouble. She was not a good student. Maddie was horrified when her daughter was sent home in disgrace for throwing a chair at one of the teachers. Kim expressed her desire to leave school and find a job. Her parents agreed, as long as she began looking for work. Maddie approached her boss at the supermarket, and after much persuasion from Maddie, he agreed to hire Kim to stack shelves.

Peter's expertise as a welder in the oil and gas industry, along with his experience in operating welding equipment on pipelines, rigs, plants, and facilities, led his company to send him all over Australia. Much to Maddie's delight, he made several visits to Carnarvon to resolve issues at the local fuel depot. Although his accommodation and meals would have been covered at one of the hotels, he far preferred being at home with his family and enjoying his mother's cooking. Maddie cherished having the whole family together again.

One Saturday, Alan, Peter, Joseph, and Maddie were watching the local ladies' dart team compete against the winners of the previous season. Approaching halftime, one of the ladies became ill and had to quit, leaving them a player short. During the break, the team's leader approached Maddie to ask her if she would play for them. She flatly refused, as the only darts she had thrown were in a friendly game with Alan and a few mates. Peter and Joseph egged her on.

'C'mon, Mum, what have you got to lose? Even if you don't get any high scores, it's better than them being down a player.'

Peter went to the bar, ordered a strong gin and tonic, and handed it to his mother.

'C'mon Mum, get this down you.'

Reluctantly, Maddie agreed to play but felt extremely anxious about embarrassing herself.

Each time Maddie took her turn, the boys cheered for her. Alan, surprised by how well she was doing, smiled to himself. 'Looks like the gin and tonic helped!'

As the match approached its conclusion, both sides needed to peg out on double one. The opposing team member, whose turn it was, happened to be the town's champion player. The team felt confident that Sally would peg out, securing their victory. Everyone in the bar fell silent; all eyes were on her as she approached the oche. Her first dart bounced off the top bar, narrowly missing the double. The second dart also missed and landed just outside the bottom bar. Her team groaned, having been so sure she would win the game for them. Sally walked towards the dartboard, reclaimed her darts, and motioned for the opposing team member to step up to the line.

One of the team members gave Maddie a gentle shove.

'C'mon, Maddie, you can do it.'

Maddie was stunned, as she hadn't realised that she was next up. After just having downed her third gin and tonic, she felt very relaxed but knew it was a big ask for her to peg out. Walking over, she positioned her toe on the line, took a deep breath, and, with her eye lined up with the dartboard, took another intake of breath. She steadied her hand and held the dart up to her eye. Her left hand lined up in front of her nose, creating a straight line to the top of the board, and she aimed the shaft at the double one. The next moment, everyone was cheering, and the rest of her team gathered around her. She was their hero! Maddie couldn't believe it. She had played in the league and knocked off the town's top player!

Maddie was persuaded to join the team. She looked forward to improving her skills and making new friends at the Tuesday evening game. She was well aware that the day she threw the winning score was a fluke, but it gave her the confidence to keep playing. Alan joined the men's team, which met on the same evening at one of the other hotels.

Although Alan's drinking habits hadn't changed, he was usually too tired to stay out late during the workweek. Weekends were the worst. One Saturday, he went into town around midday and stayed until the pub closed, barely able to walk. After unsuccessfully trying to get a lift, he resorted to walking home. Although it was less than a kilometre, once he was out of the town area, everything was shrouded in darkness. He lost track of where he was and stumbled through the bush, landing amid a group of Aboriginal people huddled around their humpies. - The humpy, known as a gunyah or wurley, was a small, temporary shelter made of branches and bark. - Struggling to stand upright, he was eager to leave, but one of them grabbed hold of him and, gabbling away in his native tongue, indicated for him to sit with them. After Alan drank the can of Emu beer that had been thrust into his hand, a younger man from the tribe beckoned him to follow and led him back onto the track toward home. Then, without saying a word, his new friend vanished into the darkness.

Joseph was working evenings for a delightful Indian couple at their newly opened fish-and-chip shop. One day, they asked Maddie if she would like to pick up a few hours with them, as they were extremely busy. She loved it there, especially being able to work alongside her son. Although she was no longer cleaning ablution blocks, she continued working at the butcher's most mornings and the newsagents in the afternoons, along with the fish shop when they needed her.

A friend of Maddie's who worked in the kitchen of General Hospital phoned to let her know that one of the cleaners on the wards had handed in her notice that morning. She told her friend that if she was interested, she should go along as soon as possible before someone else snatched it up. Maddie dropped what she was doing, changed into some decent clothes, and hopped on her Honda scooter, which Alan had bought for her a few weeks earlier. Upon arrival, she was directed to see Mary Patterson, the head of domestic staff. She was hired on the spot and agreed to start work immediately. Determined to work hard and prove her capability to take on anything, she hoped to secure a full-time position.

They rarely left the house for long, except for a quick trip to the shops, seldom locking the door. One day, they returned home to find a woman sitting in their lounge room.

'What the hell are you doing in here?' shouted Alan.

'Call me a fuckin cab,' she retorted.

'Okay, you are a fuckin' cab. Now GET OUT!' With that, Alan tugged her out of the chair and marched her to the open door; after pushing her out, he slammed it behind her.

Another time, Maddie prepared the tea while Alan read the paper; suddenly, they heard a commotion coming from the side of their house. They rushed outside and watched in amazement as a young lad ran toward the back fence, chased by Candy, who barked and snapped at his heels. Right behind them were two policemen! A few days later, one of the policemen visited them with a warrant for Candy, as the boy's family said they had a vicious dog. After handing them the warrant, the police officer informed them that, by law, he was required to deliver it, but advised them to ignore it. They never heard anything more about it.

Their neighbours on one side were not a bad family. It was usually the visitors they had that caused all the trouble. Maddie often talked to them and occasionally gave the children cakes.

One time, when they had visitors and a lot of drinks were consumed, the situation escalated into a huge fight. One of the men ended up sending the other over the fence into their garden. Alan was enraged and, grabbing a piece of two-by-two, he hit one of them over the head with it. The fight broke up immediately, and his mates carried the injured man back to the house.

Sadly, Mustard, the cat, died after being bitten by a snake. Candy had a nasty cancer on one of her ears, but that didn't slow her down or prevent her from getting into mischief. Maddie couldn't understand why she had found a metal dog dish on the front lawn for the past couple of mornings. The following day, as she was getting ready to go to work, she saw Candy coming down the road with a dish in her mouth. Upon reaching home, Candy deposited it on the ground outside the gate and proceeded to eat the contents! Their dog was a thief!

One of Alan's drinking mates brought a very young joey kangaroo into the pub. He said her mother had been run over, and unless someone were prepared to look after her, she would die. Alan knew that his wife had always wanted one, so he agreed to take it. Maddie couldn't believe her eyes when Alan unwrapped the little bundle, as she had always wanted to care for a little joey.

Phoning an animal sanctuary down south, she received all the information she needed. First, she stitched up the bottom of one of Alan's old jumpers and then hung it on a wire coat hanger. Knowing that it would likely be in shock, she lined the inside with a small towel and then, taking the Joey from Alan, carefully placed it, with its tail, head, and toes peeking out of the opening. She snuggled inside the warm, cosy pouch that Maddie had hung on the back of one of the kitchen chairs. She had been advised not to feed her for a while as she needed time to recover from the shock of losing her mother first.

Maddie was no longer cleaning the wards. She had been assigned to the kitchens, where she assisted with the patients' diets and delivered meals to the ward with the older patients. She loved her work, especially taking meals to those in need of special care, often taking far too long to complete her rounds. One day, Mary came to see why she hadn't returned to the kitchen and found Maddie helping one of the patients who was struggling to feed herself. From that day on, Maddie was permitted to divide her time between the kitchen and alleviating some of the strain on the nurses in that ward.

Every Saturday, Maddie studied the local racing page, and after selecting what she hoped would be a good bet, she went to the betting shop. One weekend, while having a flutter, there was a race in which she couldn't decide between four horses running. So, she opted to place a quartet, hoping that the horse with the best odds would win. Later that afternoon, on her way to her shift at the hospital, she stopped by to check the results and arrived just in time to see the end of the race. Peter walked into the shop just as the results appeared on the screen. They couldn't believe it when every horse Maddie selected crossed the finish line in the exact order she had picked. Standing rooted to the spot, she waited anxiously to find out how much she had won. Several punters, realising by her exuberance that she had won big, assured her that she would get an excellent return. But no one was prepared, least of all Maddie, for the return on the small amount of five dollars it had cost her: $9,963! Although eager to let Alan know about her fantastic win, she went on her way to work. It would have to wait until she finished her shift.

They paid off all their debts, indulged in a few small luxuries for the home, made a deposit on a house in Mandurah, and still managed to save several thousand. Maddie had always been quite lucky, but this had exceeded all expectations.

Josie, the kangaroo, had settled into her new environment very well. At six months, she had just ventured out of her pouch for the first time. Maddie bought a couple of pairs of baby trainer pants, and by cutting a hole for her tail, she was now able to explore around the house. She loved digestive biscuits, and when left on the table with no one watching, she would stand tall and take them in her paws before hopping away to eat them.

Alan's sister, Sarah, asked if her eleven-year-old daughter, Laura, could come and stay with them for the term holidays. A few weeks later, Amy, three years younger than Laura, joined them. Amy returned home two weeks later, but Laura begged to be allowed to stay much longer.

One evening, while Maddie and Alan were watching television, they received a phone call from a good friend. She informed them that she had just spoken to another friend, whose husband had been washed off the rocks while fishing. They had disregarded the warning signs that the area was hazardous. Although it was a popular fishing spot, it was dangerous due to the king waves in the region. Craig was fishing on the lower edge at the blowholes when a wave came and swept him off the ledge. His friend had stayed on higher ground and managed to go back for help. His wife, Marjory, and their two children could never find closure regarding his death, as he had vanished into shark-infested waters. His body was never found. Craig was an exceptionally intelligent man, a professor, and a gentleman.

It had been nearly three years since they left the South to work on the sheep station. So much had happened during that time, and although they were settled in their new home, Maddie was not entirely happy. There was little to do besides work. Occasionally, they would go fishing off One-Mile Jetty or to the mango swamp with her friend Rose in her little rowboat, setting down cages to catch delicious mud crabs.

Maddie enjoyed attending the Landor bush race meetings, held monthly in the Eastern Gascoyne area. It was a strictly amateur race meeting for local station horses and riders. There were no starting gates at Landor – all races featured 'walk-up starts.' The day was tremendous fun, with fashions ranging from moleskins and shirts to Akubras, fillies in frocks, and mares dressed up with hats, of course. Later in the evening, the men would gather around the bar, renewing old acquaintances or venturing to the 'two up' ring set up in the bush nearby. Women were not allowed under any circumstances.

She had always wanted to see what the place was like, so one day Alan agreed to take her there, provided she remained in the car. Parking a few feet away from the gambling area, he left Maddie in the dark. She sat peering out the window, watching the men standing outside the ring. Then, as the 'spinner' threw two pennies ten feet into the air, all eyes turned skyward. When the pennies landed, the onlookers waited anxiously for the spinner to call, hoping that the pennies had fallen in their favour. They frequently moved the rings to a different area because the local cops would raid them whenever they could.

For some time, Kim had been seeing a local boy. On the surface, he seemed very polite and of good character. He was the only child of a well-respected couple. Unfortunately, his parents believed their son could do no wrong. It was not until some of Alan's mates warned him that Larry was a known troublemaker that whispers began circulating in the community suggesting he was a drug pusher. Kim utterly ignored any advice from her parents, and as she was now seventeen, there was little they could do to prevent their relationship.

One evening, Maddie sat watching television, waiting for Alan to come home for supper, when she heard the sound of the door opening and closing. She was surprised to see her daughter standing in the doorway.

'Hi Mum, I need to talk to you.'

Maddie looked at her daughter, her eyes filled with sadness, knowing with certainty what Kim was about to tell her. She shook her head wordlessly.

'Please, tell me you're not pregnant?' Maddie sat there for several long minutes living in both the present and the future, watching as dreams of her daughter were being wrenched away. She knew that whatever she said at that moment would live forever in both their memories. In seconds, she could completely shatter their relationship if she said the wrong thing.

Kim was already defensive.

'Yep, I am, and don't think about asking me to terminate it. It is my baby and I will be keeping it!'

The thought had not crossed Maddie's mind, and she was confident that Alan, although not particularly happy, would take this in his stride.

'Does Larry know?'

'I told him as soon as I knew, and we informed his parents yesterday. They suggested that it might be a good idea if I went to stay with a relative in Perth until the baby is born.'

Maddie remained silent for a moment or two.

Knowing that her husband would be home late after downing too many pints, she advised her daughter, 'Let's wait until morning, and then we can discuss it with your father.' Now come and have some supper and try not to worry too much.'

The following morning, Alan, Maddie, and Kim sat around the kitchen table discussing what would be in Kim's best interest. They concluded that she would be happier if she left the town. Later that day, Alan phoned his sister, Mary, who lived in Melbourne with her husband Jim and their three children, all in their late teens. After explaining the situation to Mary, he asked if Kim could stay with them until the child was born. Much to everyone's relief, his sister said without hesitation that she would be happy to have her. A week later, Kim was on her way to the other side of Australia.

Life went on as usual until the day Charles phoned, informing Maddie that her mother had been diagnosed with cervical cancer and was scheduled for surgery in two weeks. After applying for compassionate leave from the hospital, Maddie flew to Perth the following day, where Peter met her at the airport.

Maddie was surprised to see her mother looking very well, showing no signs of illness. Daisy told her daughter that she had been offered the choice of chemotherapy or an operation but had been warned that, because of her age, there was only a twenty per cent chance of a successful outcome.

Maddie smiled to herself, aware of how vain her mother was and knowing she would have dreaded losing her hair. She admired her mother's spirit and determination to proceed with the operation, regardless of the consequences. At the age of 71, she remained stubborn and saw everything in *black and white*! Maddie was determined to look on the bright side for both their sakes and ensured that their time together was special, filled with laughter and mother-daughter bonding. During this long time together, Daisy reminisced about her childhood and her love affair with Maddie's father, Jacque. It was a special time for both of them, and although Maddie was fretful that it might be their last, she remained positive.

The day before her operation, Charles drove Daisy and Maddie to the hospital. After the necessary documents were completed, she was transferred into a wheelchair and taken up to the ward. Maddie kissed her mother and said she would see her in the morning before going down to the theatre.

Maddie was up early and at the hospital by eight o'clock. She wanted some time with her mother before they took her to the operating theatre. It had just turned eight-thirty when the trolley was wheeled into the ward, ready to take her mother down for the operation. Just as they were about to leave, Daisy started pulling at her bottom row of teeth. The nurse leant over her.

'What on earth are you doing, Daisy!'

'They're stuck. I can't get them out!' Leaning over the stretcher, one of the nurses exclaimed.

'Oh, my goodness! We didn't realise you had false teeth.' Carefully removing Daisy's hand from inside her mouth, she said, 'Your mouth is dry, preventing you from taking them out.' Then, giving her patient's teeth a gentle tug, she managed to extract them. 'Maddie, can you put these away safely in your mother's bedside table?'

Daisy and Maddie burst into laughter, followed by the two nurses who, not wanting to upset their patient, had been trying to suppress their amusement.

Giving her mother a quick kiss and hug, she assured her that she would not leave the hospital until her mother returned from the operating theatre and was back in a ward. Maddie was shown to a small sitting room, and within minutes, a member of the domestic staff brought her a cup of tea. Having taken a book with her, Maddie was content to sit and read. Now and then, a nurse would pop her head around the door to ask if she was okay and assure her that her mother was in excellent hands.

Maddie was dozing when she heard the rattle of the dinner trolley, and the dinner lady asked if she would like some lunch. She was starving, so she didn't hesitate to accept the offer. Looking at her watch, she noted that it was almost one-thirty, five hours since her mother had gone into surgery. Another hour, and then another ticked by, and as it neared four o'clock, a nurse came to let her know that her mother had been in the Intensive Care Ward for the last couple of hours. They had not informed her sooner as it was a critical time, and they needed to ensure that all was well. The nurse said that Maddie could go and see her as long as she only stayed a few minutes.

Maddie cried with relief; her mother had survived the operation!

The following morning, the hospital called to inform them that Daisy had returned to the main ward. When she and Charles arrived, the ward sister told them it was remarkable that a woman of her age, especially after such a major operation, had not only survived but was already sitting up in bed and ready to receive visitors!

Once her mother returned home and was receiving care, Maddie knew it was time to return to her home and resume work. Kim returned to Carnarvon six weeks after giving birth to her beautiful baby girl, Kayla. Maddie and Alan loved having a little one in the house and spending time with their first grandchild. Kim had stopped taking drugs during her pregnancy, but now that she was back home and back in contact with Kayla's father, she worried that her daughter would be influenced by him once again.

Joseph, now seventeen, was working on a prawning trawler, spending two to three days at sea. His boss, German Bob, was a hard taskmaster, but the pay was good, and there was the bonus of boxes of prawns and scallops. Kim was working in the prawning factory 'shucking' oysters, and even though the job required long and tiring days, she was determined to keep at it for as long as she could. Shucking fresh oysters was a delicate process of opening the shell and removing the meat without losing the oyster's nectar. Breaking into the tough shell to reach the succulent parts required a firm hand. With Alan and Maddie bringing home a good wage, they were finally able to start saving. It would have been more if it weren't for Alan's heavy drinking and forty to fifty cigarettes a day.

Maddie continued working evenings at the fish-and-chip shop and during the day at the hospital. She loved both jobs. However, she also noticed that she was developing quite prominent veins on one of her legs, and it was becoming painful. She attributed this to being on her feet for so many hours each day. One day, her leg was more painful than usual, so her sister sent her to see one of the hospital doctors. After confirming the presence of varicose veins, he scheduled an appointment with one of the surgeons to have them stripped. She was off work for two weeks. When she returned to see the doctor, he informed her that she could go back to work. She was back on the wards for two days when she started developing a high temperature and didn't feel well at all. The pain in her leg was excruciating. The sister spoke to the surgeon who had operated, and within an hour, Maddie was back on the operating table. She had septicaemia.

Maddie kept a diary recording events from her time at the hospital, such as when one of the ladies in the laundry suffered from a nasty migraine. The nurse in charge obliged by giving her two tablets. Almost immediately, the woman's pupils dilated, and she looked rather dopey. They grew concerned when the nurse rushed back into the room, telling them she had just realised she had given her two Mogadon sleeping tablets! Another time, when they were short-staffed and Maddie was helping out in the laundry, Hillary, with whom she was working, pulled a birthday card out of her apron pocket and asked Maddie if she could read it for her, explaining that she had never learnt to read or write. Maddie had not been coping with her stammering particularly well that day, and after stumbling over the first few words, she gave up. They glanced at one another, knowing how hilarious it was, and then burst out laughing. Hillary could not read the words on the card, and Maddie was unable to speak!

When Kayla was six months old, Kim told her parents that she wanted to return to Mandurah to be with friends, asking them if she could live in their house—the one Maddie had bought after winning a considerable sum on the horses. Peter had been taking care of it, mowing the lawn and ensuring that the garden didn't become too overgrown. Although she was sad to see her daughter and granddaughter leave, Maddie was pleased that they would be away from the temptation of drugs. Or… so she thought.

Alan had been at the salt mine for about eighteen months when, without looking where he was going, he received a hard knock to his head. He was taken to the hospital, where X-rays revealed that the blow had slightly misaligned his brain. They administered medication that gradually helped to realign it, and after a couple of weeks, he was able to return to work. However, it all became too much for him, as he was experiencing intense headaches that made it difficult to concentrate on his work. Since he had recently been elected as their union representative, they reinstated him at the town office.

James had left the butcher's shop in Carnarvon and was now working at a butchery seven hundred kilometres north in the former gold rush town of Roebourne, with a population of just under one thousand.

The oil company where Peter was working consolidated with another group, and he was offered a redundancy package he could not refuse. The other establishment then hired him. However, within twelve months, his department also gave its staff the option to take early retirement or redundancy. Peter accepted the money, which allowed him to buy a house without needing a mortgage. He also decided to start a business. Renting a large building on the outskirts of town, he and his partner, Stephane, eventually opened the doors to Mandurah's first indoor sports centre after many months of hard work.

After spending five years living and working in the Gascoyne area, they decided it was time to return to the south. Carnarvon offered little beyond pubs, fishing, and darts. Maddie was happy that they would, at last, be leaving.

Let's Call it a Day

During their time in Carnarvon, Maddie managed to save a considerable amount, and there was also Alan's superannuation payment from Dampier Salt. Since the house in Mandurah was fully furnished, they sold all the items they had acquired since moving to Carnarvon. The removal truck and van had been sold some time ago, and they now owned a 1974 Holden Kingswood. Kim had moved out and was living with a girlfriend who had a daughter a year older than Kayla, who had recently celebrated her first birthday.

It didn't take long for Alan to get a job with a local company renovating some of the older weatherboard buildings in town. Maddie visited the local nursing home, registered her name, and informed them she was willing to do anything. In the meantime, she secured a part-time job in the hotel's kitchen and cleaned the rooms as needed.

Maddie was over the moon when the nursing home called her to say they had a vacancy for a cleaner in the residential side. She was never late for work and often stayed even after her shift ended because she loved spending time with the residents. They frequently asked her to substitute for the occupational therapist when the therapist was experiencing health issues. Then, when she asked to take an extended leave, they asked Maddie if she would like to fill the position in the meantime until her return. Maddie jumped at the chance. She attended a training course that, although it did not provide her with a certificate, taught her everything she needed to know. She was now regarded as the nursing home's official occupational therapist.

Maddie loved her work and was eager to take on any tasks assigned to her. She drove a minibus to transport the more capable residents for outings, morning tea, or shopping at one of the local malls. On many occasions, her friends would ask to join her, which was a great help and a lot of fun for both them and the residents.

There was a moment when one of their female residents, Trudy, who suffered from irritable bowel syndrome, needed suppositories inserted into her rectum for a few days. She refused to accept help, insisting that she was quite capable of doing it herself. Then, one morning, a supervisor, upon entering her room, was shocked to see Trudy cutting the corners of the plastic coating that surrounded the suppository! The staff member snatched it from her, asking what on earth she was doing. Trudy replied that she always cut the sharp edges off because they hurt when going into her bottom! The doctor was summoned.

Then there was Elsie, another resident, who was found with the angina patch stuck to her nightie because she disliked the feel of it on her body!

Joseph showed his mother a hundred-year-old book on palmistry that he had found in a second-hand shop. Maddie was intrigued and asked if she could borrow it. She spent hours examining all the lines and islands on her own hands. One day, the Matron, Joan, saw Maddie with her hands under the photocopier lid and asked what she was doing. Maddie explained that she was learning about palmistry and had decided that the best way was to read her own hand. Joan then asked Maddie if she would take a copy of her hand and do a reading for her. At first, Maddie refused, explaining that she had just started reading the book and had a great deal to learn. Joan persisted until Maddie finally relented, telling her that she would, but emphasised that it was just a bit of fun.

Scrutinising every line and examining the breaks in the strokes and the size of the islands, Maddie became immersed, as every part of the palm revealed a person's life. She could not understand how a professional palmist could uncover everything someone wanted to know in just a few minutes. It took several weeks before she disclosed the results to Joan, but she didn't share much, as this greatly disturbed Maddie, who felt certain she must have misinterpreted what she had observed on her employer's hands.

It was almost a year later when Maddie went into work one morning and sensed an unusual quietness. Sarah, the head nurse, took her into her office and, sitting her down, told her that the matron was dead! She had been found the night before at one of the local beaches, where she had walked into the sea and drowned. She had committed suicide. It emerged that, apart from having problems in her marriage, she had been embezzling money from the nursing home over the past year.

Maddie was in a state of shock, not only because their lovely matron was dead, but also because she had kept something to herself that she was unable to share. The information she had withheld from reading Joan's palm indicated, to Maddie's untrained eye, that there were problems in her marriage, and more than that, it revealed that she would commit suicide by drowning. She was not about to reveal what she had seen to anyone, mainly because it seemed inconceivable that it had shown on her palm, but who would believe something so sinister? Everyone went about their work in a daze that day, none more so than Maddie.

Sometime later, Maddie was helping one of the nurses make the beds when she doubled over in excruciating pain in her back. She had experienced problems before, but not like this. Years of lifting heavy removal boxes and hours spent working while caring for her family had all taken their toll. When she started work at the nursing home, she stated on the form that she was unable to perform any heavy lifting. Whenever possible, she would ask a staff member for help lifting residents in and out of their wheelchairs, but with everyone being so busy, it was not always feasible. Since Maddie was always so willing, the matron had been giving her more and more responsibilities.

Maddie was off work for a week. Upon her return, the matron called her into the office and asked her to sit down. She then informed her that, since she could no longer perform the tasks for which she had been employed, she would have to leave. She walked out of the office in a daze, struggling to hold back her tears. She loved her job, the staff, and all the residents. She was determined not to let them get away with it, both for her own sake and for the protection of all the staff.

Peter was now married with two children; James was travelling the world, and Joseph was in a serious relationship. Kim had four children by four different fathers and seemed to be as happy as she would ever be. As far as the family knew, she was no longer taking drugs.

Not long after, one of the nurses at the home informed her that when she left, they had hired two people to manage the responsibilities she had been handling alone.

As a member of the Nurses Union, she agreed to take on her case. After presenting it to the Town Council, they were not surprised when the opposing party declined to accept responsibility and settle out of court. Maddie's solicitor, Graham Droppert, informed her that they expected to win the case. A trial date was then set at the Court House in Perth for 'unfair dismissal.'

Maddie had been attending a speech therapy group at Curtin University. She found it very difficult to use soft sounds and speak in a way that made her comfortable. Everyone was lovely, especially when she shared her experiences with the court case and how worried she felt about testifying in the witness box. Troy, one of the therapists, called Maddie on the day of the trial and guided her through smooth speech.

Maddie was the first witness called. Graham assisted her during the initial minutes as she struggled to articulate her responses to their questions. Then, with a few stumbles and the kind and patient judge's help, she managed to answer their questions with greater ease. Everyone was very supportive and empathetic. She was in the box for over an hour and felt relieved when they took a lunch break.

When they returned, the matron was called to the stand for cross-examination. She became inconsistent with her evidence; however, the Director of Nursing and the OT, who had recommended Maddie for the position, had nothing but praise for her. They stated her work had been above reproach and that they would find it very difficult to employ someone as capable of performing all the duties she had undertaken, and with such compassion as well. They also noted that all the residents had suffered since her dismissal. Additionally, it was brought to the court's attention that when Maddie started working at the nursing home, the matron had been made aware of her previous back injury, yet continued to burden her with extra work, ignoring her frequent requests for assistance.

Graham requested a thirty-minute break, but as it was getting late, the commissioner rescheduled the case for a later time. Two days later, at 11:00 a.m., they were summoned to the courtroom, and by 2:30 p.m., the proceedings were over. The case was settled out of court. Graham and their solicitor negotiated back and forth, and in the end, both sides agreed to a settlement. Maddie could have held out for more, but after discussing it with Graham, she decided to accept the $6,000 and close the case. Maddie was very pleased with the outcome, especially since her primary goal had been to establish a precedent for the safety of the nursing home staff.

Kim joined a dating agency, and after a few non-starters, she met Scott, who, at twenty-three, was a year older than her. Alan and Maddie were pleased that at last, their daughter seemed settled. They had been seeing each other for about six months when Kim paid a visit to her doctor, who confirmed what she already suspected: she was pregnant. When she told Scott, he was more worried about how his parents would react than about the prospect of becoming a father. He knew they would be angry and accuse him of letting them down. Scott's father, Dennis, arranged to meet with Kim's parents to discuss the situation. He told them that the right thing would be for his son to marry their daughter, as he and his wife were highly respected in the community, and he intended to maintain that respect.

Family and friends gathered to witness their marriage, which a celebrant performed in a picturesque park. Afterwards, everyone made their way to a village hall where Maddie and a few of her friends prepared a magnificent feast. They spent the evening dancing late into the night to a three-piece band that Alan had arranged. Maddie was pleased to see Kim so happy. She loved her daughter dearly and prayed for Kim and Scott to succeed now that they were married. Despite the many challenges her daughter had faced in her short life, she was kind, generous, and had a good heart.

Scott had worked with his father in the real estate business since leaving school, but now that his son was married, Dennis decided it was time for Scott to branch out on his own. He bought them a house and set up another office one hundred kilometres south of Mandurah. Maddie and Alan visited several times over the next few months and were pleased to see that they appeared happy in their marriage. Scott was doing well in business, and they were making new friends.

Their daughter was born in the early hours of the morning. They named her Amber. Now, at forty-two, Maddie was a very proud grandmother of two beautiful little girls. She and Alan were busy with their careers, making it hard to take time off to drive down and see them as often as they would have liked, but by all accounts, everything was going well. That was until they received a call from Scott long after they had gone to bed. He told them he was very worried about Kim, as she had left the house hours ago and had not returned. He said that she'd been cutting up the children's toys and behaving irrationally. Just as they were about to leave, Scott phoned back to tell them that the police had found her and taken her to Graylands Mental Institute in Perth.

The following morning, Alan and Maddie visited their daughter. Scott was there with his parents, waiting for news. They were all told to leave and that they would be contacted in the next couple of days after she had been assessed. Kim was allowed supervised visits, and the boys were devastated to see their sister looking so sad and gazing ahead as if in another world. They did not find out until later that she had undergone several sessions of electroconvulsive therapy. They were furious and demanded to know why there was a need for such barbaric treatment! Two weeks later, she was allowed home.

Kim and Scott parted ways after a few months, and following a lengthy court battle, Scott was awarded custody of Amber. Kim took Kayla and returned to Mandurah, where she found a small two-bedroom unit. She distanced herself from her family, who knew she was using drugs again but felt powerless to intervene. Occasionally, she would contact her mother or one of the boys to ask for money, but mostly they would buy her food or pay some bills.

Peter was seeing a lovely girl, and James was working down south at an abattoir because he wanted to experience the other side of the butchering process. Alan was still doing building renovations. Maddie was happiest when she was at work and away from her husband's constant mood swings and drinking.

Life with Alan was never going to change, leaving Maddie to wonder what lay ahead for her.

In 1992, there was significant discussion about asbestos, and Alan became concerned because their house was clad in that very material. Although it did not cause a problem unless disturbed, he thought they should sell before it became impossible to do so. He discussed this with Maddie, who agreed it would be for the best. Their home was just a five-minute walk to town, situated in a quiet area away from all the tourists during the summer season. It was a prime location.

Alan's drinking and mood swings were worse than ever. Maddie spent many evenings alone, but as a prolific writer, she would sit for hours writing letters to friends across the globe and composing poetry. She sent letters and poems to the Prime Minister and the royal family. She was amazed when she received a handwritten reply from the then-Australian Prime Minister, Malcolm Fraser.

One evening, alone as usual, Maddie browsed through the numerous diaries she had written over the past forty years, her thoughts drifting back to when she first met Alan.

'If only I could turn back time. Would life have taken me down a different path, a better one, if I hadn't gone on that first date with Alan? Was I a fool for waiting at the bus stop, watching as every car approached, hoping it was him? Why did I wait for so long? Why, when I knew he had been drinking and offered no apology for being late, didn't I go back home? Why?'

Slowly, she packed away the diaries, her thoughts lingering on all the adventures she had experienced since their first meeting. Over the years, many joyful moments had occurred, but now nothing held them together. She knew he had many dalliances, and while she was sure that most were harmless, she recognised that it was not always the case.

Shortly after moving from Mandurah to their new home, Maddie found a pamphlet that had been shoved into their letterbox advertising exercise classes to music for over-fifties. It appealed to Maddie because they met twice weekly at the local Community Hall. Throughout their marriage, she had fully supported Alan, but now she felt brave enough to do something for herself. His jealousy had held her back from many things over the years, but now she didn't care about what he said or did.

When she joined, the organisation was small, but its numbers grew rapidly. They held demonstrations promoting themselves in places like Forest Place in Perth city, a focal point for significant political meetings and events. Centres began opening all over the state. Maddie and her friends were the founders of an organisation that grew to over four thousand members.

Many times, while in class, she'd receive phone calls. It was always Alan asking her to pick up something from the shops or checking what time she would be home. He was ensuring that she was not somewhere else. Her friends were very protective, and whenever it became too much for her, they were there to support her. They supported one another. She knew that the friends she made would be with her for a lifetime.

Maddie always regretted the day she received a letter from a childhood sweetheart, who, after so many years, had somehow managed to track her down. They had met in primary school and remained close friends until her mother took her to Australia. Three years later, when Maddie sailed back to England alone, they arranged to meet, but a misunderstanding regarding the day and time prevented it from happening.

Maddie showed the letter to Alan, expressing her pleasure at hearing from her close friend after such a long time had passed. They corresponded for a couple of months, and each time she offered Alan the chance to read the letters. However, soon their correspondence became more frequent and personal. Richard was not keeping the reconnection at a platonic level. Maddie felt flattered, as she craved someone who would truly and unconditionally care about her. The letters continued to flow back and forth as they both got carried away, reminiscing about the lost relationship that hadn't finished but instead had abruptly or inexplicably ended. Maddie spent a lot of time daydreaming about what might have been. She hid the letters in a drawer beneath her underwear.

After several months, Maddie knew this had to stop. Despite being desperately unhappy in her marriage, she had never cheated on her husband in all those years. She may have looked at other men, wondering how different her life could have been if she had married someone like them, but she had never considered straying. Yet, she realised that, although it was only thoughts put on paper, what she was doing now was cheating on Alan. It had to stop.

Unfortunately, before Maddie had a chance to destroy any correspondence from Richard, Alan discovered the letters. She had gone next door to see a friend, and upon returning home, she found Alan sitting in the kitchen. She recognised the look on his face, having seen it many times before, but this time it was different. Before she had a chance to speak, he began hurling obscenities at her. He was manic. Her eyes darted to a rifle that lay slung across the kitchen table; Alan, following her gaze, grabbed the gun and levelled it at Maddie. Although his finger was on the trigger, he did not cock it, and within a few seconds, he threw the rifle back onto the table and strode out of the house. They never spoke of it again.

They sold the house and bought a large caravan in a nearby residential park, dividing the remaining proceeds from the sale. They added an annexe, furnishing it with a bed, a table, chairs, and a small wardrobe. A little table was set up for Maddie's word processor so she could continue her writing. Alan moved from the caravan into the annexe, which suited both of them. Although it was never discussed, Maddie knew that it was a step toward the end of their marriage.

They made many friends at the park, and on hot summer nights, numerous residents gathered on the central green for a barbecue, with everyone bringing food and drinks. One hot February evening, sixty friends and family came together to celebrate two wedding anniversaries and Daisy's 80th birthday. Steaks, sausages, and chops sizzled on the large barbecue, accompanied by huge platters of salad and celebration cakes. Husbands and sons adorned the area with flashing lights. Everyone danced and sang to the music until the 10 o'clock curfew. The evening lingered on until after midnight. It was then that Peter and his girlfriend, along with James and Joseph, wanted to continue the party. They had been trying, without success, to get a taxi to take them to a nightclub in Fremantle. Since Maddie had only had one small glass of wine, she offered to drive them. With everyone piling into her little car, they set off. Maddie had only driven about a hundred yards when Joseph said:

'Mum, there's a police car, and I think he wants you to pull over!'

Maddie glanced in the rearview mirror and noticed the flashing blue light. As she pulled over to the side of the road, they followed behind her. Two officers exited their vehicle and approached the driver's side. Maintaining a distance from the car, one of them pointed a flashlight into Maddie's eyes.

'Can I please see your license?' he asked.

Maddie's heart raced.

'I'm sorry, officer, I don't have it with me.'

He lowered the flashlight and continued asking:

'Have you had a drink this evening?'

Maddie nodded.

'Yes, one glass.'

The officer instructed her to blow into the straw, and she did so.

'You need to blow harder,' the officer said.

Then, glancing at the meter, he waved her on. Maddie thanked him, fastened her seatbelt, turned on the ignition, and began driving up the road when...

'Stop, stop the car, mum! Stop! Joseph isn't in the car!'

Maddie slammed her foot on the brake, believing she had left him behind, but she hadn't, as he was still hanging onto the car door. Maddie couldn't understand why they were all in stitches and found it so funny until Peter told her that when she stopped the car, Joseph had got out of the back seat and, with one leg still in the car, leaned across the road to speak to the other officer. Then, when she sped off, he was still hanging onto the door and running to keep up with the vehicle!

Alan and Maddie still went most places together, and aside from her husband's persistent drinking, life wasn't too bad. Maddie had reached a point where she didn't care what he did or where he went. She knew that the day would come when she would have the courage to walk away. It was only for the sake of her children that she had not done so earlier. Now they all had lives of their own and were old enough to understand, but she was worried about how they would react, as the thought of losing any of them would be too much to bear. Then, one evening, about a year after they had moved to the park, everything was about to change.

Maddie had been next door with a neighbour, leaving Alan hoping to sober up after spending most of the day at the pub. However, upon her return, she found him sitting on the edge of his bed, with the remnants of a bottle of whisky on the floor beside his feet. He looked up as she entered the annexe and, slurring his words, turned towards her.

'It's time we called it a day.' For a moment, Maddie didn't immediately comprehend what he was saying. However, once she recovered from the shock, she responded.

I fully agree; we cannot continue like this.

Instead of appearing relieved that she had agreed so easily, Alan wore a look of surprise and seemed as if he was going to say something, but then changed his mind. It was then that Maddie realised it was the drink speaking. He hadn't expected her to agree. This was the opportunity she needed. It was time for them to live their own lives. Thinking quickly, she asked:

'Do you want to stay in the van and pay me my half, or would you rather move on?' Realising that Maddie was serious, he contemplated it for a few minutes.

'Pay my share. I'd rather move away and find a place of my own,' he stated.

The next morning, Maddie went to the bank and withdrew the money, giving him slightly more, knowing he would have little left from his share of the house sale. She then told him there was no need to move out immediately and encouraged him to take his time finding a suitable place. She also offered Alan their furniture, which was stored along with a few personal items. She wanted them to remain friends.

Maddie's 1970 Ford Fiesta, although a bit battered, was mechanically sound, as was Alan's Hillman Imp. Despite his lack of qualifications, he was a skilled mechanic and took care to maintain their vehicles.

Alan bought a caravan and an annexe at a caravan park in Jandacot. He had many friends and kept in touch with the boys while spending time with Kim and her children. He visited occasionally but was always very tight-lipped about his life. Maddie found it strange at first, especially when each of the children started primary school and later left the nest to spread their wings. She spent many hours writing, attending exercise classes, and making new friends.

Maddie knew it was time for her to return home to England.

Epilogue

In August 1994, six months after Maddie and Alan had separated, Maddie received a letter from England. It was from her son, James, who was inviting her to his wedding. The event was scheduled for the beginning of the following year. Maddie contacted James immediately to assure him that she would not miss it for the world. Unfortunately, none of his siblings or his father would be able to attend due to work commitments and financial constraints.

Selling the caravan to a local dealer and having no time to haggle over the price, she sold it for less than it was worth. She gave her car to her daughter. Although it was old, it was far more reliable than Kim's old bone shaker!

Maddie packed most of her few possessions into removal boxes and stored them with friends. She took the word processor, along with the reams of paper she had written on over the past three years, which depicted so much of her life, and the books with her. This included everything she would need for the next four or five months, or possibly for longer.

A month later, in September 1994, Maddie was surrounded by family and friends at the Perth airport, waiting to board the plane home to England. As she boarded, she settled into her seat by the window of the aircraft. Looking toward the terminal departure lounge, Maddie was surprised to see everyone waving at her and blowing kisses. Then, to her amazement, they spread a gigantic Australian flag across the window.

Tears rolled down Maddie's cheeks as she waved back while the plane slowly made its way down the runway. Those were not tears of sadness; they were tears of all the love she had from so many – her family and friends, whom she would never forget or leave behind. Ever. Because we never really leave. We take what we can with us: emotions, love, memories, and wisdom, both good and bad; it's all tucked away safely in our hearts. When we set off, we also leave parts of ourselves behind, and that is most important: it's not so much about what we take with us but about the marks we leave behind, the traces we have left in people's hearts, and the colours we have painted in the pictures of their lives.

It was in that church in England, where she had walked in with a friend, that Maddie realised it was time for her healing. It was time to let go of her fears, and after rapidly blinking the tears away, she battled all that had held her back. She knew then she could finally move forward, her hope slowly resurrecting back to life.

Six months after returning to England, Maddie met Johnathan. He was someone who loved her unconditionally, just as she was. He was also the one to whom Maddie devoted all her love because it is more about giving than taking and understanding that when one stumbles, the other is there to catch them, helping them land softly to avoid bruises, going through pain together, and living the ecstatic moments side by side. Maddie and Johnathan got married to experience that sharing.

Daisy, Maddie's mother, passed away at the age of 93. Charles followed her three years later; he was 97 years old. Daisy had arranged a quiet funeral for herself—she did not want anyone to attend. She said it was a waste of money! Maddie and Jonothan flew to Australia to scatter her mother's ashes in the Swan River…

The wind swept them in every direction, just as Daisy's life had taken her.

Alan passed away in 2002 due to multiple conditions. In 2014, Kim, at the age of 49, spent her final months in a nursing home after enduring many years of suffering. Maddie was with her shortly before she passed away and was there for her funeral.

Each person's life is a painting. We start with colours. The background may be different, but it's the way you use the shades that makes your painting unique. Maddie had used different palettes, experimented with blending, never erasing anything, and never altering a single line. Yet, the painting of her life brings forth all that is in life, along with no regrets about the things that could have been.

www.ingramcontent.com/pod-product-compliance
Lightning Source LLC
Chambersburg PA
CBHW052014070526
44584CB00016B/1749